Three-Quarters of a Footprint

'The essence of good writing' – *Asian Times*

'Roberts's approach to India is refreshingly untainted by received wisdom or prejudice – he just tells it as it is' – *Calcutta Telegraph*

'Joe Roberts is a happy wanderer in India. And the rougher the road, the more cheerful he gets. Yet behind the affection you suddenly realise his eye is remorseless … it is the eye of a kindly hawk' – Christopher Hope

'A thoroughly engaging and absorbing account of an innocent abroad' – Bel Mooney

The House of Blue Lights

'Charmingly laid-back. You can see already that Roberts, even when very nearly static, is a class act' – Patrick Skene Catling, *Irish Times*

'The seductive book, shining with observation is wonderfully funny' – Nicholas Wollaston, *Observer*

Joe Roberts was born in Bath, where he now lives with his wife and son. For seven years he lived in America, working as a bookseller in Manhattan and as a baker in Austin, Texas. Returning to England in 1984, he cooked in restaurants and worked for Waterstone's. He started writing in 1990, supporting himself by making pasta.

As well as *Three-Quarters of a Footprint*, his book about South India, Joe Roberts is the author of *The House of Blue Lights*, about coastal Texas, and most recently, *Abdul's Taxi to Kalighat*, his book on Calcutta. He has written also for the *Times* and for *Harper's & Queen*.

D0669301

THREE-QUARTERS OF A FOOTPRINT

Travels in South India

Joe Roberts

PROFILE BOOKS

This paperback edition first published in 2000 by
Profile Books Ltd
58A Hatton Garden
London EC1N 8LX
www.profilebooks.co.uk

Originally published in Great Britain by Bantam Press

Printed and bound in Great Britain by
St Edmundsbury Press, Bury St Edmunds

The moral right of the author has been asserted.

A CIP catalogue record for this book is available from the British
Library.

ISBN 1 86197 196 6

Contents

I have named each chapter after the appropriate Hindu lunar month. These months begin and end just before their Gregorian equivalents; Jaistha, for example, usually begins around 22 May and lasts until 21 June. From year to year there may be some variation according to the heavens. The names of these months differ, of course, regionally; the names that I have used are those used by the Trivedi family who originate from Madhya Pradesh.

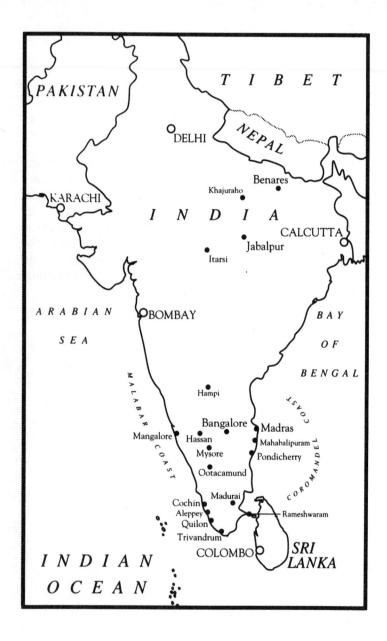

An Explanation

In the spring of 1990 I inherited some money and cleared my debts. Then I quit a job that wasn't leading anywhere and ended an affair that had grown burdensome. It seemed an appropriate moment to go abroad. I was drawn to Southern India. I'd seen a photograph of sailing barges on the Keralan backwaters; another of chillies drying in the sun, a bright crimson field. The fragments I'd discovered of Hindu mythology tantalized me. I began listening to the drifting transcendent music. Perpetually behind my interest was the hope of a dreamland. Friends assumed that I was on a religious quest (as people do when one mentions the East) but I don't think I had spiritual intentions.

I found out about a man in Woking who could arrange for me to be a paying guest with a family in Bangalore. Once I got there, I wrote letters and letters (I've never managed to keep a diary – the urge to revise hampering any progress) and most of this book is based upon those letters retrieved. Of course I've changed names. I've invented (perhaps 're-created') dialogue. Sometimes I've transposed members of families. I've juggled people and places and occasionally altered the sequence of events. This is primarily to preserve the anonymity of the originals (**my friends in India, to whom I owe the deepest gratitude and respect and to whom this book is dedicated**) but it is also because, when I started writing in 1991, I soon ceased to think in categories. If I'd been asked if I was writing a novel, I would have said that I was. Likewise a travel book. It was a book that I was working on and I just got on with it.

Jaistha

I travelled with Mrs Trivedi from Madras to Bangalore, overnight on the mail train. 'First class this time so that you are not overwhelmed.' It was my second night in India and I was already overwhelmed.

Madras Central Station, as large as any of the great London stations, was so crowded that one literally stepped over people to move forward – travellers who, despite the din, slept on the floor. It was like diving deep under water. Breathing became difficult; all one could think of was finding the right platform before the oxygen ran out.

At last we found the train. I was drenched in sweat and people were staring at me. 'It means nothing, you will be used to staring.' I must have looked strange, a dripping white man, taller than anyone else in the crowd, being led by a small Indian matron. Mrs Trivedi (educational publishing) was in her forties; just over five foot tall. Her hair was a neat bob, 'so much easier'. She had a light ('wheatish') handsome face with thick eyebrows. When she said something witty, she had a way of glaring comically – that was her smile. For a long time I kept asking myself who it was that she reminded me of, then I realized that it was Al Pacino. I didn't say so because it would have sounded rude and might have implied a masculinity in her appearance that would have been untrue; it was more the way a sister can resemble her brother, having similar facial muscles.

Mrs Trivedi disliked Madras, considered it a dirty city, 'a hotbed'. A hotbed of what? The word, like so many, had acquired different usage in Indian English.

Considering the original horticultural meaning of the word 'hotbed' – a bed of fermenting manure steaming under glass – I could see what she meant. I realized that Indian English wasn't something quaint but a language in its own right, like American English. It wasn't different because the Indians hadn't mastered an imposed tongue, they had, generations ago; it was different because it sometimes followed another logic. Indian English is full of felicities and poignant poetry. I was struck, for example, by the word 'unemployee'. An English worker is fired or laid off and he becomes unemployed, unaffiliated, faceless. An Indian worker, once an employee of a company, remains an unemployee of that company until another job comes along. A certain optimism endures, a sense of rightful position, the denial of uselessness.

There were our names printed on a sheet attached to the carriage door: TRIVEDI and ROBERET. Near enough anyway. Our compartment had four berths. The two other occupants were brothers, executives in the same construction company in Bangalore. Mrs Trivedi chatted with them; she asked where they stayed – meaning, I discovered later, where they lived – and they told her Whitefields.

'We hear there is no water at Whitefields.'

'That is what they report but we do not suffer so far. Later may be a different story.' One of them turned to me. 'Europeans always come to Whitefields, it is the home of Sai Baba.' I asked him about Sai Baba. Did he have many Indian followers? I knew that Sri Bhagwan Rajneesh was largely discredited by his compatriots. 'That is Rajneesh. Sai Baba has many, many, many followers. From all over the world, but especially India.'

'Of course,' the other joined in, 'these kinds of people attract controversy. They are in the same box as all public figures. Let me ask you, who has proved him as false? Newspapers have tried it. Nobody can say he is a fraud.'

'There is plenty of time to discuss Sai Baba,' said Mrs Trivedi sternly.

I took a handy-wipe from a packet I'd bought at Gatwick then offered them around. The brothers hadn't seen handy-wipes before and questioned me about them as if I was a representative of the manufacturer.

'How long will they last?'

'Is it pure eau-de-Cologne or diluted?'

'How are they impregnated?'

One consulted Mrs Trivedi. 'These could catch on? Something new. The fragrance, sandalwood or eucalyptus? What do you think?' Mrs Trivedi laughed teasingly. 'I think you are displaying the Indian mind at work!' As I became familiar with this sort of conversation I realized that many Indian men enjoyed dreaming up business schemes – and liked to think of themselves as entrepreneurs – but the brilliant notions generally went no further than the initial fantasy due to lack of capital.

The brothers slept on the upper berths, Mrs Trivedi and I had the lower ones. There were metal shutters that could be pulled down but we left them up. I couldn't sleep at first so I lay, listening to my Walkman and looking at the passing moonlit landscape. Whenever the train stopped at a station, men passed by with tea urns shouting 'chai, chai', and there were cows sleeping on the platform and figures stretched out like corpses, covered with grey sheets. Near the stations there were sometimes houses festooned with multi-coloured strings of lights like Christmas decorations. Then the train would be in open country again, boulder-strewn lunar wastes with mountains in the background and, long after midnight, a cool breeze started to blow in through the window and eventually I fell asleep.

The train stopped at a junction and, while we slept, a thief pushed a hooked pole through the bars of the window and stole Mrs Trivedi's bag. When she woke up and found that it was gone she was very upset, the lights were turned on and the compartment was searched. 'I can't believe it. I was even holding it in my arms,' she insisted.

'That is why I always close the windows. These thieves are very skilful nowadays,' murmured a brother who didn't sound particularly sympathetic.

'From my arms they took it! I must have been out for the count.' She turned the lights off again. Was there much in the bag? 'Money, very little, thank goodness. A cheque. That is no use to them. But there are things I can't replace. Some photographs, jewellery.' Her voice trailed away and she rested her head against the wall. The brothers had gone back to sleep and I could hear that she was crying. Because I didn't know her well, there wasn't much that I could do so I pretended to be asleep.

It was five in the morning when we got to Bangalore and Mrs Trivedi's son, Atul, was waiting for us in a taxi. It was his eighteenth birthday. He wasn't much taller than his mother and had a chubby face, the same thick eyebrows and a flat-top haircut. He wore a loose bowling shirt and baggy jeans and trainers. He greeted us and I noticed that he spoke with a slight American accent. When I commented on it, he seemed pleased. 'Los Angeles.'

'That was ten years ago,' said his mother dismissively. 'All the young people talk so. It is the influence of videos.'

'Do you like watching videos?' asked Atul. 'I can get the good ones.' Later he asked what I thought of Guns 'n' Roses. 'That is my kind of music. That and Aerosmith and Metallica. Sometimes I prefer soft. Then I will listen to Billy Joel or Michael Bolton.'

We drove through the wide quiet streets, past parks and Ulsoor Lake. What I saw of Bangalore was more modern than Madras, it resembled an American city.

'The fastest growing city in Asia,' Mrs Trivedi said but it looked much quieter than Madras. 'Madras is too crowded,' was Atul's opinion.

'Think. What is the time? Would you expect it to be busy at half-past five?'

'It's much cooler here.'

'Yes, it is cooler. We say Bangalore is a no-fan station.'

Major Trivedi was waiting at the gate. 'Welcome to your home in India!' He was a slim middle-aged man. That morning he was wearing a knitted dicky (the neck part of a roll-neck sweater) under a shirt of green and white handloom cotton (*khaddi*). He had a very straight back (he joked about 'ramrod posture') and a long thoughtful clean-shaven face. The Major's eyebrows were as thick as his wife's and his nose was fine and sculptural with flaring nostrils. It always struck me as a medieval face, he looked like a monk or a king's adviser. Sometimes he resembled a Shakespearian actor – I don't mean that he was in any way mannered or self-conscious; the pauses that he inserted between utterances gave his conversation a dramatic resonance. Quite mundane statements were somehow invested with grandeur while the lines of poetry that he was fond of quoting assumed true magnificence. He was the most dignified of men and incapable of petty or low behaviour.

(The Trivedis were Brahmins; one didn't expect to find military Brahmins but there was Major Trivedi, the son of Colonel Trivedi, married to Mrs Trivedi, a colonel's daughter. Surely the Kshatriyas were the military caste? When I asked the Major about this, he smiled patiently. 'Nothing is as fixed as you think.') Mrs Trivedi had told me that her husband had left the Army for reasons of ill health; in his twenties he'd fallen from a horse and a nerve had been pinched between two discs of his spine; it had been painful but not considered a serious injury. One morning, nearly a decade later, he'd woken up and, with no forewarning, found himself completely paralysed (a nightmare straight out of Kafka). He was in military hospitals, in and out of operating theatres, for two entire years. When the family moved to America he underwent more surgery in California.

'He is a brave man,' his wife told me, 'never has he complained of pain. There are some who cannot even bear a headache.'

Was the pain constant? 'Now not so much. But for years it was very horrible for him. Newcomers see him and have no idea what he has been through.' I don't think I would have guessed; he did move around slowly but it seemed more out of choice (a reflection of his contemplative nature) than disability. I got on very well with Major Trivedi; he was very scholarly and his great interest was history, specifically history repeating itself. He was still the official archivist of his regiment. The textbook-publishing business he'd recently set up with his wife occupied most of his time but in the evenings he liked to sit and chat. Some of his views were eccentric. He followed a strange dietary regime, a combination of Ayurvedic and European nutritional theories, strictly avoiding 'stimulating' foods. The list of these forbidden stimulants was a long one, it included tea and coffee, eggs, red meat, fish, chillies, most pickles, sweets, a wide variety of fruit; other foods were less harmful but not to be combined. Often he dined on curds and rice, sometimes a gelatinous gruel called *sat isibgol* or fleaseed husk.

The area of Bangalore where the Trivedis lived was called Bhagpur Extension, a recent development (or 'colony' in the Indian parlance) built along a stretch of the airport road; apartment buildings, some one-storey dwellings, the occasional larger house; a bazaar, a post office, a temple; small businesses: *darzis*, barbers, cafés, motor workshops, tiny kiosks that served as general stores and a pharmacist called Abishek Medical Hall.

The concrete structures, as square as children's toy blocks, were not attractive in themselves but the sunlight and palm trees improved their aspect; tradesmen's boards, enormous painted advertisements and political graffiti enlivened the drab texture of the walls and the individual embellishments of various householders (a pair of stucco columns, perhaps, or a moulded balustrade) did much to relieve what might have been architectural monotony. Drying saris fluttered like banners from balconies. There were water-towers and pylons.

Pedlars and costermongers pushed barrows through the streets, hawkers of every description went from door to door, children played; cows, buffaloes and goats grazed the scrubby verges or plunged their heads into the circular concrete rubbish bins; pariah dogs scratched and slumbered through the day to reclaim the streets at night in savage disputes over sex and territory. There was film music, the sound of television, the noise that crows make, traffic grumbling on the airport road and raised voices, often laughter, in the background.

The Trivedis inhabited the ground floor of a four-storey block of flats; the ground floor was considered the most desirable. An iron fence and a narrow border of garden, mostly paved, encircled their property. Against the wall, beside the front door, was propped a square terracotta roof tile bearing the impression of a long narrow foot, like the handprints of film stars outside Grauman's Chinese Theatre. The footprint was incomplete, the edge of the tile ran through the heel; what there was extended across the tile from just above the lower right corner towards the upper left. The roof of the Trivedis' building was flat and asphalted though other buildings in the neighbourhood had tiled roofs – therefore I assumed the tile to be placed beside the door for superstitious reasons and for months I pondered over the symbolism of the three-quarter footprint; I had seen blue handprints on walls and horned demonic scarecrows guarding building sites. It was rather disappointing to discover that the tile was simply an *objet trouvé*. Visitors tended to leave their chappals in front of the tile before entering the flat.

Over the front doors of some of the neighbouring houses hung strings of dried mango leaves, a predominantly Southern custom that the Trivedis, as transplanted Northerners, ignored. Nevertheless their threshold was decorated with white chalk patterns, *rangoli*, applied daily by the ayah, Anasuya, a local woman who considered their design a part of her general housework. The Trivedis had little idea what the markings signified as all Anasuya would say was 'lucky'. The designs were rarely, if ever, repeated and she insisted that she'd learnt each one as a girl, they were never improvised; swirling loops overlapping, intricate tracery, usually symmetrical.

One entered a living-room that ran the length of the apartment. A kitchen led off to the right at the far end. To the left ran a small passage with one shelved alcove behind a curtain and another alcove that served as a shrine – where joss-sticks smouldered under soapstone representations of deities. Off this passage were two bedrooms, whose windows faced the front and rear, and a bathroom, whose tiny high window faced the side. The living-room was simple and uncluttered with a linoleum floor and plain white walls, lit in the evening by flickering neon tubes. There were four low rosewood armchairs, box-shaped, with square beige cushions. Next to Major Trivedi's tidy desk stood three grey filing cabinets and above it hung two paintings by his wife: a turbaned officer in dress uniform and a green landscape under a gathering storm. There was an alcove in the living-room, broader but shallower than the two in the passage, with sliding glass doors, that housed souvenirs: framed photographs and certificates, typed poems, mementoes such as a pair of china Disney chipmunks and a linen tea-towel depicting a leprechaun with 'May The Road Rise With You' in green Celtic script and a border of shamrocks. Just outside the kitchen was the dining area: a circular table, four chairs and a dresser. The plates and beakers were made of stainless steel.

At the back of the living-room was another door that led outside to a shady yard, a banana tree, a tall papaya and a cubic tank for rain water. In the strip of flower-bed between the fence and the path grew hardy plants such as mother-in-law's tongue, members of the *Agave* family, their dark glossy leaves coated with fine red dust.

Atul's bedroom, where I would sleep (Atul himself unrolled a pallet in the living-room), was like the study of a sixth-form boy at a boarding-school. The walls were decorated with pictures, cut from magazines, of Western pop stars and sports cars. Against one wall was a desk and some shelves. On the top shelf were some bronzes of deities. Underneath were two shelves of school books and another of 'leisure reading' (books on cars and aeroplanes, the *Limca Book of Indian Records*, other works of reference, joke books), several rows of cassettes. A home computer, a stereo system and, against another wall, a large grey metal cupboard, its doors covered with decals and bumper stickers. This cupboard, called an *almyrah* (a word of Portuguese origin), contained clothes and valuables and was always locked. The bed was a thin mattress which was rolled up during the day; it was covered by a quilt called a *razi*.

Anasuya made us breakfast. I had a boiled egg, some chapattis and jackfruit pickle. There were tiny intensely flavoured bananas. To drink there was very thin coffee. Mrs Trivedi asked, 'Do you have bed tea at home?' I said that I sometimes made a pot of tea or coffee and took it back to bed with me.

'Here Anasuya will bring it. In the North we call this *chota hazri*. It started with the British. You see, *hazri* is

17

really an offering to a god, like *prasad.* I suppose the servants felt that bed tea was an offering to the sahib, to put him in a peaceful mood.'

All day long Atul's friends popped in to wish him a happy birthday. Only boys came as it was customary for teenage girls to be chaperoned. The boys used somewhat archaic slang, expressions like 'smooth' and 'ace'. Mrs Trivedi was right about their 'American' accents but what struck me most was how ruly and unrebellious these teenagers were; their clothes were tidy, they didn't smoke or drink, they were respectful to their elders (addressing Major and Mrs Trivedi as 'Uncle' and 'Auntie') and generally seemed too clean-cut to be real, like the students in advertisements for bank accounts. Atul's friends dropped by to play computer games – Atul was usually the winner – or to hear the new Phil Collins tape or to read *Archie* comics and, later in the afternoon, one brought a video. It was a pirated tape of *Honey, I Shrunk The Kids*, a juvenile choice, I thought, for a group of eighteen year olds, but it was a great success. Even Major Trivedi enjoyed it. 'You see, it refreshes the soul to return to the world of childhood.'

That evening the Trivedis had a small party. I presumed it was for Atul's birthday but Major Trivedi told me it was an informal gathering for no particular reason. 'We run an open house.' A schoolfriend of Mrs Trivedi's called Arun Dandapani, a manufacturer of photographic equipment, was visiting Bangalore on business from Jabalpur. His wife, Syreeta, was with him and his two young sons. They arrived at seven. Atul took the little boys off to play Space Invaders. Syreeta went into the kitchen with Mrs Trivedi; they were preparing *bhel poori*, the snack that is sold from carts all over India, and a favourite meal of Atul's. It seemed a strange birthday dinner. Later I discovered that Mrs Trivedi forbade Atul to buy *bhel poori* on the street (though he often disobeyed this edict) so this was a special treat.

Arun – who was knowledgeable about a range of subjects, none of which particularly interested his host – sat and talked about current affairs. The Major steered the discussion to the writings of Nostradamus. My opinion was that the prophesies were too vague. Arun agreed. The Major insisted that it was necessary to acquaint oneself with the imagery. Drumming the arm of his chair, he intoned solemnly: 'First the call of the unwelcome bird will be heard from the rooftops ... bushels of wheat will rise so high ... men will devour their fellows.'

Arun looked alarmed – which was no doubt the Major's intention – and, turning away from doom and eschatology, started to talk about India's relationship with other countries. I hadn't been aware of the tension between India and the United States.

'It goes way back to the 1960s,' he told me. 'We know now that with America there is always something hidden behind whatever gesture is made. You may remember that Johnson and Mrs Gandhi fell out.'

The Major refused to be drawn into this digression and kept on with Nostradamus, quatrain after quatrain; he had the most extraordinary memory, I'm sure that he wasn't making them up.

A widow called Mrs Sen arrived, with her teenage children, Ajay and his sister Suchie, who talked for a while (Suchie had been to England) then went into Atul's room. Mrs Sen was about fifty and the author of textbooks for very young children. She had brought a square cake with blue icing. She had darting eyes and large, very white teeth that caused her to whistle a bit. She sat beside me and spoke in a conspiratorial whisper. From her interrogative manner, I could tell that she liked organizing people. 'What plans have you made?' she hissed. I replied that I had arranged to use the Trivedi household as a base from which to explore Southern India. 'That we understand. What I want to know is, where first? There is no time to waste.' I told her that I was going to sit down with a map and a guidebook the next day. 'At what time?' Off the top of my head I said ten o'clock. 'Then I will be here.'

Major Trivedi declaimed, '. . . the coast will be deserted from Monaco to Sicily . . . no cities or towns will the barbarians leave unpillaged.'

Arun coughed. 'Do people in UK still read Maugham?'

Suchie told me her impressions of England. 'It was small and very pretty. I didn't like the food. Oh, Cadbury's I liked but that was all.' Ajay, coming into the room, sniggered. 'That is so typical of her!'

'What about Jerome K. Jerome?'

Atul said that he could get another video. Mrs Trivedi, who was putting steel bowls on the table (little puffed *pooris*, rice crispies, chopped onion, chopped potatoes, green lentils, herbs, various chutneys and tamarind water seasoned with sulphuric salt) said that one video a day was enough. 'But, Auntie, it is his birthday!' protested Suchie. The three teenagers went off to the video shop which was just around the corner. The two little boys were quietly going through Atul's collection of comics.

Major Trivedi declared that, '. . . the plains of Ansonia, rich and wide, will spawn so many grass-hoppers that the sun will be clouded over . . .'

Mrs Sen and Mrs Trivedi drew up a month's worth of excursions for me. Mrs Sen brought a large envelope stuffed with brochures. Maps were spread on the dining table. The names of hotels were found in my *Lonely Planet* guide. Down to the hour, itineraries were planned. Major Trivedi said that Mrs Sen would make a great military commander.

So the first trip that I made was a Karnataka State Tourism Development Corporation tour to Sravana-belagola, Halebid and Belur. It meant starting early and returning late in the evening.

I'd been in India less than a week and had mild diarrhoea, nothing to worry about – a couple of Lomotil would sort it out. Mrs Trivedi packed me a picnic of bland food; boiled eggs, bananas, delicious curds and rice, Horlicks biscuits. Major Trivedi told me not to drink anything except coconut water, 'nature's electrolytes.'

I set off from Badami House, the tourist bus station in downtown Bangalore. There were three children begging with notices that they thrust into one's hand. The printed notices, the same in each case, said I AM A DUMP. I AM BORN WITH OUT TONGUE IN THE MOUTH. They opened their mouths to display the little pink stubs – it was clear that these children had been mutilated.

The journey to Sravanabelagola was a long one. I noticed how red the soil was. Trees at the roadside had white bands painted around their trunks. We passed a lorry, loaded with people who waved at the bus. 'Are they farm workers?' I asked the man sitting next to me. 'They are poor, heading for new life in the city.' It rained a little. 'Monsoon,' said the man and I thought how anticlimactic the monsoon was if that was typical.

Sravanabelagola is a celebrated religious site for Jains[1]. Leaving my shoes at the ticket booth I walked barefoot up the 600 steps of Vindhyagiri Hill. On the way up I passed various medieval Jain temples (or *bastis*). Old pilgrims were carried up the steps in covered litters called *doolies*. The doolie-wallahs raced up and down the steps, their passengers looked terrified. The majority of those making the climb appeared to be tourists rather than serious pilgrims; there was a lot of stopping and laughing and puffing; it was a muggy day. At the top of the hill there stood a colossal statue, a 57-foot-high image of a saint, Lord Gomateshwara[2]. The statue was strange, monolithic

See *Notes* on pages 315–348

and quite unsettling, as if an extraterrestrial had been abandoned on earth. The silence became melancholy and there was a sense of time passing with agonizing slowness. A weird sad grandeur. The saint stood naked, an androgynous white giant gazing northward through the still white air. Vines twined around his smooth limbs, ending just below his shoulders in clusters of fruit. At his feet was a lotus; beside his great legs were ant-hills from which emerged serpents. His hair was a mat of flattened ringlets, the lobes of his ears stretched with large rectangular holes.

Halebid was once the ancient city of Dwarasamudra, the capital of the Hoysalas who ruled the area from the eleventh to the thirteenth century. Hoysala temple architecture is considered very fine indeed; they went in for double temples, like reflections or Rorschach's ink-blots, in dark stone. The temples at Halebid were solid, squat, polished buildings covered in a riot of the most intricate carvings: among them was Brahma sitting on a goose, Vishnu dancing with the skin of an elephant and, again, stamping on a dwarf, Krishna playing a flute. Literally thousands of dancers, hand-maidens, musicians.

Between Halebid and Belur it rained, seriously this time, for about half an hour. When we got to Belur the rain had stopped but the temples there, a compound of green chlorite buildings, were steaming – a sinister effect. We passed through a gateway lined with venerable beggars and people selling garlands of marigolds and little bags of fruit to be offered as puja. The outside of the temples positively crawled with tiny carved images (lions and elephants; lovers copulating; maidens beneath trees, gazing into mirrors or getting dressed; dancers; foot soldiers and horsemen; all kinds of deities and demons) and smelt like a swimming-pool. There was an old guide who jabbered a high-speed mixture of English and Kannada. Sometimes I could understand him, sometimes he went too fast.

'God is three, ha?' He raised three fingers. 'Three, ha, ha? What names?'

A woman answered: Brahma, Vishnu, Shiva; the Hindu trinity.

'Acha, ha! Governor! Operator! Destroyer! G—O—D, acha? One God, three names!'

Later the guide said that he had seen a boot, found near the temple, so large that he could stand inside it. The boot had gone to a museum in Delhi. It was proof enough to him that giants had inhabited the region. He also pointed out the image of a Poison Girl[3].

I went inside the sanctuary. The resident deity was Narayana, an incarnation of Vishnu as the son of Nara, the original man, the Hindu Adam. It was a noisy place. There were people with trays of fruit, flowers and coconuts that they handed over to the bare-chested priests, who took them away into the inner sanctuary as offerings. The priests returned half the trayful to the worshipper, having split the coconut by bashing it against the wall. The flowers and fruit were thus blessed and the priests kept the other half, decorating the deity with the flowers and eating the food themselves. You could give the priests money as an offering, which I did, then I cupped my hands over a little flame and the priest rubbed ash on to my forehead. On the way back to Bangalore the bus hit and killed a dog.

One of the framed photographs in the glazed alcove was of Major Trivedi, in parade uniform, leaning forward to shake the hand of a senior officer. The senior officer, barrel-chested and mustachioed, loomed over the Major. 'Who is this?' I asked.

'That is General Kapur, you must know of him, the hero of India's war with Pakistan, 1965? Kapur of the Uri-Poonch Bulge?'

'I was only seven years old.'

'All the same . . .' muttered the Major and he opened the sliding glass and took the picture out. 'If men of

Kapur's stature were running this country today! Soldier, of course, and swimmer, all-Indian crawl champion. Witty . . . a great talker always. Repartee for all occasions! I think I will move this to my desk.' General Kapur was evidently the beau ideal of Indian soldiery. Major Trivedi smiled at the photograph. 'Old Crashy! He must be getting on now.'

Mrs Trivedi had found some green cloth, gauzy cotton similar to cheesecloth, and asked if it would be of use to me. 'There is enough for a shirt certainly, maybe pyjamas.' I said that I would like a shirt. 'Then let us find Mr Prakash.' Anasuya set off in search of the *darzi*. Mr Prakash was a thin man with an embarrassed expression who knew very little English. He measured me and said to Mrs Trivedi that he would make me a shirt exactly like the one he was wearing, a skin-tight tapered affair that would have looked awful on me. So I gave him one of my own shirts to copy; it was ready the next day and cost less than a pound.

On Sunday the Trivedis had a visitor, a big shapeless scowling man wearing an olive-green safari outfit. The visitor wore a wig that wasn't well fitted, a poor-quality nylon-strand toupee, tilted like a hat. He had an unusual dark-grey complexion and bulging eyes with a green tinge to the whites. All in all, he didn't look very well. His arrival, which was unannounced, caused a stir. Mrs Trivedi stooped and touched the visitor's feet. Major Trivedi displayed the greatest courtesy.

The visitor sat and drank coffee. He was like a leader of organized crime, the way he inspired fearful respect. I asked Atul, who'd retreated to his bedroom to use his computer, who the visitor was. He answered, 'Nagaraja Naidu. A real big shot. He has headed government committees here in Bangalore.' I asked if he was a politician. 'Not a politician. He is somebody the politicians must consult. Fingers he has in many, many pies. So it is the same.' I asked what he was doing in Bhagpur Extension. 'He stays near here. This is his neighbourhood. Sometimes he comes. My parents like him.'

'You know that's a wig, don't you?'

'Oh yes. Sometimes he goes without it even.'

Nagaraja Naidu wasn't very friendly. He wouldn't speak to me at all and didn't say much to the Trivedis either. He just sat, without smiling, in the Major's rose-wood chair. I noticed too that his feet were irregular: one was wide and blunt and the other was much narrower and pointed; this might have been because he was wearing very shiny, probably hand-made shoes – it is perfectly possible that irregular feet are normal and the symmetry of mass-produced shoes is misleading. He seemed to be chewing something but when he opened his mouth there was no red staining to indicate betel – the chewing might just have been a ruminative habit, his inner cheeks were probably hardened with calluses; along with his grey skin, his odd feet and reptilian eyes, it made him seem creepy, almost inhuman. Nagaraja, I worked out, meant Cobra King. Although the visitor didn't resemble a snake, the name suited him. I imagined him commanding a secret army of snakes.

Mrs Trivedi said that her brother was about to arrive. Nagaraja Naidu gestured his approval. I went back in to talk with Atul. 'Your uncle's coming?'

'Yes, Uncle Vijay. He is passing through. He's in the Army.'

An hour later, Uncle Vijay arrived. There was a striking family resemblance – he looked exactly like Al Pacino. As soon as he was introduced to the Cobra King he became very tense and deferential. Uncle Vijay told the visitor that he'd been in Sri Lanka. This interested me so I asked Uncle Vijay about the Indian army's presence there and he snapped at me. 'Do you think I would tell you, a foreigner, what we are doing?'

I hadn't realized that I was touching on military secrets.

Nagaraja Naidu stayed for another hour and the Trivedis grew more and more tense. I thought he was a most exasperating guest, a thoroughly unwelcome presence. He had a way of curtailing every attempt at conversation while he sat and brooded. Eventually a young man knocked on the door and said that he had come to collect him and, when Nagaraja Naidu left the flat, the relief was palpable. 'A very great man,' said the Major and Mrs Trivedi said, 'It is an honour that he chooses to visit us.'

'What a big shot,' said Uncle Vijay.

'He looked ill,' I said.

The Major shrugged. 'Yes, he has had bad luck with his health in the past.'

Mrs Trivedi served a wonderful rice pudding, with almonds in it, called *khir* and Uncle Vijay loosened up considerably and turned out to be a most talkative and funny man.

Much later, perusing Dowson's *Hindu Mythology and Religion*, I came across an entry for Naga. Besides meaning the Hooded Cobra, it was the name of a 'mythical semi-divine being, having a human face with the tail of a serpent, and the expanded neck of the cobra'.

The Trivedis' bathroom took some getting used to. There was a small wash-basin with one tap. There was a Western-style lavatory but the cistern was kept empty so, before one could flush, it was necessary to turn the stopcock until there was enough water. There was a tap at heel-level just beside the lavatory and a small plastic bucket: water for one's left hand. Paper was considered insanitary. 'Think about it. Does it clean at all? No, it just smears.' Many Indians were horrified at this disgusting Western practice. There was neither a bath nor a shower but a tap over a sloping tiled area leading to a drain. On the floor was a red plastic stool and a large plastic bucket and a little jug. If you wanted to wash thoroughly you took a bucket of hot water into the bathroom (Anasuya would heat it in the kitchen) and blended it to the right temperature with cold water from the tap. Then you sat on the stool and poured the water over yourself with the jug.

I caught the night bus for Mangalore. It left from Badami House and, even as late as ten o'clock, the 'dump' children were there. The bus pulled out at ten-thirty. I had an aisle seat near the front next to a man with a peculiar physique, like a reflection in a distorting mirror: a small head on a thin neck, narrow shoulders, but everything expanding from the chest down so that, in effect, he appeared conical. Each of his thighs was the width of a normal man's torso – it was like sharing my seat with an extra passenger.

Across the aisle sat two boys wearing disco fashions who smoked – though it was forbidden – all the time that they were awake. They both had haircuts similar to Ian Botham's: layered on top, close-cropped at the sides, with a thick hank bobbing out at the back. One wore a T-shirt that said: *This little cat is rough and tough but inside my heart is filled with love.*

Most people went to sleep immediately. The windows were clamped shut. I tried to sleep but couldn't. My seat wouldn't tilt and the movement of the bus was erratic and the horn kept sounding. The smoke from the disco boys irritated me. It was horribly stuffy. The inflatable neck-pillow I'd bought (but not used) for the plane was no use at all; it might have provided some comfort if it had been possible to lean against something but the only option was to lean against Cone Man – who was himself leaning against the sweating window and thrusting his enormous buttocks towards me – an altogether unpromising arrangement. I decided to give up the attempt and put a cassette in my Walkman, *Sun Label Rockabilly.* I looked out of the windscreen, the only unfugged window. The driver enjoyed racing trucks. There weren't defined sides to the road. Many vehicles were unlit. I never even saw a set of traffic lights. At every crossroads it was a game of chicken. I saw brothels, mean hovels indicated by single red light-bulbs, with trucks parked in front of them. Just outside Hassan we stopped at a level crossing and there I saw another of the houses festooned with Christmas lights. Two musicians (at least, men carrying musical instruments) were going in. I decided that those places must be honky-tonks.

The other side of Hassan the bus stopped for petrol and there was an all-night *chai* stall. An albino lunatic accosted me, circling and gibbering, gesticulating wildly. He was a spectral figure, dressed in a winding-sheet; I never worked out if he was begging. All through the encounter I was listening to Jerry Lee Lewis performing 'Crazy Arms'.

I worked out that we'd reached Coorg; for hours on end we descended towards sea level. Down and down we went, zigzagging through the dark, until dawn broke. We were in a thick forest. With daylight came the rain; not the soft drizzle with sporadic downpours that I'd expected but great glassy walls of water through which the trees defracted and shimmered like marine vegetation.

I got off at a place called Kankanaddy, stepping into a marsh. Within seconds I was soaked through. I'd never seen such rain, it was just as if someone was emptying great tanks. I managed to get an auto-rickshaw to take me to Ullal. The absurdity of heading for a beach resort struck me as I sat shivering and dripping. The rickshaw-wallah took a circuitous route, not from dishonesty but because many of the roads proved impassable.

The motel Mrs Sen had recommended was a compound of cabins among palm trees, deserted and steadily flooding. I asked the receptionist, who wore an oilskin cape, if the rain was likely to ease off. 'Sir, understand. It is first week of rains, what we expect.' A bearer in a clear plastic Tyrolean hat showed me to my cabin. There was a slight leak in one corner of the living-room, otherwise it was fine; I thought what a pleasant place it would be in better weather. I lay down and fell asleep to the sound of the swimming-pool swaddling out across the lawn and, further off, the churning Arabian Sea.

I woke up at lunch-time, feeling quite hungry. The path to the restaurant pavilion was a deep red stream. The food was excellent. First I had a peppery soup called *rasam*. It was the only thing on the menu that I'd ever heard of. After the *rasam*, I ordered at random; there were no descriptions given of the dishes. I chose *karkumbuda puli koddel*, a sort of pumpkin curry with lots of grated coconut, rice dumplings called *pundi* and raisin chutney like fiery Branston pickle. A crow, fluffed out by the rain, begged at my table.

I asked the receptionist about going to Udipi, a temple further up the coast. He didn't think it was possible. Not even by taxi? 'Sir, if they take you they'll charge you much more. Understand, flood waters damage engine. First week of rains.' I realized that I was marooned. Would I be able to get back to Bangalore? 'That should not pose a problem.' That afternoon I wrote letters and read a book by Thomas Love Peacock. The electricity kept failing.

Early in the evening I heard a muezzin's call. There were many Muslims on this stretch of coast, the descendants of Arab traders or of those converted by them[4]; the Moguls hadn't reached these parts. And, miraculously, as the muezzin wailed, the rain stopped. I decided to walk into town. It meant skirting great lakes. I passed a warehouse that stored *bidis*, the tiny laurel-leaf cigars. A half-painted (I should think abandoned) advertisement for Usha ceiling fans. Men strolled together hand in hand, skipping nimbly over puddles. Rickshaws were parked in a line and the drivers sat and smoked and joked while lissom adolescent boys pranced from one lap to the next with peals of shrill laughter. At a bazaar women sold dried fish. Schoolchildren surrounded me and asked me for pens. A teenage girl said 'silly buggers' and her companions covered their mouths in amused disbelief. There was a woman selling twisting snake gourds and ridge gourds (*peeree* in the local Tulu dialect) and the small aubergines, called *baigan* in Hindi, she called *badan*. It started to rain again so I dashed back to the rickshaw rank and found a driver who could be torn away from the catamitic flirtation. A doe-eyed Ganymede, clad in green nylon pyjamas, called after us as we sped towards the motel. That night I had an egg curry with coconut (*tethi paladya*) and *pooris*.

The next day the rain was worse. Most of the time there was no electricity at all. A woman in old-fashioned football boots, several sizes too big for her, came to sweep my room. 'Ginger biscuit,' she said, meaning, 'change your bedsheet.' I asked the receptionist to reserve me a ticket on the bus to Bangalore but the telephone was dead so, at great expense, a boy was sent into Mangalore to make the reservation in person. I had a splendid lunch of bitter gourds in a mustard seed sauce (*kanchala gasi*) and finished *Headlong Hall*.

The whole town of Mangalore was blacked out, the bus station lit by candles and battery lamps. I had a window seat this time. I was prepared for another sleepless night but found myself drifting off easily. We stopped at a café in the forest; film music boomed out through the rain. The café was run by tribals, dark-skinned men stirring cauldrons of mutton stew and dhal. I bought some biscuits, ate a couple, then fell back to sleep.

At five in the morning we got to Bangalore and, when I reached Bhagpur Extension, Major Trivedi was up and about. He rose early as a rule, well before dawn – when the milkman came down the street shouting *'pol, polloo!'* – and spent an hour in prayer. 'How is your stomach?' I said it was fine, that the food had been the high point of my trip. He puckered his lips and breathed through his nose. 'Just take it easy, my friend.' After he'd finished praying he made some tea. 'What did you make of Udipi?' I told him that I never got beyond Ullal. He shook his head sadly. 'What a pity you gave in so easily.'

Just before lunch I was sitting outside the Trivedis' flat, on the narrow patio, writing another letter and enjoying the sunshine – there had been some drizzle but nothing compared to the coastal weather. The ironing man, called the *ishtri*, was working our section of the Extension; his iron was huge, a Victorian museum-piece that contained hot coals, and his trolley was an upholstered table on wheels. Ayahs and housewives brought piles of clean laundry out to him and, for a few rupees, he'd return them pressed and neatly folded. He did this round once a week, the rest of the time he worked at his house which was just along from the temple. Anasuya often carried a basket of rumpled clothes over to him. I passed the *ishtri*'s house most days. Sometimes his wife and mother sat on the step, oiling, combing and plaiting one another's hair. His wife often wore a green turmeric preparation on her face. '*Haldi*,' explained Mrs Trivedi, 'so that her skin glows', but it looked strange to me.

I was used to the various vendors who passed the house and knew their cries. The onion man shouted *'Erulli! Beliulli!'* The rag-and-bone man shouted 'Batlee! Pie pie!' (only later did I realize that the cry was in English). The man who sold toys squeaked a half-blown balloon to make a noise like a parrot's squawk; it certainly attracted children but I never saw him sell anything. So I sat writing my letter and the ayah from next door (a grinning Spanish-looking girl

31

with flashing eyes, like a painting by Russell Flint) came out and stood, with her hands on her hips, flirting with the *ishtri* and around the corner came two musicians leading an ox. One carried a drum and the other a *shehnai*, a long reeded pipe. The piper wore a scarlet puggaree, a large loose turban. The ox looked very pretty with a shiny orange cloth on its back and a decorative bridle; its horns were bound with different coloured ribbons and had little bells on their tips. I gave them some change and the drummer started drumming and, once a rhythm had been established, the piper joined in with a series of very random-sounding blasts (like 'free jazz' or the way James Brown plays keyboards on instrumentals – without a melody as such, just 'statements' above a riff) as if he was testing the drummer's tenacity. Little by little, between them, they found a haunting 'Arabic' tune and, when they both knew its twists and turns and variations, they sped the whole thing up. The next-door ayah clapped and swayed and broke into a little formal jig and the *ishtri* clapped and I clapped too and tiny children came out to feed the ox with slices of fruit. Major Trivedi came to the door smiling and wagging his head and told me that I must marry an Indian girl and have a traditional wedding.

There was a good deal of construction going on in Bhagpur Extension, it was by no means complete. The men on the building sites were the rural poor who came to the city – and building jobs in particular – to make ends meet; a similar situation to the Irish labourers in Britain. They wore khaki shirts undone over vests and checked lungis doubled above the knee like short kilts; an old towel might serve as a shawl or a headcloth. The women who worked on the sites alongside their husbands wore hard hats and pastel saris, a bizarre combination. The younger clerical workers and shopkeepers wore tight white shirts, fitted slacks and chappals. The garments would be made locally, possibly by Mr Prakash, and there was a deliberate attempt to 'move with the times' that, because of corners cut, failed, giving the clothes a tatty, disposable look. Much smarter were the outfits of the older men; some wore kurtas and dhotis (starched and tied formally so that they formed loose tubular pantaloons) and, in the early mornings after cool rainy nights, coarse woollen waistcoats. These older men carried umbrellas – whatever the weather – and had great dignity. The real dandies were Atul and his friends – the gilded youth of the airport road – who wouldn't have looked out of place in a Californian shopping mall. Some of their notions were strange: jeans with three pleats at the waist and an inset pleated panel from the knee to the hem, snow-bleached jeans with suede patch pockets. Because designer labels weren't readily available they dreamt up their own variations on a Western theme – there were certain hip tailors around Brigade Road who could be trusted – or relatives travelling abroad brought back a longed-for shirt or a pair of trainers. There was a branch of Benetton in Bangalore and a very trendy boutique called Wearhouse. It was harder for teenage girls to be quite as fashionable; the restrictions were greater and the *salwar-kamiz* was pretty much *de rigueur*. A few wore long dirndl skirts, a 1950's High School look. Some girls did wear jeans, I even saw a denim miniskirt. Tracksuit bottoms and loose over-sized sweatshirts were a safe bet, keeping the basic idea of a *salwar-kamiz* but nodding towards a Western image as well. These girls carried themselves in a curious way; an almost boneless flop was the ideal deportment. Whenever and wherever it was possible to lean (backwards or forwards, propping one's head against a wall or one's spine on the side of a door) they would, rather than stand unaided.

There was a pan stall on the airport road and sometimes after dinner I'd go there to buy three sweet pans. Mrs Trivedi and Atul liked an after-dinner pan and I had acquired the taste. The Major considered pan-chewing a bad habit but tolerated our indulgence. The pan-wallah (a jokey man who called me Mr Johnny, I've no idea why) would spread a paste of powdered lime and water on to the open betel leaf, scatter slivers of betel-nut, green cardamom seeds, coconut, sweet rose-petal jelly, aniseed, a little tobacco. He'd fold the leaf into a neat triangular parcel, held in place with a clove. Sometimes there were bits of silver in the mixture. You put the parcel in your mouth and chewed and all the flavours would run like Opal Fruits. Betel is supposed to be mildly stimulating but I never noticed any effects.

A pi-bitch that lived at the end of the Trivedis' street had whelped just before I'd arrived. The local children played with the four puppies, carrying them around; they were like beagles to look at but a deep chocolate brown. The bitch put up with the children but wouldn't let me near her offspring; I was too obviously a stranger, too tall and too pale. One of the puppies gashed the top of its muzzle. It was a nasty wound. I suggested to Major Trivedi that we call a vet. 'A vet would not come for pi-dogs. These dogs are nearly wild. Who do they belong to?' I could say they were mine. The Major waved the idea way. 'Believe me, a vet wouldn't come.' Later, when the subject came up again, he said, 'The mother will lick the wound clean. These animals are tough. Look at how they survive!' But the puppy's muzzle swelled and his eyes began to weep pus and he got thinner and looked very ill. I spoke to Mrs Trivedi. She said, 'I could take you along the street to a child even that is dying, his parents are too poor. This side of life you must get used to.'

I'd brought a blue Lacoste shirt with me that Atul admired so I gave it to him. He was very pleased. 'You can tell this is a real Lacoste,' he said, 'because the alligator is small. Pirated versions, they make it so big – this is a real one,' and he put it on immediately. Whenever he looked in the mirror he had a special expression. He'd raise one eyebrow and turn up the corners of his mouth; nothing as definite as a smile, just a suggestion of amusement. Atul asked me if I liked Arnold Schwarzenegger. I didn't much. 'He is a great star,' Atul insisted. 'Do you know how much money he has made? Lakhs of millions!' He confided in me that he would like to be a film star. I told him he should go to Bombay. 'Not in India. Not Hindi movies. Hollywood!' He thought it would be easier to break through in the American system. I wasn't so sure. 'No, no. You tell me, how many Indian stars are there in Hollywood? None at all. So I go there and I corner the market, it's that simple.' Had he done much acting? 'A little, it's not so necessary. It is business you must know. That is Schwarzenegger's secret – he knows business. And, you tell me, is Schwarzenegger American even?'

The rest of that day Atul wore the shirt. He visited friends and he went down to Commercial Street. I asked him later if the shirt had been a hit. He was slightly nonplussed. 'Do you know, all the time they are saying it is fake? The alligator is so small for them. I said, "This is real," and they ask me, "Then why do they make the alligator that size?"'

I was going to the jungle beyond Mysore to stay at a nature reserve. I'd booked it all from an office in Bangalore. They'd arranged everything, including a car to pick me up from Mysore. I took the morning train to Mysore, then waited for a Mr Bhose at the Metropole Hotel. The Metropole was the sort of hotel that one expects to find in India but, in fact, rarely does. Threadbare but still functional, it was straight out of a Paul Scott novel; there was an atmosphere of wartime India – the last and somewhat austere days of the Raj, when jazzy American touches like cocktail bars and floodlights were creeping in; it was easy to imagine men and women in uniform, dancing to gramophone records, in the high-ceilinged dining-room but when I ate lunch there, beneath a faded portrait of the Maharajah of Mysore, I was the only guest. There was an aged and nervous waiter, who poured sugar syrup into my lime soda even though I'd asked for salt, and an hysterical *maître d'hôtel* who was unnecessarily angry with the old man, then apologized profusely to me, wringing his hands. I had a greasy Hyderabadi biryani and some rubbery naan bread and an ice cream called 'cake roll' and some thin black coffee, not a very satisfying meal.

Mr Bhose had arrived and was waiting in the lobby. He was a small neat man smelling of roses. He looked up at me and, smiling sweetly, said, 'Please just relax. Everything is seen to.' A driver would take me all the way to River Lodge whenever I was ready. I said that I was ready. 'But you have not relaxed yet,' said Mr Bhose. 'Why not take it easy for an hour?' I said that I'd rather make a move and that I could relax in the car but Mr Bhose just smiled at me as if he was a nanny dealing with a recalcitrant little boy.

An hour and a quarter later the driver arrived. I said goodbye to Mr Bhose who held both my hands (I noticed that his own were immaculately manicured) and sighed. 'There, you see how much better it is to be fully relaxed.' Soon I was leaving Mysore in the back of a small grey car. It was a lovely day. A warm, light breeze (that, I believe, is called a *loo* in Hindi) played through the trees and I decided that a private car was the best way to travel in India. Having said that, a lot depends on the driver. Mine was a moody young man with pitted skin who was extremely keen on sounding the horn. Ox-carts, strolling elders, goatherds and their flocks, all were alarmed by loud continual blasts of at least a minute's duration. Still, the frondy trees looked very pretty. The people resting under shade trees and the farmers with their white oxen ploughing the rice paddies and the peasant women in their colourful and billowing saris gave the scene an Elysian quality, like a painting by Watteau. I felt that I could put up with the blaring horn for the rest of the journey. After some time, and when I thought that we should be getting near River Lodge, I asked the driver when we would reach the jungle. He raised his eyebrows at such a stupid question. 'Sir, can you not see? All around it is jungle!' I was taken aback. I suppose I had been expecting a rain forest. What I saw was just uncultivated land[5], almost less 'jungly' than an English wood. But then we turned off the main road and on to a *kutcha* track and the trees did get denser. We passed through bedraggled villages. The driver pronounced their inhabitants to be 'very, very backward'. I saw a wild peacock. The driver pointed out a herd of spotted deer. So it was a jungle but a jungle of little trees and dappled glades; I half-expected to see a unicorn. I certainly couldn't imagine tigers or even elephants in such surroundings. Were there such creatures in this part of the jungle? The driver raised his eyebrows again. 'Many, many, many!' he snapped. I think that I seemed backward to him as well.

River Lodge had been a nineteenth-century Maharajah's *shikar-ghar* (hunting quarters), a cluster of red-brick nineteenth-century buildings like a school. I walked down to the water's edge and found a circular pavilion and, inside, a party in full swing. Some middle-aged men, in lurid double-knit leisurewear, were getting tipsy on Indian 'Scotch'.[6] Their wives and teenaged children were drinking Limca and Gold Spot. Everyone was laughing and jolly. Trays of snacks were passed about: *wadas*, *bhajis*, samosas and bowls of mix. I was offered a soft drink and invited to join them. I talked to a girl called Padmashri who described herself as 'American-born', a student at Boston University. She was staying with relatives in Mysore. It was her first time in India. She told me that she was beginning to understand her parents; ideas that she had assumed to be neurotic in a North-American context (obsessive cleanliness, a whole set of taboos concerning food and personal hygiene) she now realized were cultural. The party, Padmashri explained, was a public relations exercise. A successful wholesale fruiterer had invited some valued customers and their families to a picnic. It had been going on for several hours by the time I got there and was drawing to a close. A coach had already arrived to take them all back to Mysore. We were joined by her cousin, a very tall young man with a head no bigger than a mango. His name was Vinny and he was a student of literature and philosophy at Mysore University. He had an irritatingly smug expression. 'English? Then you do not like music, you only like the sound it makes, am I right?'

'Are you fond of debate?' he asked me, seconds after this introductory sally.

'Aw, c'mon, Vinny, it gets so tedious!' groaned his cousin.

'It is not you that I am asking, Padmashri, it is our friend from the UK.'

'Don't,' she warned me.

'You may choose any subject. The existence of God in the light of modern science, perhaps, or American foreign policy?' I told him that I wasn't in a debating mood. 'Then you are surely fond of riddles?' He was a determined fellow.

'Yes,' I answered, more politely than truthfully.

'Acha! You are indeed lucky for it is my hobby to invent riddles!' Padmashri was fed up. 'Jeez, this guy is such a nerd.' Vinny called for silence. 'I must think for a moment.' The whole party, including the whisky drinkers, froze in anticipation. Vinny's expression grew even more irritating. He screwed up his eyes and scratched his tiny head. 'Yes, yes, yes,' he announced, 'I've got a good one for you. Are you ready?' I nodded. 'Very well. Tell me, please, what is the heaviest substance in the world? So heavy that even Hercules cannot hold it?'

'I don't know, what?'

'Shit,' he cackled. 'Not even Hercules can hold shit!' Vinny's parents and their friends chuckled proudly. The joke was translated into Kannada and into Hindi and successive waves of restrained applause ensued but the only real laughter came from Vinny himself. Padmashri just scowled and muttered, 'That was so dumb.'

Colonel Bridgewater drove up in a jeep. I'd heard that an amazing English 'character' ran River Lodge, a true *burra* sahib. He turned out to be a stout elderly Eurasian with curly dark eyelashes and a fine waxed moustache, dashingly dressed in a camouflaged flak jacket and a knotted silk scarf. I got into the front next to him. Also in the jeep were three lawyers from Bangalore – Mr Chellaram, Mr Daryani and Mr Lakhani, keen photographers with expensive equipment around their necks. There was a very dark Tamil who was a professional jungle guide. His name was Sonny and, confusingly, he called Colonel Bridgewater 'Daddy'. The Colonel had two distinct ways of talking. To the Bangalore lawyers and Sonny he spoke Indian English, similar in rhythm and accent to Major Trivedi's. But when he spoke to me he used a very old-fashioned English English, soft and clipped and precise, like a voice in a black-and-white film. There was something unconvincing about his conversation when he used the English voice. 'Bath, eh? Oh, yes, I know it well. Just down the road from Hereford, what? Weren't at All Hallows, were you? I knew a chap there called Roberts. Great rugby player. Played for England Schoolboys. I expect that was your father.' Colonel Bridgewater had attended Blundell's in the 1930s. Those schooldays had been his only experience of 'home', as he called it. He'd been cold and unhappy and hopeless at every subject except games. I don't think he realized how much British life had changed since the war. Although he hadn't known my father, it turned out that he had known an uncle of Mr Chellaram's so they chatted happily in the Colonel's Indian mode. 'Those were Calcutta's golden days. I tell you. The Three Musketeers, everybody knew us as. It was Bridgewater, Chellaram and Croaker Singh. What trouble we would cause!' We were moving further into the jungle. There were lots of uprooted trees, like jumps for horses, that apparently signified elephants. We saw several monkeys, both macaques and langurs. Sonny was standing up in the back of the jeep, looking through binoculars. Every so often he'd whisper 'Daddy, to the left' and the Colonel would stop the engine and peer through a pair of opera glasses. He would announce something like 'chital' or 'sambar' and the lawyers and I would click away. It was dusk by now and beginning to drizzle. We saw wild boar and enormous bison that stood at least seventeen hands and then we came across a herd of wild elephants. They were making a terrific racket. The herd consisted mainly of cows and calves but there were a couple of tuskers, one of whom objected to our presence and, trumpeting ferociously, charged towards the jeep. It was quite alarming but Colonel Bridgewater did something that I thought most impressive. Raising one palm, he spoke firmly to the furious giant. 'Now just stop it!' he said. 'Don't be so silly!' And the tusker, reprimanded, turned and skulked back to the herd. Sonny was shaking his head and giggling and, for a moment, I wondered if the display of sang-froid had been staged. But, of course, it couldn't have been. We drove to a place where a tiger had been observed earlier in the week. We waited and waited but, alas, in vain. Sonny climbed out of the jeep and found a pug. The tiger had passed by about an hour ago. Altogether we were in the jungle for nearly three hours and when we returned to River Lodge it was dark.

* * *

I slept very well. A bearer woke me at half-past six with a pot of sweet milky tea. At seven the jeep arrived. Sonny was taking us to a lake to watch birds. He recited a rapid litany ('Great black woodpecker, serpent eagle, honey buzzard, grey-headed fishing eagle, pied hornbill, cormorant, teal, duck . . .') that sounded like a menu. Mr Daryani whispered in my ear, 'If you don't mind me saying, my friend, it is my opinion that your camera is not a good one.' We drove through a stretch of jungle and when we got to the lake there were some men with two leather coracles, as round as bowls, to row us out on. The lake, in the soft morning light, was serene. Dead trees stood in the water and, on the bare branches, were hundreds of species of birds, all colours and sizes, but, as Sonny drove away after dropping us off and the coracle men spoke no English and the lawyers were more interested in photography than ornithology, I can't tell you any more than that. I expect the average visitor to River Lodge was more familiar with the serpent eagle and the honey buzzard than I was. Mr Chellaram spotted a crocodile which he called a 'mugger'. I looked where he was pointing but saw nothing. Breakfast was served in the pavilion – *pooris* (puffed bread) and *aloo sabzi* (potato curry) and sweet white coffee from an urn. After breakfast the lawyers departed for Bangalore.

Later that morning I went back into the jungle, with Sonny, to a camp where trained elephants were used for hauling timber. Sonny had arranged for me to ride one. This meant sitting on a sack-cloth blanket on the animal's back, behind a mahout. The mahout was a toothless old soldier wearing a puggaree and a gossamer-thin but lovingly ironed parade uniform and a row of medals. He saluted me before I climbed the step-ladder that one used as a mounting-block and then, when I was settled, talked to me (I guessed about the provenance of his medals) in what I presumed to be a dialect of Kannada, without seeming to mind (or perhaps not realizing) that I couldn't understand a word he was saying. We lumbered off, swaying rather, and I could feel the elephant's backbone beneath my bottom, a bit uncomfortable. The old soldier spoke to the elephant, a cow called Swati, from time to time as we trundled along and seemed to be actually saying 'mahout, mahout, mahout' in a peculiar voice, as if 'blowing a raspberry' and talking at the same time. He carried a metal steering implement with which he gently tapped Swati behind either ear. An elephant calf, called Beauty, followed us as we shuffled through the undergrowth. When the ride was over I got into the jeep. In the back was an otter in a small cage. There was a bloody wound on its back. It had been fighting over territory with another otter and Sonny was moving it to a different stretch of the river.

I sat on the verandah reading *The Castle of Otranto*. Two ayahs were sweeping the tiles in a dreamy manner and chatting in pretty giggly voices. Suddenly they fell silent. A tall and very dark woman, wearing a black pyjama outfit was approaching. She was middle-aged and had a sinister manner, like an Ian Fleming villainess. Parting her lips to reveal several gold teeth, she said, 'So, you are Mr Roberts.' I stood up and smiled at her while she gestured to the ayahs to get on with their work. 'I am Mrs Bridgewater. Your room is, I hope, to your liking?'
    'Oh, yes.'
    'So you have no complaints?'
    'None at all.' She burst into loud wheezy laughter. 'Lunch, Mr Roberts. Come along.'

At lunch (a curious meal – chicken curry and roast potatoes) I sat next to the Colonel. First we talked about dogs; his two retrievers were lazing on the lawn. We had a most interesting conversation about the East India Company and its army. The Colonel's ancestors had been in India since the early eighteenth century, generation after generation; mostly as soldiers, to a lesser extent as planters. He told me that an ancestor of his had fought in nearly every battle that had taken place on the subcontinent. Sometimes (because before the mutiny there had been no stigma attached to taking a native wife and still wasn't as far as the Bridgewaters were concerned) on both sides of the conflict. Sonny asked if I found the food too spicy. I said that I was used to chillies, that I ate plenty of them at home. 'Ever been to Veeraswamy's?' asked the Colonel. I replied that I hadn't but knew that it was one of London's oldest Indian restaurants. 'Used to be good,' he said.

'Veeraswamy is a Tamil name,' Sonny told me.

We heard a woman shouting in the kitchen. 'My wife,' explained the Colonel sheepishly, 'she's telling the cooks that she ordered rice not potatoes.' Sonny shook his head sympathetically. 'Can't say that I mind in the least,' murmured the Colonel, after a pause. 'I love spuds.'

I returned to Walpole. Three monkeys chased across the lawn, up into the branches of a tree, then clattered across the verandah roof. One of the Colonel's dogs, who'd followed me back to the guest quarters and was now dozing at my feet, looked up and barked half-heartedly. I thought of my own terrier at home and how thrilled she'd have been at such a disturbance. The ayahs were lying down outside a room they had just cleaned. The softest possible rain was falling. I felt like drifting off myself, it was so peaceful. But, just as I'd put the book down, the calm was shattered by a Klaxon playing 'Happy Birthday To You' and I saw a car, decorated with coloured streamers, pulling up. The guests to replace the Bangalore lawyers had arrived: they were two couples, both newly wed, and the husbands were brothers, close in age, weedy and anxious looking. The older brother had a streaming cold. One of the wives was short and plump and pretty in a doll-like way, wearing a salmon-pink sari. She smiled a lot and I guessed that she was responsible for the Klaxon. The other wife, a few years older, had a rash on her forehead and looked fed-up. She wore an electric-blue *salwar-kamiz* and a white knitted cardigan. I never managed to work out which bride was which brother's. They told me that they had had a double wedding in Poona. Their honeymoon was mainly being spent in Ootacamund with this trip to the jungle as an additional treat.

Colonel Bridgewater didn't take to the honeymooners at all. He warned the women that their outfits were too bright for the jungle twilight. The husband with a cold was staying in his room. The younger husband wanted to bring a portable tape player so that we could listen to film songs as we drove along. Colonel Bridgewater coldly explained that it was out of the question. Sonny, following Daddy's example, was disdainful and off-hand with them, answering their questions in a curt manner and quashing any attempts they made at general conversation. I felt sorry for them. We certainly saw less than we had the day before. This might indeed have been due to the colours the women were wearing which, in the crepuscular gloom, seemed almost fluorescent. We saw some chital and, a long way away, a retreating elephant, surprisingly well camouflaged for such a huge creature, and we heard, but didn't see, a barking deer. We were able to get close to a herd of nilgai but the wife with the rash started to scream hysterically and the herd scattered. The Colonel, I could see, was livid but too polite to say anything. The waxed tips of his moustache quivered. The other wife burst into uncontrollable laughter. The embarrassed husband put his arms around each wife in turn. 'Please, I am most sorry.' There was a frosty silence for a moment and Colonel Bridgewater said, 'Do not mention it,' and turned the jeep back towards River Lodge.

There was a powercut, 'load shedding' as it's called, and it was raining. Dinner was served in the pavilion by the light of a smoking fire. The food, fried chicken and stodgy rice, was cold and tasted of petrol. The honeymooners weren't having any dinner so I sat there on my own. I went to my room and tried to read by candlelight but found it difficult. So I blew out the candle and decided to have an early night. At one in the morning the power came back and the light went on and woke me up. I had to get out of bed to turn it off. I was amazed at how noisy the jungle was! Ticking, whirring, chattering, hooting. I lay back down thinking what a strange place I was in, how far from anything familiar, and it was as if I was a swimmer who suddenly realizes how far from the shore he is and panics. I felt myself being swallowed by a great whale of loneliness. That was the first time in India that I felt homesick. But it wasn't true homesickness, more of a general self-doubt. I wondered if I really liked the country and, if so, enough to stay until October? Could I cope with the people? They were pleasant enough and kind to me and much politer and more considerate of each other than people at home . . . but who could I talk to and, more to the point, laugh with? The Indian sense of humour seemed completely incompatible. I wondered if I'd ever get used to the squalor, the beggars, the flyblown pi-dogs and the ghastly fæcal smell of the streets. And then I considered the myriad inconveniences and inefficiencies of everyday life, the difficulty of making a telephone call or buying a railway ticket, for instance, or the days without running water, and this line of thought made me feel disappointed in myself. Such gloomy considerations led to a general malaise and I found myself unable to go back to sleep. I tried to read but couldn't concentrate so I turned the light off again and gave in to depression and the hours whirred and chattered by and soon the bearer was knocking at my door.

It started to rain just after dawn and, by the time the driver arrived to take me back to Mysore, it was bucketing down. The journey back was unpleasant. The driver was as surly as before and just as obsessed with sounding the horn. 'Listen, there's no need to make so much noise.'

'Then you would like me to run over a child, is that it?'

'Don't be ridiculous. I just don't think you need to sound it so often. Or for so long. That's all.'

'All right, sir. I will abandon caution and hit all I come across. That is what you would prefer.' There was no point in continuing the argument.

In Mysore bus station I gave a beggar a packet of glucose biscuits but he wanted money and went on bothering me. I found my seat on the bus to Bangalore. It was next to the window. A man selling sandalwood souvenirs came to the side of the bus and tapped my arm. '*Beda*,' I told him, which is Kannada for 'go away.' My rudimentary Kannada amused him and he tapped my arm again with a wooden elephant. '*Hogo*,' I told him, which is stronger. He cackled and whacked me hard on the elbow. I'd had enough. 'Just fuck off,' I said in English, which he did. The bus was crowded. A little girl sat beside me and, within ten minutes of leaving the bus station, was sick on the floor. I felt utterly dejected.

I was pleased to see the Trivedis though and there were some letters waiting for me and, towards the evening, my despondence lifted. Atul had rented a video called *Look Who's Talking*. Kirstie Alley was in it; I liked her, she was funny and sexy, the best combination.

Asadh

Dr Lal, a sericulturalist, was returning to Bangalore after more than a year abroad. Most of the time he'd spent in the United States and Central American countries like Colombia and Panama, but he had attended conferences in England and Japan as well. His was the flat at the very top of the building. The Trivedis were excited about Dr Lal's return. Major Trivedi informed me calmly that the doctor was a very great man. I was getting rather accustomed to great men by this point. Mrs Trivedi told me that Dr Lal was divorced. That was certainly unusual. 'It is very sad,' she said, 'that such tragedies are happening even in India now. It is, without a doubt, the influence of America upon our society.' Atul told me that 'Dr Lal is often visiting America. He is well known in New York.'

'United Nations,' specified the Major proudly, straightening his neck and flaring his nostrils. 'He is the man to solve America's drug problem.' But surely a sericulturalist is an expert on silk? What does silk have to do with narcotics? All three Trivedis looked at me as if I was very dim. Major Trivedi was the first to say anything. 'You are surely familiar with the slogan *Cocoons Yes, Cocaine No*?' I had to admit that I wasn't. Atul was astonished. 'But it is even on T-shirts. There are badges! Bumper stickers!' The Major explained that Dr Lal's mission was to persuade the coca-growing nations to turn instead to silk production. 'But silk isn't an addictive drug,' I reasoned feebly. 'Not an addictive drug, no, but certainly a luxury product. Research has proved that it is because of its expense and its luxury status that many American people are attracted to cocaine to begin with.' Mrs Trivedi warmed to the theme. 'These people have so much money that it is just shoot-shoot-shoot.' (I thought that she was referring to guns, or possibly hypodermics, but she made a gesture like somebody dealing cards very quickly.) 'That is the real foundation of their problems.' Major Trivedi flared his nostrils again. 'We must agree, my friend, that it is a country full of *nouveaux riches*. Let them spend their money on silk.' I wasn't convinced.

Dr Lal joined us for dinner that evening. His hair gleamed with oil and he was extravagantly scented. Atul recognized the fragrance. 'Old Spice,' he noted appreciatively, savouring the vapour. Dr Lal was quite tall and as wheatish as Mrs Trivedi herself. A puffy Chinese face. His clothes were an advertisement for silk: a sumptuous iron-grey suit and a cream shirt, a dark-blue shantung tie. 'You have put on some weight,' remarked Major Trivedi. The doctor had a very protrusive stomach but the rest of him was slim. Mrs Trivedi and Anasuya had prepared a special 'non-vegetarian' meal. We had green chilli chicken, *kheema*, bitter gourd, *bhindi*, curds, rice and chapattis. Custard apples that looked like hand grenades. The Major unscrewed a bottle that was labelled Bangalore Wine; that was all the label said, like a jar of home-made jam. It was, in fact, a type of ruby port, a tiny glass was taken as an aperitif. We all sat down to eat. 'Go easy, my friend,' the Major advised the doctor, 'your stomach is not yet back to our Indian food.' He stuck to curds and rice himself but the doctor ate heartily. Mrs Trivedi asked, 'How is the American food, Doctor-Sahib?' Dr Lal slapped his pot-belly as an answer and everyone laughed. 'Which is better,' asked Atul, 'in your opinion, Wendy's or Burger King?' Dr Lal thought for a moment then gave a cryptic answer: 'I believe America is whatever you are looking for. It is there to be found.' Atul nodded, like the follower of a guru, absorbing some great wisdom.

After dinner (and pan) Dr Lal asked to use the telephone as his own had not been reinstalled yet. He wanted to reach a friend of his staying at the Taj Residency Hotel, an actress called Tiptoe who was filming in Bangalore. 'A star of many movies,' explained Mrs Trivedi – she dropped her voice – 'now more often the heroine's mother than the heroine proper.'

'An old friend of the doctor's,' said Major Trivedi. Dr Lal was having some difficulty getting through. The receptionist kept connecting him to the film's director, who was also staying there. The doctor grew impatient. 'It is not a man I am after!' Atul went out to get a video. He came back with an old Peter Sellers film, *Where Does it Hurt?*, which broke after twenty minutes. Dr Lal chuckled. 'Now I know I am back in India!' Mosquitoes kept biting me so I said good night and went to read on my bed, under the net.

When I saw Dr Lal again a few days later, he was wearing a pleated peacock-blue Mexican shirt and a Panama hat. He stood out against the scrubby grass and rubble. Had he been able to get hold of Tiptoe? The phrasing of my question caused a howl of salacious laughter. 'Oh yes indeed! Yes indeed!' He shook his hand from the wrist as if trying to work it loose and told me that his ears were still ringing. 'Such stories she tells me! Ouch, ouch!' Then he asked me what I presume was a riddle. 'Tell me, why does a woman talk so much? Because she has two mouths!' I smiled because I didn't want him to think me a prude but it wasn't particularly funny. The doctor was in a wild talkative mood and kept sniffing. 'Allergies, so much dust and smoke in the air.' A vendor passed selling jackfruit segments. I bought some and shared them with the doctor. 'These will remind you of England,' he said. I answered that I'd never noticed jackfruit for sale at home but I imagined it was available at certain markets, possibly Brixton. Dr Lal, who knew England well, corrected me; jackfruit was popular and widely available all over the country. 'In many pubs, you will find them. Pickled, in big glass jars.' 'Those are onions', I said, but he was adamant. 'Onions there are, I know, but also there are jackfruit segments. Jackies, they are known as. A pint of best bitter and some jackies.'

In England, did I know the town of Paisley? A town of outstanding beauty and great sericultural significance? Paisley's in Scotland, I told the doctor. 'Of course, of course, you are right. Before partition it was England but now it is Scotland. You are right.' I could see that the doctor's knowledge of British history was shakier than he'd have one believe. He sniffed loudly and changed the subject. 'Now you say fifty peas, don't you?' I didn't understand. 'Money. Now you talk of pounds and peas.' Before I could say anything, Dr Lal started to reminisce. 'Of course, I remember the old system. Pounds, shillings and dees. A cup of rosy lea for six dees.' Surely he meant sixpence? 'Such formality!' The doctor scoffed. 'In Paisley we were more relaxed. A tanner, we might have said. Six dees was more usual.'

Later that day Dr Lal sat drinking tea with Major Trivedi. The Major was riveted by the conversation and invited me to join them. 'Many famous people have been sericulturalists. This I had no idea of. For instance, Dr Lal tells me that President Eisenhower kept silk-worms. Did you know that?'

'Your Prince Philip! A most zealous sericulturalist.'

'There!' exclaimed Major Trivedi.

'Many of the Queen's dresses are made from silk produced in Buckingham Palace. Mulberry trees abound in London, do they not?' I nodded. 'And 90 per cent of them are the personal property of the Duke of Edinburgh. You must have known that already! No?

But it is well known, well known.' The doctor sniffed scornfully. 'Perhaps you are against the Royal Family?'

Mrs Sen was talking to me about ghosts. In rural Karnataka, she told me, the villages and paddy fields are full of ghosts, all kinds of spirits and demons. Certain colours are worn, dishes of specific food are offered, different measures taken to keep these *rakshasas* away. 'They are a problem,' she whistled. I asked where they came from. 'Sometimes they are unhappy spirits of deceased family members.' She told me that if an unmarried man dies he might choose to haunt a married younger brother; he'll make the brother's life miserable because he is jealous, his own life was 'never so fulfilled with happiness'. So when a bachelor dies it is customary for his spirit to be married, as quickly as possible, to an inanimate object, a water pitcher or a gate post. This marriage is intended to protect the living male relatives. Young men are, however, always at risk from *mohinis*, the wandering ghosts of unmarried women who search desperately for sexual satisfaction. They seduce and murder young men, leaving their bodies at the roadside or face down in the paddy. This, Mrs Sen assured me, was a fairly common death and a reason for boys to avoid drunkenness.

I found an easier way of making travel arrangements. There was a travel agency called Kamadhenu. Kamadhenu is the name of the original holy cow, it means 'the cow that grants desires'. The travel agents were three identical brothers who looked like pigeons. They always hedged their bets by saying it would be nearly impossible to find a place on such a train or bus (usually because it was a religious holiday) but they would see what they could do. That way, if they got you a ticket you were grateful and if they didn't, they had a good reason. Generally they managed to get me the tickets I wanted.

Mrs Trivedi was going to Hospet to visit a school that used their computer-training system and I was to travel with her by train and spend the day visiting the ruined city of Vijayanagar at nearby Hampi but, because of some difficulty, she had to cancel her journey at the last minute. 'All is not lost for I will give Atul my ticket and he can accompany you to Hampi. He has not seen it.' There was some concern as to whether Atul would be able to use a ticket issued in his mother's name but it was settled that he'd explain the situation to the ticket inspector. The journey was overnight. The train would get to Hospet at nine in the morning, then in the evening we'd catch another overnight train returning to Bangalore.

We set off for the railway station late on a Sunday evening. I was hesitant about going and would will-ingly have postponed the whole thing; I was suffering from diarrhoea, the worst so far, a strain too virulent for Lomotil to cope with; but Atul's enthusiasm persuaded me. The ticket inspector wouldn't allow Atul to use his mother's ticket so we had to buy a new one; our berths were quite far apart. Mine was a top berth and below me were two middle-aged men. I asked the man on the lowest berth, perfectly politely, if he'd swap places with me as I knew I'd have to keep going to the lavatory and didn't want to disturb their sleep by climbing up and down all night. 'It is against railway law,' he told me. 'This berth is allotted to myself only for the duration of this journey. That is the law, I'm afraid I have no powers to change it.' And, just as I predicted, I did have to keep climbing down. I did my best not to wake the other passengers but some disturbance was unavoidable. The train rolled and lumbered along. Squatting over the hole-in-the-floor loo was tricky and sickening. Indian public lavatories are nearly always vile, even those in decent restaurants (whereas domestic bathrooms are immaculate) and it took me a while to work out why they let them get so bad. It is to do with the caste system and 'pollution' laws; public lavatories are cleaned by *bhangis* (sweepers), the lowest of untouchables and very little concern is shown for them and their repellent livelihood. Something nearer contempt prevails. The attitude seems to be: what difference does it make to a *bhangi* whether you shit down the hole or on the floor? So there I would crouch, in the reeking hellish midden, swaying perilously, weakened and tired and miserable; then I would heave myself up to the very top bunk. 'Good God,' the man who couldn't change the law would mutter in exasperation and, within an hour, I was climbing down again. The two men got out at Bellary. I was exhausted. Stomach upsets wear one out with indignity – there's not much pain or fever involved but it's miserable to be ruled by one's bowels. I found Atul who'd slept soundly. I suggested that when we get to Hospet we check into a cheap hotel so that I could get a few hours' sleep.

Hospet was a dusty place. There were cycle-rickshaws instead of motorized ones. The town is famous for the Tungabhadra dam. We found a taxi which we commissioned for the entire day. Atul could speak good Kannada and was able to haggle with the driver. This naturally attracted a cluster of spectators. A wild-eyed old fakir came forward and opened his mouth for my inspection, as if I was a dentist; the interior was bright red from betel and his tongue was divided into two independent pieces. The driver took us to a Tourist Home. Atul ordered himself a slap-up breakfast while I feebly slumped on the bed. I asked Atul what he'd do while I slept. 'Don't worry about me,' he said. 'I'm going to look around a bit.' His breakfast arrived and I drifted off. When I woke up, about an hour later, Atul was chuckling over a stack of Asterix books. 'Did you buy all those?'

'No, no. I rented them from reception.' Starvation had effectively cured my stomach. There didn't seem much point in trying to sleep again now that I was awake so when Atul had finished the book he was reading ('Please don't hurry.' 'No, no. Many times before I've read this one.') we went down to find the taxi.

The Tungabhadra River, the colour of rust, that flows through Hospet also flows through the ruined city of Vijayanagar. The Tungabhadra was once called Pampa and was considered divine; Shiva himself took the river as a wife. The still active Virupaksha temple (also called Pampati in connection with the river goddess) at Hampi predates Vijayanagar and has drawn pilgrims for at least a thousand years. The region is rich with legend and history and the weird combination of the two that is an Indian common-place. In England, such a merging of verifiable fact and myth can be found in places like Glastonbury – in India it is everywhere. Partly it's due to a very diverse set of chronologies; calendars varied from kingdom to kingdom and events were difficult to date precisely; this vagueness allowed a good deal of fanciful historic interpretation and the interpreters of history were invariably priests with an outlook attuned to the divine and miraculous. The area is believed to be the ancient monkey-kingdom of Kishkindha. Kishkindha was ruled by the monkey-king Sugriva ('Handsome Neck'). At one point Sugriva was dethroned by his brother Balin. Rama defeated Balin and reinstated Sugriva as king. Sugriva, with his chief minister and general, the heroic Hanuman[1], supplied a monkey army to fight beside Rama in his war against Ravana, the demon-king of Sri Lanka. All this is, of course, recounted in the *Ramayana*. Just outside Hospet there was a village of tents, inhabited by people that I took at first to be migrant Rajasthanis. 'Lambadis[2],' said the taxi-driver.

The country was craggy; granite boulders every-where. The Vijayanagar rulers favoured this forbidding terrain because it offered natural protection, because building material was all around and because of the existing divine associations. When a city came into existence is hard to say; perhaps it grew around the temple as the modern village of Hampi clusters around the Virupaksha temple. A city called Vidyapuri (the City of Learning) existed which became Vijayanagar (the City of Victory) in 1336 when a sage called Vidyaranya appealed to two princes of the Sangama dynasty, Harihara and Bukka, to establish their capital there. Islam was sweeping down through India and Vidyaranya persuaded the princes that a great Hindu city would serve to defend their faith and culture. Vijayanagar flourished for nearly two hundred and fifty years; a wealthy cosmopolitan city. The central position on the Deccan allowed the kings to control the traffic of spices from the south-west and cotton from the south-east; both commodities had to pass through Vijayanagar to reach the northern markets. An enormous army was maintained and often hired out as mercenaries. The kings encouraged and sponsored any number of Hindu cults, tolerated Jainism and even, to a small extent, Islam. The great fourteenth-century Vedic scholar, Madhavacharya, was an early prime minister and used his influence to attract the most learned Brahmins to the city. Lavish festivals and processions took place; the most spectacular was the Mahanavami celebration, a great durbar when all the local chieftains assembled to pay their rents to the Vijyanagar kings; it lasted three days – there were parades, sporting contests, fireworks, armour-plated elephants and bejewelled camels. Visitors from Persia, Russia, Portugal and Italy acknowledged the splendours. The greatest king of all was Krishnadevaraya who ruled from 1509 to 1529. In 1565 the Vijyanagar army finally suffered a defeat at the battle of Talikota; a confederacy of Deccan sultans had the Hindu city ransacked and smashed; the pillaging lasted six months. 100,000 citizens were slaughtered.

The taxi took us to the Virupaksha[3] temple. A towering *gopura* (gate tower) formed the eastern gateway, 170 feet high, swarming with coloured sculptures. Krishnadevaraya commissioned this gateway in 1510. We went through and found ourselves in a colonnaded courtyard. In the middle of the courtyard was a temple with columns carved into prancing elephants.

In the shade of the colonnade was a real elephant, chained to a column. His dark-grey skin was decorated with painted symbols. He was eating bananas and didn't, to be honest, look particularly unhappy. I asked Atul if temple elephants were ever unchained. 'Oh, yes. Every day he would be brought here by his keeper. He doesn't stay.' We went inside the temple and did puja. It was busy in there. The priest was giving a *prasad* of banana *lassi* and we smoothed *tulsi* water over our foreheads. When we stepped out again Atul said, 'Perhaps you are really a Hindu.' I said I didn't think so. 'What I mean is just this life you are British but all your others are Indian. Why not?' The courtyard was suddenly full of chattering monkeys. We went into a separate chamber; it was dark in there and a chink in the stone wall let in a solitary beam of light. As this beam hit the wall it projected an upside-down shadow of the eastern *gopura*. 'So, you see, the principle of photography was known in India even in those days.' There was another *gopura* on the north and through that a large tank with steps going down to slimy green water. A priest sat on the steps reading a newspaper. Atul and I sat down as well. I asked if he'd ever considered becoming a priest. 'Never!' he answered sharply. 'You tell me, what kind of life is it?' We walked back through the courtyard and retrieved our shoes at the eastern *gopura*. I gave a few coins to the aged sannyasi who begged at the gates. 'Will you become a sannyasi, Atul?'

'Are you kidding me? You see, these are strict Hindus only.'

Major Trivedi had told me about the ideal Brahmin life, according to orthodox doctrines. There are four stages, called *asramas*. The first is Brahmacarya, the period of schooling and discipline; then comes Garhasthya, the period of active participation in society, the life of a householder; the third *asrama* is Vanaprasthya, retirement, when the bonds are loosened, the reins handed over; finally comes Sannyasa, the hermit's life, all worldly goods renounced.

At the Aspiration Stores, we bought cartons of mango juice and browsed through the books; I bought one called *Everyday Processed Foods of India*. We wandered up through the bazaar. Stretching beyond the bazaar was what would have been a great boulevard, the location for temple chariot processions. It was vaguely Pompeian. The ruins of merchants' houses were transformed into shanty dwellings. One building had become a makeshift café with a cardboard hoarding announcing BREAK FAST. FRIED EGG. FULL FRY EGG. HALF FIRED. We asked the taxi to wait while we wandered, following the course of the Tungabhadra, past the Kodandarama temple below Matanga Hill; it was on the site of this temple that Rama recrowned Sugriva. I asked Atul if he honestly believed in monkey-kingdoms, the *Ramayana* generally. Wasn't it all just allegorical, like the story of Noah and the flood? 'No, it is history. It seems unusual but that is because it has happened before our history begins. That you must understand.' There was another temple (the Narasimha[4]) and a swarm of monkeys and down at the riverside a party of dhobi-wallahs beating white garments against boulders. There was a cave with painted stripes emanating from the entrance. This is where Sugriva is supposed to have hidden the jewels that Sita dropped as she was being carried off by the wicked Ravana. Out of the cave came the weird split-tongued fakir that I'd seen by the station. The Vittala temple is fairly complete but inactive. There is a stone chariot. I couldn't tell if it was real or just a stone representation. There are pier-like structures; clusters of heavy columns joined together; these can be slapped to produce a sort of xylophone sound. Atul was keen to climb Matanga Hill and to see the view over the whole ruined city. He'd once seen a photograph taken from the summit and was keen to take his own. So we walked back the way we came and started to climb.

The hill is really an enormous pile of boulders, you have to scramble to the top. I stopped three-quarters of the way up. No food and very little sleep was making me dizzy and I wanted to rest. I sat on a ledge and Atul went onto the top. It was very hot and the sky was bluer than it had been for days. A vulture hovered – perhaps he thought I was dying? I felt peaceful and happy; I felt as if I could suspend my disbelief and believe that on this very mountain Sugriva and Hanuman hid when Balin took over Kishkindha. It was as if a cloth could be draped over modern India and this cloth was the stuff of fantastic events. The vast majority believed in those events. I could let myself. Atul said there was a temple at the top, dedicated to Virabhadra. Virabhadra is a terrible emanation of Shiva, springing from his mouth in anger; he has a thousand blazing eyes and a thousand legs and a thousand arms with a different weapon in each hand. Sharp tusks sprout all over his body. I asked how he was represented in the temple. 'It was just eight arms or so. I think. I didn't pay much attention.'

We went by taxi to the other side of the city. We saw the charming Lotus Mahal, the Queen's pavilion. Near by was a small temple, more of a chapel. It was covered in carved friezes depicting episodes from the *Ramayana*; it's known as the Hazara Rama temple (a thousand Ramas). There was an open parade ground with military buildings on one side and the great elephant stables along another. The stables were huge loose boxes, ten domed chambers where the elephants stood manacled. The chambers were linked by doors for grooms to pass through and there was an upper storey, reached by a central staircase.

We went back to the Tourist Home. Atul ordered a plate of fried chicken and settled down with the

Asterix books. I wrote postcards and fell asleep. When I woke up it was time to leave for the station. I drank some coffee and immediately had diarrhoea. At the station I saw the split-tongued fakir again and it occurred to me that he'd been on a day trip. I slept peacefully on the way back to Bangalore.

The Trivedis had a friend called Krishnarayan who ran a boarding-school near the Nandi Hills. Krishnarayan had suggested to the Trivedis that I visit the school and give a talk. I was hesitant – what would I talk about? Major Trivedi dismissed my qualms. 'Life in Mrs Thatcher's Britain, why not?' Mrs Trivedi had an idea. 'You could point out that the grass is not always greener.' I asked how old the boys were. 'All ages, eight to eighteen.' A few days later I met Krishnarayan. He was a charismatic man who'd taught Asian History at an Ivy League university. He was still quite young, in his thirties, and he spoke slowly and precisely to me, almost as if I didn't know English. He told me about the school. In America he'd met many Indian immigrants who felt that their American-born off-spring were being assimilated too quickly and were worried that these children ignored their own culture. Krishnarayan's idea was to start a boarding-school in India for the sons of the expatriates – a co-ed boarding-school would have been too progressive – following a curriculum that would be compatible with American university entrance requirements while stressing Indian history, religion and culture. The school had existed for five years but, as yet, no American boys at all had enrolled; currency regulations made the payment of fees almost impossible. Instead the school was attracting parents who wanted their sons to win places at American colleges.

'A straightforward factual lecture with room for discussion,' was what Krishnarayan wanted. So I went to the British Council Library on Saint Mark's Road and there I gathered a wealth of information and statistics that were just as new to me as I hoped they would be to the audience. I managed to turn the information into a short speech which I gave to Major Trivedi to read. He read it carefully and commented on it; I got the impression he was disappointed. He asked me several questions such as, 'What is your own view on that?' and, 'How would that affect your life?' Finally: 'What have you told me of yourself?' I defended my speech by reminding him that the subject was Great Britain not Joe Roberts. Mrs Trivedi read it and she looked disappointed as well. 'It is perfectly good as far as it goes but you say nothing of the problems. These boys should be told of racialism, for example.'

The school was in a very rural setting. The buildings – some designed by Krishnarayan himself – were influenced by Le Corbusier. Besides the private school, there was a free village school just by the gates; Krishnarayan was a progressive liberal and his idealism was infectious. I was shown around the school; we entered classrooms and I remembered visitors coming to the various schools that I had attended. It seemed a happy place. There were two hundred and fifty boys. The school uniform was a white kurta and chappals; some of the boys wore grey woollen sleeveless jackets, which seemed unnecessary as it was very warm. There was a school zoo; mainly birds and reptiles but there was a big sambar doe in a smallish enclosure. 'She will not stay here,' said Krishnarayan, 'we have nursed her back from sickness and she will return to the wild.' The sambar had frightened rolling eyes and very loose bowels, the floor around her was plastered with slurry.

I joined the boys for tea (a *wada* and sweet coffee) in the dining hall which resembled a pavilion in a world's fair. The boys wanted to discuss the World Cup. Many of them asked for my autograph, not because they assumed I was famous but because they collected autographs in the old-fashioned way, as a souvenir of friendship. The three members of staff that I met were younger than me. The art teacher, a Malayali called Mr Thomas, was interesting; he told me that it was difficult to be a painter outside Bombay, Calcutta and Delhi, there was simply nowhere to show your work. And even in those cities the galleries mainly sold art that tourists wanted; he told me the only way out of the trap was a scholarship to a Western art school with the possibility of establishing a reputation abroad. He was very knowledgeable about European and American painting. There was a music teacher who said that he liked Western folk music. I remarked that I'd often heard similarities between traditional Celtic music (as performed by the Chieftains or Alain Stivell) and Indian music – but what the music teacher meant by folk music was non-electric pop music, singer-songwriters. He mentioned James Taylor and John Denver, 'very gentle music'. A young woman with round steel-rimmed glasses taught English literature. She had a strong jaw and a battling nature. At first I took her for a radical of some kind. Then I realized that she was quite shy and that her questions were just questions, not the challenges they came out as. I stayed in the school guest-house. There were no screens on the windows and as soon as the sun went down I was attacked by mosquitoes.

My speech was after the evening assembly, which took place in an outdoor theatre. The boys sat cross-legged on the floor and the teachers sat on tiered seats at the back. The assembly started with the boys intoning a passage from the *Bhagavadgita* then, switching seamlessly from Sanskrit to English, they chanted (rather than sang) 'Lead, Kindly Light'. Krishnarayan introduced me. After I'd spoken for five minutes, the boys in the front got very restless. One called out, 'Sir! Be careful! There is a snake!' and there was – a thin red snake had dropped from the proscenium. It looked to me as if it wanted to be ignored but a teacher rushed forward and put it in a box. 'This is a good snake,' he told us, 'it is young, a tree viper. It will not poison.' I carried on and when I'd finished, the boys clapped and I asked if there were any questions. A hand went up. 'Sir, would you tell us about Alton Towers, please?'

Then a much younger boy asked, 'What is your height?'

Then another: 'Your weight, please, sir?'

The English teacher came to the guest-house holding a very ragged paperback, a collection of essays. She said, 'I hope I am not disturbing you, sir.' I replied that she wasn't and asked her to call me Joe. 'Well, Mister Joe, please. I would like to ask you if the Government of England still proposes cannibalism in Ireland.' It was clearly something that upset her. She was referring, of course, to Swift's 'Modest Proposal' and I told her it was intended as a satire. The English teacher looked puzzled. I said that Swift hadn't meant it seriously, that it was black humour. 'Acha, black humour. He thought the Irish were like Africans, therefore cannibals, acha.'

Not at all, I said and tried to explain black humour.

'But that is not amusing,' she stated flatly.

I wasn't doing very well. Eventually I just said that although the proposal was horrific if taken literally, for it to be taken literally wasn't the author's intention. 'Oh, but it is most logical.' I said that that was precisely why it worked as satire. 'Satire,' she repeated. It was a new concept.

I slept well but woke up with mosquito bites on both eyelids, making my face look weird and mask-like. A bucket of hot water was brought for my bath. At breakfast, the English teacher came to me even more puzzled. 'Mister Joe, are you telling me that Swift was not a human being? Or perhaps that he was sexually insatiable? If that is so, what has it to do with his proposal?' I had no idea what she was talking about. 'I found that word in the dictionary. It means a creature with long ears and the legs of a goat or it can mean the masculine equivalent of a nymphomaniac. Please let me know which is the case.'

When I arrived back in Bangalore the Trivedis were entertaining Dr Lal, his friend Tiptoe and Tiptoe's niece, a girl of nine or ten, called Sweetie. Dr Lal wore the trousers of his silk suit and a smart dark-blue shirt with pearl buttons; he looked handsome and relaxed and was much quieter than usual.

Tiptoe was extraordinary. She had a long mane of glossy hair and lots of gold jewellery. She wore a leopard-print *salwar-kamiz* and soft gold leather sandals. She was well into her forties and had an almost ghostly beauty – that is, her beauty was still a young woman's; it hadn't matured but it had survived stubbornly, fading very gradually, as if holding on just to torment its possessor. Tiptoe had great big eyes, made up like a raccoon's, and a perfect Cupid's bow of a mouth; in fact, she looked like Theda Bara. The Trivedis behaved as if Tiptoe's fame was incidental, the politest way in such circumstances. Dr Lal was besotted and so was Anasuya (a great movie-goer). Tiptoe smoked heavily, which was slightly scandalous, and had a loud rasping voice. She called Dr Lal 'Lally Boy'.

Sweetie was an Indian Bonnie Langford. Two plaits and a pink party dress. Atul asked her if she liked computer games and she turned her nose up and said grumpily that she'd prefer to watch videos. 'You must have *He-Man*? I want to watch *He-Man*!'

'Sweetie darling, don't be difficult. I want doesn't get, does it? What did I tell you?'

'If you can't say something nice, don't say anything, Auntie,' Sweetie recited in a singsong voice. Anasuya went out to buy vegetables. Tiptoe noticed the photograph on the Major's desk and asked, 'Is that my darling Crashy?'

The Major harrumphed. 'Yes, yes indeed, that is General Kapur.'

Tiptoe squealed with delight. 'He is such an old lovebird, isn't he?'

Major Trivedi coughed quietly, flared his nostrils and turned to Dr Lal.

Tiptoe told me that her dream was to act in a British film. 'With Roger Moore!' She crossed her hands across her heart and fluttered her eyelashes wittily, her head tilting backwards. It was a gesture I'd seen in Hindi musicals but Tiptoe exaggerated it minutely for effect. She hadn't been to Britain at all. 'Even just to go there would be fabulous. Shopping at Harrods, Buckingham Palace. Lally Boy,' she turned to the doctor and simpered, 'you could take me, couldn't you?'

'Oh ho,' he said, 'first you find me the money.' We talked about Ooty. I was going there in a few days. Tiptoe said, 'There is only one place to stay – the Fernhill. That is, if you want the real flavour. But they are spoiling Ooty, Major, don't you think?'

'It is a long time since I've been there,' answered the Major, still rather disapprovingly.

After some time Anasuya came back with the shopping. She must have told people in the bazaar that the Trivedis were entertaining a 'filmi'. A small crowd had gathered outside the house when Dr Lal drove Tiptoe and Sweetie back to their hotel.

The puppy with the swollen muzzle was now just a ragged fur sack and rattling bones. He had distanced himself from his siblings, occupying a stretch of roadside about 50 yards away. Sometimes he crept about wretchedly but most of the time he lay on the warm stones, tormented by insects. I couldn't bear to look at him. I knew it would be tactless to talk to the Trivedis. One morning the puppy was surrounded by crows and, realizing that he was dead, I felt a momentary relief; then I went back to wondering if I couldn't have saved him.

* * *

One afternoon the *ishtri* had just started his ironing, not far from the Trivedis' gate, when down the alley lumbered the Cobra King. The *ishtri*'s jaw dropped and he stopped ironing mid-sari. Nagaraja Naidu made a weird, almost feline, hissing noise and started reciting a list of statements that sounded to me like threats and the *ishtri* quickly pushed his loaded trolley away, back in the direction of the temple. Nagaraja Naidu continued this tirade until the *ishtri* was out of sight. It was an unpleasant spectacle. Anasuya was standing at the door and she nodded sadly. I wondered if the Cobra King was the local gombeen-man. I asked Atul if he was a money-lender. 'That I don't know. But, you see, many people have gone to him for help, all kinds. Nothing is free with such operators. He may ask for something, not money always, in return.'

I'd visit Gangaram's bookshop on M.G. Road. Mr Gangaram sold many imported books, including paperbacks that hadn't been released yet in Britain, at less than half the printed price. It was a big, disorganized shop but it was always possible to unearth something you wanted to read. In the bookshop I sometimes saw an American woman in a sari. She had grey hair full of pins and a sari didn't suit her; it was like material wound around an old wooden doll. She lacked the swaying grace of an Indian woman, her carriage was different. The American woman looked like Emily Dickinson and also like a nineteenth-century folk-art portrait; a solemn, plain, small face with intelligent, unfriendly eyes. She bought academic books – scholarly works on Hinduism and comparative religion – and novels by Iris Murdoch. Because she had a forbidding manner, I never spoke to her but Mr Gangaram told me that her name was Dr Stickney and that she was a university professor on a year's sabbatical. 'Do you know of Saccinanda?' I didn't. Mr Gangaram sucked the stem of his spectacles. 'It's near

Trichy, beside the Cauvery. Father Bede? No? I am surprised.' I asked who this Father Bede was, assuming he was a missionary. Did he run a hospital? 'Oh, no, no, no. You have the wrong end of the stick. This Father's a sannyasi. A Christian monk who has embraced the Hindu ideas. Saccinanda is really an ashram. He's not a missionary, he's some kind of mystic. An old, old man now.' Mr Gangaram said, 'I may be wrong but I believe this lady is writing about Saccinanda. That is what I can gather. She does not chat.'

Sometimes I'd take my book and sit at the Indian Coffee House next to the offices of the *Deccan Herald* or Chit-Chat, a swanky joint with a marble fountain. Near Chit-Chat there was something called the Bangalore Ham Shop. It didn't look like a delicatessen. The dusty windows were boarded up but there were always customers, usually young men, going in. I asked Major Trivedi if it was a ham radio shop. 'No, no. It is the actual meat. There are those with the taste. This ham shop is famous state-wide.' Then I might look at the papers in the British Council Library and have samosas or potato *wadas* for lunch at K.C. Das.

From time to time the Trivedis employed a typist called Asunta. Asunta was nineteen years old, tall for an Indian girl and very dark skinned. A sloping forehead, a weak chin and bulging cheeks gave her face a formic appearance – but her large sparkling eyes and shy smile made her a very pretty giant ant. Asunta arrived early in the morning, around seven, and would stay until four. She invariably wore pink and black – Elvis Presley's favourite colours, I told her, but the name meant nothing to her – sometimes a *salwar-kamiz*, more often a sari. Asunta called Major and Mrs Trivedi 'sir' and 'madam' and worked quietly and thoroughly in their presence, sitting at the dining table, tapping away on a 1950s typewriter, triplicate letters on onion-skin paper with dusty black carbons between each sheet. The letters were single-spaced with ragged right margins, words (as short as 'many' and 'even') were broken in two and hyphenated on to the next line, her spelling was disastrous. As soon as the Trivedis left the flat Asunta relaxed, the typing slowed right down and long giggling conversations with Anasuya and me occupied her time. Asunta was a Roman Catholic ('RC,' she told me and I misheard her, thinking she said 'Parsee') but she decorated her brow with a *tika* mark like a Hindu woman. I asked her about the *tika* mark and she told me that only a red mark had religious significance, black was purely cosmetic; hers was, in fact, a stick-on patch. I told her that eighteenth-century Englishwomen wore velvet patches. 'This Madonna? That is, you think, such a patch?' One day she wore a larger patch decorated with a silver cross. Indian Christians have arranged marriages but the suitor has to be approved by the prospective bride. Asunta's parents were trying to find her a husband – without much success. Asunta repeatedly found fault with her suitors. Whenever I saw her I asked her if she was engaged yet.

'He was too fat for me.'
'They think I will marry such an old man!'
'His breath smelt eggy!'

I travelled to Ooty, via Mysore, by super-deluxe tourist bus. From Bangalore to Mysore it followed much the same route as the train: Ramanagaram, Channapatna, Maddur, Mandya, Srirangapatna; a lot of the way the road and the railway line ran parallel but the bus passed right through the towns and countless villages and the places became more than names on the map or the painted signs on platforms. From time to time the bus stopped at roadside cafés where one could buy *idlis* (cakes of fermented rice) and *dosas* (pancakes), drink coffee from a cloudy glass or the juice of a tender coconut. A tall Sikh, in a light-blue turban and matching shirt, approached me. '*Ich möchte mich mit Ihnen, bitte, auf Deutsch unterhalten.*' I was forced to plead ignorance of the language but he remained convinced that I was German. 'Don't you believe that I know German well? Five years I have studied.' I told him that I'd taken French at school. 'That you have studied in England I can tell. *Ihr Englisch ist gut, fast fliessend. Wie Sie feststellen werden, ist mein Deutsch flüssig.*'

'But I can't speak German. I'm sorry.'

'You are a reserved man. Such aloofness in India is unreasonable. We do not expect it. I, however, understand your national background and am not surprised.'

I was getting a bit irritated by all this. Again I protested that I was English, not German. The Sikh looked me in the eye. 'The English are known for their intransigence.'

At Mysore I stayed put. Peanut-sellers, sandalwood-souvenir-wallahs came to the window. A beggar-woman with a baby mewed '*Bap, mabap*' and touched her cracked lips. I shared the sandwiches Mrs Trivedi had given me; the tinned cheese was better than I'd expected. Some chickoos that looked like boiled potatoes but had a sweet musky flesh. The beggar-woman snatched through the window – I noticed her elegant hands – putting the food into a cloth bag. I gave her some coins and biscuits and she moved to another bus.

Between Nanjangud and Gundlupet, it was flattish plain; scrubby bushes, shade trees with painted hoops. A sizeable nullah was the bed of the Nugu River. On the horizon were brightly lit mountains and the sky behind them was dark petrol blue. I asked my neighbour if a storm was approaching. 'Nilgiris,' he answered. I explained that I was referring to the sky behind the hills. 'Sir, you cannot see behind the hills.'

He was right. As we approached Gundlupet, I realized that the mountains were just foothills and that the petrol blue was the great wall of the Nilgiris, their peaks cut off by cloud. Gundlupet was a shabby place. Several passengers got on for the ascent. Bandipur, on the edge of the jungle, had a roadside temple. The bus stopped and a priest came aboard with a camphor flame, a bowl of *tulsi* water and some bougainvillaea petals, all on a brass tray. He moved down the aisle, blessing those of us who tipped him and went back into his temple. 'You are in the habit of making puja?' asked my neighbour, who hadn't bothered himself, so that I felt rather affected. 'Not a Christian?' I replied that I was. 'I am friends with Roman Catholics. They don't make puja,' he informed me and turned away disapprovingly. Soon we were in the jungle. Billboards of wild animals announced the Mudumalai reserve. Under a picture of a tiger was written *Don't look at me with that tone of voice* which caused some amusement. The tall Sikh boomed, 'I like it!' Monkeys swarmed over the roof of a deserted bungalow. We were in the jungle for some time, slowly climbing. A herd of wild elephants was seen to the left of the road. At Gudalur it started to spit with rain. All the windows were clamped shut. As it was a luxury bus, the glass was tinted; the little damp town looked even drearier through a film of grey. Small sodden goats huddled in doorways with mouths shaped into smiles and cold yellow eyes. Dogs, horses, cows, even cats, have eyes that we can recognize emotion in, emotions that we imagine correspond with our own; not so with goats, they are inscrutable creatures. Is that the reason for the old demonic connection, that alien gaze? The landscape started to change, the jungle had subsided. The climb was steeper now. Great boulders lined the road, painted with evangelical graffiti. It would seem difficult to misspell JESUS SAVES but I saw JESES SAVES, JESUS SAVS and JUSES SAVES. Then there were no more boulders and we seemed to have left India. Some

Eastern European country stretched ahead of us with conifers and bright green meadows. It wasn't like Britain at all. In the drizzle it looked how I imagine Transylvania would look and ought to have been peopled by woodcutters – slab-faced, raw-cheekboned peasants, muttering prayers and carrying talismans to ward off horseflies and vampires. The other passengers were reacting badly to the change of temperature, sneezing and spluttering. My neighbour wrapped a woollen scarf around his head. It was certainly colder. I put on a sweater.

In 1602 a Portuguese priest called Jacome Ferreira became the first white man to travel up into the Nilgiris. He set out from Calicut, having been sent by his bishop to confirm the rumour that Christian tribes were living up there, cousins perhaps of the Syrian Christians of Malabar. The journey took several months. The jungle was alarming enough but what struck him most, as he started to climb, was the cold. The porters, used to the balmy Keralan climate, became ill. Eventually the party reached a village and the first priority was to barter for warm clothing. The inhabitants of the village were Todas, the most mysterious of all Deccan tribes, who were perfectly friendly and forthcoming with blankets but obliged to disappoint the shivering explorer – no, they had never heard of Christianity. Father Ferreira went back down the hillside, promising to return.

But he never did and the Todas weren't to see another European for two hundred years. A Scot called Francis Buchanan[5], prospecting territories that the British had recently annexed from the defeated Tipu Sultan, reached the Toda settlement of Ootacamund in 1800. He spent one day there, 24 October, was unimpressed and went back down again. Twelve years later two British surveyors, Keys and Macmahon, showed up. They went about their job methodically and departed with a similar lack of excitement. In 1818

Messrs Whish and Kindersley, two young assistants to John Sullivan, the Collector of Coimbatore, were chasing a gang of tobacco smugglers. Apparently they were great sportsmen; chasing smugglers would have been a popular diversion from desk-bound duties. The smugglers made off into the mountains and Whish and Kindersley (no doubt hallooing and whooping) followed. The gang eluded them but, curious as to the strange cool surroundings they found themselves in, the pair decided to explore further. Some Badaga tribesmen offered to act as guides and led them through the thickest bush. To their astonishment, Whish and Kindersley were shown a plateau, eight thousand feet above sea level, some fifty miles long, with rich fertile soil. Not jungle at all but downland that reminded them of home. A sportsman's paradise, riding country and every thicket bristling with game. So they turned and galloped back to Coimbatore to inform Mr Sullivan. An account of their discovery was published in a Madras journal but didn't arouse much interest; perhaps it was considered an unlikely story, the sort of yarn young sportsmen spin.

The Collector, however, was intrigued and decided to see for himself. The following year, Sullivan set off on a twenty-day tour. He took with him a French naturalist, M. Leschenault de la Tour, who was far from well, brought down by fever and barely strong enough to travel, and an assistant-surgeon called Jones, just in case. Passing up beyond the jungle, they reached the plateau. As if by magic, the Frenchman's health was restored; invigorated by the clear cool air, he amassed a collection of over two hundred plants, including some that were new to botany. Sullivan was thrilled. The next year, 1820, he made the trip again, taking his wife along. He approached the Government in Madras and suggested that Ootacamund would make a splendidly healthy hot-weather retreat for both soldiers and civilians. The Government responded by constructing a pass into the mountains, work which began in 1821. By 1823 Sullivan had built his own bungalow up there. Another of Sullivan's assistants, a Mr Johnson (less gallivanting, one imagines, than Whish and Kindersley), planted an English apple tree and grew strawberries. Fruit and vegetables flourished in the rich soil and clement sunshine. The first settlers were private individuals who purchased land off the bemused Todas for just one rupee an acre. In 1828 the Government started to build a sanatorium for military invalids. In 1830 a Military Commandant was put in charge of the entire settlement. Ootacamund, the Queen of Hill Stations, was born.

The bus stopped beside a small lake. Friesian cows grazed at the water's edge. Under a tall tree stood a rustic *chai* stall. The rain was no more than a damp mist now and the tea was sweet and strong. I wondered if the other passengers would survive the final stretch of the journey, they seemed to have developed all the symptoms of chronic influenza, streaming nostrils, hacking coughs. We didn't stop long. Tea bushes, surprisingly pretty and ornamental, grew in tiers on the hillsides and the women picking them were ghosts from my childhood, the picture on the Brooke Bond packet. To the sound of noses blowing a melancholy fanfare, we chugged into Ooty. It was frankly disappointing. Perhaps my expectations had been too high. I'd imagined Regency villas, Victorian *cottages ornés*, certainly Edwardian mock-Tudor residences. Instead I saw hideous 1950s boxes, squalid and cramped-looking hotels of recent provenance and already dilapidated, a town centre obscured by enormous misspelt advertisements. Stepping down from the bus, the first thing I saw was a squashed puppy being devoured by crows. Various hotel touts rushed to my side. I told them that I had a reservation at the Fernhill.

'Not possible. Fernhill closed, sir.'

I know that old trick, I thought. The Fernhill wasn't

closed at all. Major Trivedi had telephoned the hotel from Bangalore. They would be expecting me. 'Sir, I speak truth. Fernhill is closed down. The Taj Group has bought it. Many alterations they are going to make. It will be a modern five star. Now it is empty. Work starts later in the year. Southern Star, I show you.'

'Southern Star, very expensive. I show you better,' offered another tout and a row broke out in Tamil. Sides were taken, soon all the touts had joined in. A group of Tibetans had gathered to watch the argument. At the same time a young man rode by on a chestnut mare. He was riding bareback and jogging along at a very fast trot. The mare kept throwing her head about, her eyes rolling sideways. I could see he was having trouble. Frightened, no doubt, by the noise and traffic and the angry voices of the touts, the mare broke into a canter, then a gallop, dispersing the crowd as she bolted up the street. The rider clung to the mare's neck. The Tibetans looked at one another with broad smiles and started to clap as horse and rider disappeared from sight. I managed to flag down an auto-rickshaw. 'Fernhill Imperial, yes, sir,' and off we set.

The Fernhill Palace was about a mile away. Its iron gates were closed and the rickshaw-wallah got out to open them. I thought that a bit odd but he acted as if it was customary. A gravel drive led through a splendid garden. The Palace itself was an enormous, silly building, very high Victorian, a gigantic Swiss chalet in red and white stucco. It really had been a palace, the summer residence of the Maharajah of Mysore, Krishnaraja Wodeyar IV. We stopped at the front door. I paid the rickshaw-wallah and he sped off. There was no-one around as I carried my bag up the steps. The dark panelled hall was also deserted. I started to wonder if what the tout had told me was true after all. I shouted hallo. No answer. So I walked into the next room, what must have been a ballroom but was now a combined lounge and dining-room and shouted again.

'Sir,' said somebody behind me. 'Please. What do you want?' A thin man, with an upright shock of hair, peered at me with a pained expression, touched his temples very gently with the fingertips of both hands and shook his head slowly. He seemed to be suffering with a migraine. I introduced myself and told him that I had a reservation. We walked in a gingerly way back to the desk where he flicked a book open. 'No reservation, sir.' I told him that Major Trivedi had telephoned from Bangalore. Holding his throbbing head, he repeated firmly, but *sotto voce*, 'No reservation.'

'Well, have you a room?'

'Yes. There are no guests now.'

'The hotel is open, isn't it?'

'You can see it is.'

'How come there are no guests?'

'It is the rainy season,' was his answer which didn't convince me, the town centre had been full of tourists. The thin man rang a bell (wincing as he did so) and a bearer appeared – a sprightly old Tamil wearing a white cotton uniform, nautical in cut, which he'd probably retained after serving on an ocean liner in the 1930s – to take my bag and show me to my room.

I followed him along dusty corridors. Chintz wallpaper, faded photographs of lawn meets and tennis parties; the light was too dim to look at them properly. It was all dismal, mice running everywhere, like Miss Havisham's wedding reception. The first room that I was shown was a great vault, the gloom pierced by a single light bulb. It was rather magnificent, fitted with sturdy rosewood furniture, everything just too big to be comfortable. I thought of the great railway hotels of the nineteenth century – in London, of course, but also stretching across chilly Canada – and the baronial mansions that industrialists erected in the Scottish Highlands. The bathroom floor, however, was completely flooded and had been for some time – thallophyta bloomed on the water's surface.

The next room he showed me was smaller, presumably intended for female guests; the furniture less grandiose, everything softer. There were cushions, floral-print curtains, more chintz. Dust, like grey velvet, on every surface, but the bathroom was dry. I said that I'd take it. The ancient cabin-boy left me and I sat down on the bed and dozed off and it was early evening when I woke up again, freezing cold, with a horrid taste in my mouth. The bathroom turned out to be too dry. There was no hot water at all. I tried the cold tap. A judder, a few brown drops like tobacco juice, then nothing but a ghoulish sigh, something between a whistle and a death-rattle. So, unable to wash, I changed into clean clothes and wandered through the musty corridors towards the dining-room.

More guests had arrived. 'Well, hello! I can't *believe* it. Another paleface! We didn't think *anyone* else was here at all.' The man at the bar was in his forties, ginger-haired, paunchy, a close frizzy beard and hair tied back in a small tight knot. He extended a plump little hand like a pink flipper. 'I'm Michael. *Who* are you?' The barman was reading a Bible. A muskrat edged along the skirting board. Michael and his friends were on a month's holiday. They'd travelled up from Cochin ('*fascinating* place') and were going to Mysore next. 'We've done the Malabar. It's across to the Coromandel. Aren't the names *heavenly*?' I wondered if he was putting the voice on; it was prewar 'theatrical', every bit as anachronistic as the setting. 'Tony's in the bath! I think he's too young for India. Doesn't like it, *at all*. Whereas I'm *mad* about it. He *will* moan on and on. Nothing works properly. Oh, of course it doesn't. Don't be so feeble, I tell him. Enjoy the atmosphere. This place, for example. It's quite Anglo-Irish, *purest* Molly Keane.'

'More House of Usher, if you ask me.'

'Oh, don't mock. What will you drink?' He was an antique dealer with a shop in the Cotswolds. We talked for a while about Burford. Tony joined us. He was barely twenty years old. Fair hair shaved above the ears and a bright orange tan. He spoke with a grumpy Black Country accent. 'Bloody bath was cold and all. What a bloody dump.'

'Oh, do stop. This poor gentleman has no water whatsoever.'

'Then you should bloody complain.' I guessed that, twenty-five years or so ago, Michael had been similarly befriended by an older man, a protector who had passed on all the cunning of the antique business along with a characteristic mode of speech and manner. In another twenty-five years would Tony sound like Michael? Are such chains forged? They were the first white people I'd spoken to in India.

We moved into the ballroom for dinner. The white tablecloth was dirty – so (more disturbingly) were the napkins. The hotel staff occupied the half of the room that was used as a lounge; some clustered around a crackling television, others were bedding down for the night on sofas.

'A bloody dosshouse,' opined Tony.

'What a splendid room this is! Can you *imagine* the parties there've been?'

It was a fine room with a gallery running around it. A man in a khaki greatcoat and a black balaclava helmet brought some printed menus to our table and went away again. 'Who the fuck was that, the Cambridge Rapist?'

'I expect he finds it nippy in the evenings, my dear. Let me see. Why don't we all go Tandoori?'

But when the man in the balaclava came back he said, 'No Tandoori. Pork fry or head curry only,' and shuffled back to the television.

'What *can* he mean by that?'

'What the bloody hell is head curry? Or pork fry? They're not even on the fucking menu.'

'Perhaps pork fry's a Chinese dish,' I suggested optimistically. Head curry[6], I presumed, was a curry made from the head of either a pig or a goat. 'Are you serious?' asked Tony. We all chose pork fry. What arrived, to be fair, wasn't bad at all; a minced pork and green-chilli stir-fry, served with cold white rice. Tony, predictably, wasn't happy. 'It's bloody cack,' he sniffed, pushing his plate away and lighting a cigarette. As Michael and I were eating, the old cabin-boy appeared at the table. 'Sirs like fires in room? I light them now? Eighteen rupees.'

The eighteen rupees were wasted because when I went back to my room there was one damp log in the grate, impossible to ignite. I felt cold and slightly depressed. Michael and Tony had started to bicker; by the time the meal had ended Michael was twitching with restrained pique. The light at my bedside was bulbless, the main light too dim to read by. I walked back to the ballroom to ask one of the staff for a bulb. Our plates had not been cleared away. Most of the staff had fallen asleep. Why didn't they use the empty rooms?

The shock-headed receptionist was still awake and he went to find a bulb. I thanked him and went back to my room. The bulb gave off the faintest conceivable glow, certainly not enough for reading. So I walked back again and asked for a more powerful one. 'All are the same.'

'But it's useless.'

The receptionist's voice rose. 'You want to read. You want to read! All right.' He accompanied me back to my room then asked me if I had a knife. I gave him my pen-knife. He slashed the lampshade open. 'All right? Now can you read?' I complained about the fire. 'No charge,' he screamed and slammed the door before I could say that I'd paid the bearer cash already. It was so cold that I slept with my clothes on.

When I woke up I decided I'd had enough. I'd have some coffee, then pay and leave. I sat in the ballroom among recumbent snoring figures. The dishes from the night before remained on the table. The coffee, which was surprisingly strong and good, was served in a silver pot, the size of a trophy, by the barman who asked me if I was going to church (it was a Sunday morning) and was disappointed when I said I didn't think so. 'Saint Stephen's, very old.' The receptionist scowled at me as he drew up my bill. I noticed that he'd included 20 per cent 'Luxury Tax'.

'I'm not paying that.'

'Sir, you have to.'

'Tell me what the luxury was.'

'This is a luxury hotel, full stop. There is no need to elaborate.'

'Get me the manager, please.'

'There is no manager.'

'What do you mean, no manager?'

'New manager is coming with Taj Group. Two months' time.'

'Well, who's running the place?'

'You can see. I am.'

'But it's a shambles.'

'It was your choice to stay here.' After a longish argument about basic requirements like running water –the receptionist's view was that I'd had a bathroom, whether it was functional was irrelevant – the 'Luxury Tax' was removed. It was still expensive, considering that I'd spent the night in what amounted to a squat.

I moved to the Savoy. The receptionist there was amazed that I'd stayed at the Fernhill. 'It is closed down, not reopening until later in the year. How can you have got in?' My room at the Savoy was a cottage in a rose garden. I sat in the little parlour, eating warm rolls and honey. As I wrote a letter, the rain stopped and the sun began to shine and the sky turned from blotchy grey to a hard implausible Kodachrome blue. I could smell eucalyptus trees. I arranged for a car to drive me around that afternoon and to ride early the following morning. I'd noticed that the Ooty Club[7] was near-by. Was it possible, I asked, to visit? The receptionist said that he'd telephone the secretary. No sooner had I returned to my cottage than the phone rang. 'Sir, if you would like to visit the Ootacamund Club, please go now.' So I put on a tie and strolled down the lane.

The Club Secretary was a retired colonel, a dapper man in a tweed jacket and grey flannel trousers. He told me that he wasn't well but that his ailments were simply due to advanced age. There were leopard-skins, tiger-skins, mounted heads; photographs of Churchill, the Queen, Mahatma Gandhi; Snaffles prints but none, surprisingly, of the Ootacamund Hunt. I was sure that I'd seen pictures of the Ooty hunt in a *catalogue raisonné* of Snaffles' work but, checking later, discovered that they'd been illustrations to his book *More Bandobast*.

A bearer called Silver showed me around. The men's bar was full of jackal masks, like those of foxes only flatter, more feline; honours boards listing the masters of the Ootacamund Hunt, annual winners at the point-to-point. I was shown the room where Lieutenant Neville Chamberlain defined the rules of snooker – it had actually been invented at Jabalpur the year before. There were separate rooms for various card games. I got the impression that Silver regularly made this tour and was reciting memorized lines.

The Club Secretary introduced me to a member, a rear admiral from the naval staff college at nearby Wellington, who had been cub-hunting that morning. I said that we didn't hunt on Sundays at home. 'We don't have those restrictions here.' He told me that he'd been riding a young horse, unsure of hounds, who slid about on the gorsy slopes. 'Thought I was going to come a cropper once or twice.' Soon we were discussing horses and hunting in England.

The rear admiral's wife joined us. She wore a beige cashmere shawl over her sari and was very interesting about Kerala and Keralan food. Considering this couple and the Club Secretary, I was struck by the

Englishness of their manners, their speech, the men's clothes; even the choice of a beige shawl seemed to be informed by some British instinct for restraint. I thought that this Anglophilia had probably been preserved in the Indian Armed Services more than elsewhere. It wouldn't be so evident in lofty political circles nor among the business grandees of the great cities. In some ways it resembled the adherence of certain French people of the *haut bourgeoisie* to *le style anglais*; as an ideal, quite removed from the coarser realities of contemporary English life.

The Secretary invited me to stay at the Club. I felt greatly honoured and, furthermore, it was good value, much less than a hotel and the flat rate included one's meals. I said that I'd better stay that night at the Savoy but that I'd like to stay on Monday and Tuesday.

In the dining-room of the Savoy were two young Englishmen, spending the year between school and university working for a Christian organization in Trichy. They were staying a week at Coonoor and visiting Ooty for the day. They'd attended matins at Saint Stephen's. They asked me if there was a bus tour of the town. I said that I didn't know but they were welcome to share the car that I had hired for the afternoon. Nigel and Martin were the fairly typical products of a minor public school. If they'd been more aggressive they'd have been radical Young Conservatives but they were gentle creatures, talking of C.S. Lewis, Cardinal Newman, organ music. At eighteen they were already middle aged, inhabiting a cosy sexless world. I could picture them in a few years' time. They would hold administrative jobs by day; in the evenings they'd have Radio 4, the *Spectator*, novels by Robertson Davies and A.N. Wilson, Fry and Laurie on television.

First we went to the Botanical Gardens, fourteen acres designed in 1848 by Mr McIvor from Kew. There was a bandstand and a floral map of India and a shop that sold cuttings and shrubs in pots. It was extraordinary that so many European species could flourish in Southern India; at first glance it was easy to take it for granted and forget that to most of the visitors it wasn't 'just like Bournemouth' but unlike anything they'd ever seen before.

The boating lake was pretty dismal. Snuffling tourists in overcoats, shawls and headscarves crept about. Ancient ponies stamped and coughed. I hoped that the horse I'd ride in the morning would be a better specimen. Spectacular views from Dodabetta Peak, the light beaming down in shafts between clouds, illuminating patches of the landscape. Men were selling peeled hard-boiled eggs.

Nigel and Martin had to get back to the bus stand so we headed back towards the town centre. The main street was called Charing Cross and there was an 'English Sweetshop' but we resisted.

'We're booked for a game of golf at Coonoor.'

'Trouble is neither of us can play.'

'That won't stop us!'

I told the driver that I'd like to see some Todas[8]. We set off for Sylks Road, quite near the Club, where there was a permanent Toda settlement that consisted of several small dwellings like scaled-down aeroplane hangars. As soon as we got out of the car an old Toda woman came rushing to the gate. She was tiny with a bright wizened little terrier face. Her hair was in shiny ringlets and her teeth were crooked and pointed. She grinned and grabbed my hand and jabbered at me. The driver said, 'She is asking us to have coffee with her. Come.' We went into her hut. It was like going into a gypsy's caravan. We sat on a wooden chest with a blanket over it. The woman smiled all the time and went to the stove to heat the water, talking so rapidly that the driver could only translate the odd sentence at a time.

'She is saying that an Englishwoman called Mrs River has sent you to visit her.'

'She is saying that she has three sons but two are dead.'

'When the cold weather comes her lungs are filled with blood.'

'She used to have many English visitors but not many now.'

'She is asking if you are the son of Mrs River.'

The coffee was strong and sweet and bubbles of grease floated on the surface. The Toda woman asked us to stand up for a moment and she opened the chest and brought out a cardboard box. Inside the box were photographs and a large French paperback book about Southern India. First we looked at the book which contained a picture of her with her husband and their three boys. It was taken twenty years ago but she looked exactly the same. She pointed to one of the boys and the driver said, 'Only that one is alive.' We looked at the photographs, many of which were extremely old. A laughing woman in a tweed suit turned out to be 'Mrs River'; on the back was written, *Phyllis Rivers, October 1950*. 'Mummy?' asked the Toda woman, pushing the photograph at me. I was sorry to disappoint her. Before we left she showed me a wad of prescriptions. The driver said that the medicines she needed were expensive so I gave her 100 rupees. 'She is asking you to visit her tomorrow.'

Very early in the morning a bearer came to wake me and said, 'Horse boy here, sir.' I was a tiny bit alarmed to see that the syce was the boy that I'd seen being run away with at the bus stand. He was leading two horses; one was a very scruffy creature like a tonga pony and the other was a fine speckled (what's sometimes called 'fleabitten') grey mare, a sturdy thoroughbred. The tonga pony had very ragged tack but the grey mare's was multicoloured and ornamental, not in the least practical. The syce introduced himself as Edward. The grey mare was called Nilgiri Queen. As I prepared to get on I noticed that the stirrup 'leathers', though long enough, were coloured ropes and the saddle was two wooden boards, resting on a numnah, covered by a bright blanket over the top of which ran the girth. Nilgiri Queen seemed kind and responsive. I commented on the tack. 'Special wedding bridle,' said Edward as he mounted and off we set. Trotting was difficult, at first, with the wooden saddle. I chatted to Edward. I told him that I'd seen him with the bolting cob. 'That is a bad horse, Master. No use.' It was odd to be called Master. We rode along Tudor Hall Road into a wood called Aramby. It was very pretty and wild and brightness seemed to fall from the air and catch all the different leaves. We cantered up the paths and jumped a small fallen tree. At one point the trees cleared and there was a grand view. 'All the way to Mysore, Master,' said Edward, exaggerating somewhat. We left the wood and passed a lake and rode along beside conifers and silver birches. Edward told me that he'd taken some Australians on an eight-hour ride but we only stayed out for three hours. I arranged to ride the next morning as well.

I moved to the Club. My room was spartan and neat with checked blankets on the iron bed and Peter Scott prints on the wall. Before going into lunch I had a drink and met Admiral Kuruvila, the MFH (MJH, perhaps?) and his wife. We discussed Jack Russells; they were trying to find a puppy in India. They'd been to England and had been particularly impressed by a shop in Hampshire called Calcutt's where they'd found good quality second-hand riding clothes. 'I wear a green coat,' Mrs Kuruvila told me. 'Oh, I know, strictly speaking, it's for harriers but it's awfully smart.' Two hunting women from Lynchburg, Virginia, had recently been out with the Ootacamund Hunt. 'How did they describe it, darling? What was that word?'

'They said it was merciless,' smiled Admiral Kuruvila proudly. Hounds only stayed out for two hours. That seemed a very short day to me. 'That is long enough, I can tell you.' Mrs Kuruvila told me of the unique hazards they faced: steep gorse-covered slopes, bogs and rushing nullahs, panthers hiding in the undergrowth, the Toda buffaloes that have been known to kill both horse and rider ('If you see one you must crack your whip like billy-o,'). Most of the field were naval officers studying at the staff college, many new to riding. Wasn't that dangerous? Admiral Kuruvila roared, 'Yes, yes. But they are expendable,' and Mrs Kuruvila snorted happily at the joke. The dining-room was lined with framed photographs of the hunt's masters, ending with one of Admiral Kuruvila. There was mulligatawny soup (not unlike the *rasam* I'd had at Ullal) with toast, followed by chicken pie and cabbage, then jam tart and custard.

Later I went into the kitchen, expecting to find a gleamingly preserved Victorian range, bright pans and pudding basins. Instead I found a practically bare room with four gas rings and the minimum of equipment, what was there was entirely Indian.

I spent the afternoon browsing in the library. There was a good selection of memoirs, generally sporting and military. Between *Character-Building in Kashmir* by C.E. Tyndale-Biscoe and *With A Camera In Tiger-Land* by F.W. Champion, I noticed *Bring Me My Mule* by Brigadier-General Rajesh Kapur. I flicked through it and, when I reached the index, I looked for Trivedi. He wasn't listed but I did find Bridgewater and, turning to page 75, read that,

> . . . Young Kumar Chellaram, Walter Bridgewater and Rohit 'Croaker' Singh, all from well-known military families, the so-called Three Musketeers, though I thought Crazy Gang of Calcutta more fitting myself, entertained us after dinner with the Whiffenpoof Song . . .

The older volumes (late nineteenth, early twentieth

century) were interesting, almost like oral histories; one could hear the writers talking, their realistic breezy voices, not slangy but decidedly informal as if a book would begin, 'Unaccustomed as I am to the writing game . . .' Was it the surroundings that brought the books to life? Discovered in a Cheltenham jumble sale, would they seem dull and blimpish?

Next to the library was a reading-room containing the club records and some cabinets of rare and prized books. I looked through the hunt memorabilia and some volumes of photographs. The photographs, mainly from the early 1920s to the late 1950s fell into three distinct periods.

The earliest pictures showed gaunt erect figures, still Victorian in clothes and attitudes. They take their pleasures formally; the women ride sidesaddle, tennis is played with a marionettish stiffness and Indian servants stand in faceless attendance. There is a certain grandeur but it is standardized; all Englishmen are fair-haired, lean and athletic. India is ruled by the set example.

With the Second World War comes a great loosening. A group photograph in front of the Club reminds me of Happy Valley Kenya. The clothes are much less formal; some men wear boating jackets, some wear tweeds, some wear uniforms, hats are various and optional. The hairstyles of both sexes vary considerably; the women wear shorter skirts and look generally younger. There are even one or two bashful Indians among the members, politely trying to fit in. The club servants are more distinct now, they look directly at the camera rather than to their employers. I imagine that the photograph I'm describing is of soldiers and their wives on leave, which would explain the relaxed house-party atmosphere.

The post-war photographs make up the bulk. The British appear stouter and older; less soldierly, more bourgeois. They are presumably tea planters. There are rugby dinners, fancy-dress balls (the usual pirates and Frenchmen but also a pair of hilarious Todas), children's Christmas parties. A dinner to celebrate the Coronation. Elegant Indians attend these occasions dressed in long achcan coats and jodhpurs, their wives in sumptuous saris, looking altogether sleeker than their dowdy white friends. Now *they* set the tone, for the British have surrendered their monopoly on grandeur. And something else occurred to me: that, despite the remains, the British presence in India was historically little more than an interruption.

I was on my own in the dining-room. Just as I was finishing my pudding, a middle-aged couple, a judge from Hyderabad and his wife came in. 'Not exactly a *tamasha*, this evening,' remarked the judge. His wife commented that 'these clubs can be real morgues'. The judge had been educated at Harrow and Oxford, as had his father. Now his own son was at Shiplake. 'A very happy school,' said the judge's wife. The judge said, 'Bath. That's in Wessex.'

'What does it mean, Wessex?' asked his wife. I said that it was an ancient kingdom, King Alfred's kingdom, and now it's used to describe the West Country. And, of course, there's Wessex as the setting of Hardy's novels. 'So it's not a county?' No, I answered, it's like talking about the Deccan. 'You put it on the address then, so there,' grunted the judge. I said that it wasn't necessary to do so. 'It jolly well is,' he contradicted. 'I've a friend there who absolutely insists that I put Wessex on my Christmas card.' Perhaps his friend was a Wessex Regionalist? There is a pressure group, I said, not a terribly serious one, led by Lord Weymouth . . . 'That's the fellow I'm talking about! Alexander!' guffawed the judge, clapping his hands. 'There! What a small world it is!' said his wife. 'I used to visit Longleat,' the judge told me. 'Can't be the same now, with lions and giraffes and what have you.'

A bearer woke me early and I walked down to find Edward waiting with the horses. We set off in a different direction than before and found ourselves riding through the town centre. We passed through a scruffy residential area and dogs came out to bark at the horses. Nilgiri Queen was frightened and kept shying, I had to kick her on. I suggested to Edward that we head for a more open space.

'We're going to charge, Master.' Taking that to mean gallop, I said it was a crazy idea.

'No, no, Master. Not crazy! Catholic charge, I show you. Beautiful big charge, very near here.'

The church was unusual; not a building at all but a garden with a raised stone altar beneath which ran a passage with painted sculptural tableaux behind glass. 'South India, many RCs,' said Edward. We rode along the old Mysore road. Black-and-silver creepers, red soil. A row of great trees with gaping scooped-out trunks, big enough for a man to enter and sit down. 'You could live in one of those.'

'Yes, yes, Master,' Edward answered, clearly puzzled, 'but I have a good house.'

We passed small man-made lakes that reflected the sky, giving the illusion that the earth's surface was a thin and ragged membrane; above and below it, the deep chromatic blue. We cantered over powdery ground where conifers had been uprooted.

I left Ooty on a private video bus which was cramped and uncomfortable. Sitting near me was the tall Sikh but he pretended not to recognize me. He was wearing a magenta turban this time and his beard smelt of violets. There were two Chinese girls speaking Hindi. We descended thirty-six numbered bends. At Fifteen, a skeletal naked sadhu was meditating on top of a wall, a gust of wind would have toppled him. When we reached the jungle at the bottom it was like returning from a trip abroad. I took my sweater off. I was 'back in India' and the heat felt good. The videos were long (at least three hours each) and tedious; terrible acting, terrible singing. I was hoping to spot Tiptoe but didn't.

In Mysore we stopped for lunch at a hotel with a rose garden and, just in front of the gates, a man was being pelted with rocks. He had a weird mincing walk as if he'd shat in his trousers and he covered his lowered head with his arms. The people throwing stones at him (men, old women and children) formed a circle, jeering and shouting, and round and round toddled the victim, bleeding now, confused and giddy. The odd thing was that it seemed a casual affair and people passed by as if nothing unusual was going on.

When I got back to the Trivedis they had a suggestion. Every year Mrs Trivedi visited her family and her husband's family in Jabalpur and it had occurred to her that I could accompany her. 'You'd find the north different.' It was a splendid idea.

My hair was getting quite long so I visited the barber, Mr Shekhar, who had a curling moustache like a character from the televised *Mahabharat*, and afterwards I sat outside the Hotel Pushpa drinking coffee from a stainless-steel beaker. The traffic was at its most intense on the airport road, it was the evening rush hour. Tiny motor-scooters would tootle by carrying two, sometimes three, passengers – even an entire family: father, mother, two small children. Crowded buses, auto-rickshaws, small grey cars and ox-carts. A boy in brown rags led a chained performing monkey dressed in a tiny red waistcoat and pantaloons and carrying a toy gun. 'Cowboy, cowboy,' the boy muttered and prodded it with a stick. The monkey pointed the gun in the air. 'Bang, bang, bang!' said the boy enthusiastically. A dog trotted by holding a length of intestine in its mouth. An old woman was collecting cow dung. I'd seen her before, she had a very straight back, great agility for her age and a quizzical, vaguely patrician expression – a retired Girton professor who'd taken up dung-collecting as others might take up mycology or lepidoptery – each dropping seemed to have the fascination of a rare specimen. She shaped the dung into round cakes that dried in the sun; then arranged them in neat piles for sale, as fuel for cooking fires.

I went on another of Mrs Sen's outings, a bus trip to Somnathpur. Back again to Badami House, too early, at half-past six, for the tongueless children. The bus station was crowded. There were several excursions leaving at the same time and lines were forming at different counters. A tiny official stepped out of the office in an elaborate drum major's uniform. Gold braid hanging in swags, KSTDC emblazoned on his collar and epaulettes and even the enormous buckle of his belt. He was no more than five foot tall and a lot of that was created by soft leather riding boots with Mercury wings flashing out at the two-inch heel. His lofty pompadour was oiled and coiffed so precisely that it was more like a gleaming hat than hair. A moustache as thin as a pencil line ran along his upper lip and on his forehead were three red and white lines (the *nammam* marks of the Saivite) stylized into a neat sergeant's chevron. The whole effect was most dramatic, pure rock and roll, like Prince walking on stage before an audience of thousands. There was a hush. He watched us all for a moment, rapped his clipboard moodily, spun on the winged heels and returned to his office. Would he appear again in another costume? A sequined cape?

The bus arrived and we could get on. The other passengers fell into two groups: a large family picnic and a group of old people. The family picnic consisted of a middle-aged couple and their children – or, I'd imagine, a mixture of their children and their children's friends – many of whom were married, with their husbands and wives, a cluster of strikingly pretty teenage girls and an assortment of very young grandchildren, including one baby girl of about six months, passed about like a cherished doll, wearing smudgy mascara. They were a jolly bunch, chatting and laughing, swopping seats all the time and sometimes the teenage girls would sing with sweet clear voices and the others would clap or they'd giggle so much that their black eyes would fill with tears. The other group, eight retired friends, four couples in their late sixties and early seventies, were rather strange. My first impression was that they were Canadians or Americans of Indian descent on a trip to the old country. They all wore Western clothes and spoke to each other in English and had names like Brian and Daphne and Lenny. The men wore plaid shirts and crewcuts. The women looked comparatively ungainly in their knee-length skirts, much less elegant than they would have in saris; they were all quite stout and, with their hair cut short (one even had a blue rinse), they bore a curious resemblance to the buxom black matrons of the Southern United States.

At Mandya we stopped for breakfast at a canteen run by the tourist board; two big, bright, light-blue halls and stern notices in English and Kannada: *Let Not Your Conversations Be A Nuisance To Others* and *No Political Activities Will be Tolerated.* I had some *idlis* and *sambar* (a thin soup to dip them in) and two cups of weak coffee. The retired people sat near me and expressed disappointment at the limited menu. I listened for North American references, tried to detect appropriate inflections in their speech – but there was nothing to go on. At a pinch they could have been Australian. I was fascinated by them. It had crossed my mind that they were Eurasians but I'd seen Eurasians in Bangalore and, both physically and in their dress and manner, they were quite different. Eurasians were, by and large, much sallower and tended to wear very old-fashioned British-style clothes, maintaining a strong identification with their British ancestors. These people were as dark as the darker North Indians (not as dark as Tamils) and there was none of that almost totemic Britishness about them.

Two more buses pulled in and soon the dining halls were full. Before getting back on board I went to the lavatory and there was another European in there, a tall, red-bearded, overweight man with no shirt on. He was very pale and his flabby back and chest were covered with crimson welts, an inflamed rash, that he was dabbing with cold water. I attempted a conversation but he couldn't understand me very well; he was Portuguese. Had he seen a doctor? He said he'd hoped that the sunshine would burn the rash off but he hadn't found any, not even in Goa. He'd been in India four weeks and was going home in two more. He'd had the rash since his first night in Bombay; it was 'like a burn with fire'.

There was more singing from the teenage girls. I'd guess the songs were from films; they were definitely improved by the a cappella treatment. Up until this point there'd been no communication between the two groups. Now one of the retired men stood at the front of the aisle and started to sing 'Clementine', waving his hands like a conductor and encouraging everyone to join in the chorus. As that proved popular, we had 'She'll Be Coming Round The Mountain'. Then, an unexpected choice from a septuagenarian, 'Yellow Submarine'.

After an hour or so we stopped at Sivasamudram to visit a hydroelectric dam, built in the 1920s, that stood at the bottom of a deep canyon through which the Cauvery River flowed. Hawks wheeled in the air and, down by the churning water, fishing birds gathered. We bought our tickets to look at the engines and our cameras were impounded – for security reasons, photography was forbidden. If it was so strategic, why were visitors admitted at all? We descended to the engines on a funicular railway. The baby girl had been decorated with garlands of marigolds and looked very sweet, a tiny temple deity. One of the singers sat next to me and introduced herself. Her name was Parvati. She was remarkably pretty, 'a dear gazelle', and her movements (a slight tilt of the head or a descriptive sweep of the hand) suggested Bharata Natyam[9], the classical Indian dance. The great hall that we entered was like the engine room of a ship. On the sides of the engines were metal plates saying, *Boving and Company, London.*

'Come and look at this,' said Parvati. Just beyond the gravel drive was a fenced and padlocked enclosure, very overgrown with weeds and yellow grass; a row of wooden crosses, splintered and blistered by the weather. On one of them a name was just legible: Donald Clark.

The next stop was a car-park overlooking Shimsha Falls. The falls were very impressive; the huge wall of black rock and white streamers of water, the roaring mist. I took some photographs. The other passengers preferred to use the falls as a backdrop for group portraits. I was asked to take some of the pictures, then to stand with Parvati and her siblings; I was conscious of being so much taller than anyone else but flattered to be so accepted – I was even given the baby to hold. On our way to Somnathpur we came to a bridge that the driver suspected wasn't very sturdy so he stopped the bus and asked all the men to get out and walk across it. This was considered a great joke. 'Don't you go drowning all those womenfolk,' said one of the plaid-shirt men. We passed bullock-carts, smoking brick-kilns, flocks of sheep being driven through small villages. Once I glimpsed, edging along the side of a rice paddy, a single-file procession like an Egyptian frieze, carrying a small stretcher covered with flowers. It was a funeral (a child's, I guessed, from the size of the stretcher) but it didn't look solemn at all.

Somnathpur is another Hoysala temple, built in 1268 by a general called Somanatha. The temple, set on a platform, has three star-shaped sanctuaries emanating off the main hall. As at Belur and Halebid, bands cover the walls: marching elephants and horses, marching geese, weird sea monsters called Makaras[10].

There are larger figures beneath carved trees: Vishnu and Lakshmi riding on Garuda (half man half vulture and the king of the birds); Indra, the god of the firmament, and his wife Shachi riding on an elephant; Vishnu dancing merrily with Ganesh. Life-size carvings of Krishna and the cowgirls. The temple is inside a cloistered courtyard and the cloisters and little cells, because they seem familiar to European eyes, give the place a monastic calm. This contemplative atmosphere could just be because the temple's no more than an archæological site; if there were priests and bells and chanting worshippers and coconuts cracking, things would certainly be different. The temple is dedicated to Keshava, an aspect of Vishnu renowned for the beauty and abundance of his hair. I walked around with Parvati who pointed out the different figures and told me about them. There were several *mithuna* carvings (couples making love) that seemed to fluster her so I pretended not to notice them.

When we returned to the bus I saw that the retired people had stayed on board the whole time. Hadn't they wanted to look at the temple? asked one of the family group. 'All that business doesn't interest us!' replied the woman called Daphne cheerfully. It occurred to me that they might be Jehovah's Witnesses, a group notoriously wary of entering places of worship other than their own.

Ranganathittoo Bird Sanctuary was next. It was very crowded. Boats went out on the river but there were so many people on each one that I couldn't believe you'd see that much so I stayed on the bus and read a book called *The Yellow Wallpaper* by Charlotte Perkins Gilman. Some people were cooking on a primus stove set up on the flatbed of a truck, a worrying arrangement. An old beggar pestered them and they threw him torn-off pieces of chapatti as if he was a crow. The driver and his companion grew anxious that the party was spending too long at the bird sanctuary. 'They are told forty-five minutes, nearly twice that it is already.'

And it was another forty-five minutes before they returned. A trip to the ruins of Srirangapatna had to be cancelled. This decision caused some outcry. 'Then we will get a damn refund,' said the man who'd led the singing.

When I told Major Trivedi about the strange Westernized people, how I couldn't work out where they came from, he shook his head. 'Why should they be from anywhere other than right here? Would you ask where Atul comes from? Aren't his clothes and habits also American-influenced? And likewise those of his friends? Perhaps these people caught on early to whatever it is?' But they had Western names. 'Nicknames, I would think.' The Major said that just across the airport road there was a frozen meat stall that was run by people who fitted that description. I asked what caste they were and the Major shrugged. 'Who knows?' he said. 'Let me explain something about caste. You probably think there are just four? Here in the South there are possibly hundreds and most would be considered untouchable by Northern-caste Hindus. The caste definitions most Europeans know apply simply to those of Aryan descent, the Sanskrit people. That notion your forebears kept because they could grasp it, it corresponded to their own class system. Come down to the Deccan and all is muddled, nothing's that simple. Besides, the Indian population has more than doubled in even my lifetime. People forget, or choose to forget, these rigid systems. Maybe they always did. British scholars wanted to watch us as specimens, they would say, "So-and-so's a Brahmin therefore his beliefs are A, B and C," but it was never that simple. Human nature was overlooked. Oh, I'm not saying caste does not exist nor that it does not apply. What I am saying is that it can't be understood so easily. Whereabouts, local history, family fortunes, all these are factors. This is a large country, almost a third of the world's entire population is living here, would you expect it to follow such simple patterns?' If it's such a muddle, why does it survive? The Major said that Gandhi had wanted to revise the system so that all men are born Sudras and would rise by self-determination to their appropriate level. That had been rejected as too radical a solution. 'But what the solution is, who can say? This is the *Kali Yuga*, the Age of Darkness. Very little light shines upon us. We can only fumble around, make what sense we can and hope that God is benevolent.'

Sravana

The evening before our journey to Madhya Pradesh, Mrs Trivedi was rushing about. She went to Brigade Road to have her hair cut. She sent Anasuya to chivvy Mr Prakash the *darzi*, who was late with her new *salwar-kamiz* of lime green and orange cotton. She bought presents for her parents and her parents-in-law. She prepared a vast quantity of food for us to take (*parathas,* boiled eggs, chapattis, little pots of jackfruit pickle, *aloo sabzi* – 'Fruit we can buy when the train stops'). She packed her own bag, travelling surprisingly light ('Oh, my sisters have plenty of saris') and then cooked dinner. There was a powercut so we ate by candlelight. Dr Lal came downstairs and joined us. Mr Prakash came to the door with the *salwar-kamiz* at ten o'clock. Mrs Trivedi scolded him for being so slow but he laughed as if he wasn't taking her seriously. Dr Lal told me that he had been presented with a crocodile skin in Singapore. He'd had a pair of shoes made, with a matching belt and hat. I was intrigued by the hat (though I'd come to expect a certain eccentricity from the doctor) and asked him about it. He seemed surprised at my interest. 'It is a trilby. Have you not seen such hats? They are the in thing.' I hadn't seen a crocodile-skin trilby before.

When the lights came back, Major Trivedi produced a marvellous book of cave paintings from Pachmarhi, a hill station near their hometown of Jabalpur. 'Every one of these we have seen ourselves.' They were extraordinary pictures, like the black figures on Athenian vases. Some of the paintings resembled X-rays. There were pictures of deer with tubes that ran from their mouths to their stomachs. Others were of pregnant beasts with embryos shown in their wombs. Battle scenes, war dances, strange orgiastic celebrations that veered into brutality – scenes of homosexual abandon after a victory in battle, human sacrifice, ritual rape. As a teenager the Major had accompanied an elderly British archæologist around the caves and later, as a young husband, he'd taken Mrs Trivedi there. The whereabouts of these paintings were almost secret, very few guidebooks mentioned them. I checked in *The Lonely Planet* and, sure enough, they weren't listed under the entry for Pachmarhi. Then, as if to tantalize, Major Trivedi told me that the caves would be impossible to enter during the rains. 'Completely impossible?' I asked. 'Completely impossible.' He clapped the book shut loudly, as if to finalize the enquiry, and went to bed.

The Major, Atul and Anasuya waved us off as we bundled into an auto-rickshaw. It was a damp, sunless morning. 'In the North it will be worse. Monsoon proper you do not get in Bangalore.' I was beginning to wonder if a journey into such weather was going to be worthwhile. Mrs Trivedi insisted that it was. 'It is beautiful in the rains, so green and fresh. And it is comfortable.' She made an expansive fanning gesture. At Bangalore Station we boarded the Madras train. We were early, the train wouldn't leave for another fifteen minutes. We found our seats and sat down. I discovered, too late, that my seat was covered in water (I hoped it was water anyway), soaking the back of my trousers. I swore quietly, annoyed at the prospect of a wet bottom for the next hour or so. Seeing my plight, Mrs Trivedi clapped her hands and laughed girlishly. 'Even before we leave Bangalore, your troubles begin.' She handed me a cloth. Just before the train departed, we were joined by three students. Two of them were returning to university in Benares and would therefore be catching the same connecting train as ours from Madras. The other was studying at Saint Joseph's in Bangalore and knew Atul, whom he pronounced 'a fine fellow'. In fact, with his Americanized accent and cool manner, he was rather like Atul. He was on his way to visit relatives in Madras. 'You will please excuse me,' he said and climbed up on to the top berth, where he stretched out. 'Always I take this journey easy. Never sit when you can lie down is my motto.' He reminded me of Top Cat. The two Benares students were considerably less casual. They chatted earnestly and Mrs Trivedi bombarded them with questions about qualifications and post-graduate opportunities. One was called Dilip, small and shy, a bespectacled chemistry major. He seemed flustered. The other was called Mohan who, as if by contrast, was tall and handsome, sure of himself and talkative. He had attended Bishop Cotton's in Bangalore, a very smart school. Now he was studying metallurgy but he planned to join his father in the property business. His hobby was weight-lifting and he was carrying some American body-building magazines. He had the relaxed swagger and self-confidence of someone born to succeed. I actually found him a little too pleased with himself. Mrs Trivedi was impressed. She admired go-getters, 'the future of India'. Top Cat asked if I had seen *Dick Tracy* yet. 'You are probably a Madonna fan.' Travelling on my own, I reflected moodily, I didn't have to spend the journey talking. I preferred to look out of the window, read, listen to my Walkman. There was a lull in the conversation so I put the headphones on. 'What are you listening to?' asked Top Cat. 'Bob Wills and the Texas Playboys,' I replied. 'Is that similar to Huey Lewis?'

'It was recorded in the 1940s.'

'Acha,' said Top Cat, 'it is classical music.'

The further from Karnataka, and into Tamil Nadu, we went, the less grey it became. Coastal Tamil Nadu wouldn't get the monsoon until October. The train took us away from grey skies and green paddies into a brown boulder-strewn landscape. Green parrots, like bright leaves, flew about. Mrs Trivedi kept up the conversation with the Benares students. Top Cat dozed. I moved over to the ticket inspector's empty seat beside an open door. I was polite and friendly to everyone so there was no suggestion that I was being surly and unsociable. From time to time Mrs Trivedi unwrapped things to eat. Because we were in the South coffee-vendors went up and down the aisles; on a Northern train it would have been tea. The coffee was always very weak. People sold fruit and peanuts and horrid-looking *wadas* made of chickpeas, something like falafel. A blind beggar boarded the train and sang religious songs. He had a rasping bluesy voice and the songs made me think of a record I'd heard by the Reverend Gary Davis. Once, when the train halted between stations, two Lambadi women got on – recognizable as such from the Lambadis I'd seen outside Hospet. They wore patchwork skirts and embroidered bibs and their arms clattered with bracelets. One was carrying a harmonium and I hoped that she'd play but they just sat on the floor and tapped my knee and asked me for money. A coffee-vendor was passing so I bought them both a cup. We passed through a range of mountains called the Javadi Hills. We also passed a small town clustered around a tannery. There was an awful chemical stench and a lake the colour of methylated spirits.

We got to Madras in the middle of the afternoon. It was as airless and noisy in the station as before. We found out that our train to Jabalpur was cancelled due to industrial action. This was potentially disastrous. Mrs Trivedi, Dilip and Mohan went off to talk to the station manager. I was told to guard the baggage. They were gone a long time. Despite the heat and the uncertainty of our situation, I was happy to sit there. The crowd fascinated me. A group of women with shaven heads passed by, pilgrims returning from Tirupati. Women often go there to ask the resident deity, Lord Venkatesa, for a son; shaving the head shows the sincerity of the prayer. Families sat on the floor to eat. Little children stared at me but, by and large, I wasn't the centre of attention. A shifty *badmash* prowled around on the lookout for unattended bags. He looked like a thin wolf and I guessed that he was driven to petty crime by hunger. A very weary-looking sannyasi lay down beside me. In no time at all he was covered in flies – it seemed odd that they weren't on anyone else. A notice was stuck on a pillar. It was in English and Tamil and concerned a missing seven-year-old boy. The most poignant detail was that his complexion was described as 'Bournvita'. That struck me as particularly heartbreaking, so obviously a loving mother's notion. I was reflecting on the poor mother's agony when a tall beggarwoman approached me with a printed card. It was a catalogue of misfortunes, all misspelt. The first couple of lines said that she was an epileptic, that she had fallen down a well and had been struck dumb with shock, that her parents were too poor to support her ... I got the drift and, still saddened by the 'Bournvita' child, gave her ten rupees – a generous amount when fifty paise is the normal donation, though ten rupees is less than fifty pence. She must have spread the word among other beggars because soon I was being approached from all sides by ragged figures. The pleasant anonymity that I'd been enjoying evaporated. I very quickly ran out of small change. I wasn't going to hand out hundred-rupee notes so I hardened my heart. I'd been in India long enough to ignore most beggars, particularly able-bodied ones. I'd give a few rupees to genuine lepers and to the old sannyasi around temples and I'd give food rather than money to children because, too often, the money would be taken from them at the end of the day. As a rule, the beggars with tales of woe were fraudulent, or so the Trivedis told me. If so, and I'm fairly sure that most of the time this was the case, then, in a way, they were intriguing. Where did they come from? Where did they go to at night? It was an instance of the nineteenth-century quality of so much of Indian urban life, a world that Gustave Doré, Charles Dickens or Victor Hugo would have recognized.

Mrs Trivedi and the two students came back. 'Well, all is not lost,' she announced. 'We will travel this evening on the Grand Trunk.'

'That is the good news,' said Mohan, 'here is the bad news. We do not have berths. Madam is all right, for she can sleep in a ladies-only compartment. We three must share one berth between us. It will certainly be a hardship but no matter.' Dilip looked very distressed. 'Now we must take a cheap hotel room somewhere and rest,' said Mrs Trivedi. I suggested the retiring rooms there at the station. 'Already they are full,' said Dilip fatalistically.

We asked a taxi driver who took us to a large modern place not far from the station. As we approached it, Mohan said, 'Acha, I have heard of this place.'

'What did you hear?' asked Mrs Trivedi.

'Oh, that it is reasonable value and all that.'

The receptionist, who might have been the manager but was more probably one of his relatives, was reading *Eyeless in Gaza*. He wore a grey silk suit and a red rose in his buttonhole. He was in his fifties, with a careworn and patient expression, clearly a sensitive soul. This cut no ice with Mrs Trivedi who banged on the counter, demanding a discount for short-term occupancy of a double room with a bathroom. I felt that she was being unnecessarily assertive as the man was perfectly agreeable. I'd noticed her taking that line before, buying fabric in Bangalore. It was a pity because it made her appear bullying rather than efficient and 'no-nonsense' as she intended.

The room was right at the top of the building. The lift was broken so we lugged our bags up several flights of stairs. One bearer helped us as much as he could. The room was painted sky blue. There were greasy palm prints all over the walls. 'What has been going on?' exclaimed Mrs Trivedi. Before she let the bearer leave she demanded fresh soap and clean towels for the bathroom. She unpacked a box of sweets and handed them around, saying, 'Please, take, take.'

Mrs Trivedi was dozing on one of the beds. Dilip, who'd grown more and more anxious, had collapsed on the other. Mohan was reading his muscle magazines, sitting lotus position on the floor. I sat on the chair reading *Melmoth the Wanderer*. I decided to visit 'Giggles', the bookshop, in the Connemara Hotel where I'd spent my very first night in India, to buy some English papers and books for the journey. There was plenty of time and I didn't like sleeping in the afternoon so, telling Mohan where I was going, I set off, travelling through Madras by auto-rickshaw. As we went along I recognized the smell of Madras, burning rubber and low-octane fuel, that I'd mistaken for the chimerical 'Smell of India'. Since then I'd come to the conclusion that there were distinctive smells that one associated with particular cities or areas of cities and that a generalized Indian smell would be as hard to isolate as a generalized Engish one, though it seems to have become a literary convention that the whole subcontinent has a uniform pungency. The Connemara was calm and dark and cool. The bookshop was full of interesting new titles. The owner (whom I thought of as 'Giggles' though it probably wasn't her name) was as gracious and friendly as she had been before. 'What a pity you have chosen the rainy season to visit Madhya Pradesh for Kanha Kisli will be closed.' Was she sure of that? 'Yes, yes. I'm afraid so.' I remembered that she was keen on wildlife. I bought *The Sunday Times* and a Saturday *Independent* and the latest *Granta* and three novels. I asked her what the weather would be like. I'd been near Mangalore when the monsoon started, I told her.

Would it be like that? 'Oh, no, no. Not so bad. That is the coastal monsoon, you see.' Did it ever stop raining? Giggles giggled. 'Of course, of course. But you should be more like us. We love the rains, it is a time of year that we look forward to.'

'My home is Kerala,' she went on. 'This is the time of year I always miss it most. There is a wonderful aroma everywhere, it is beautiful. Oh and you should see the skies when the rain clouds come rolling in.'

I had a glass of *lassi* in the hotel coffee shop. There was a party of unsophisticated Americans whom I discovered, by eavesdropping, to be missionaries, evangelists with bovine expressions and big white teeth, corn-fed and God-fearing, wearing dark suits and muttering grace before eating. It would be just as hot as this in the Southern United States. What I heard of their conversation, with its inherent assumptions of racial, cultural and moral superiority, I found intensely irritating. They sounded far less educated and open-minded than the average Brahmin priest whose teachings they had come to refute. Then I went back to the hotel near the station.

Mrs Trivedi and Dilip were still asleep. Mohan was reading *Melmoth the Wanderer*. He told me that he'd already had a bath. I went into the bathroom and washed and put on a clean white shirt, one that Mr Prakash had made me. When they woke up, we rang down for a pot of tea. Mrs Trivedi produced some *parathas* stuffed with *methi* (fenugreek leaves), quite delicious and better, I thought, cold than hot. Dilip was ravenous after his nap and, because Mrs Trivedi loved to feed people, more and more food was unwrapped. Chapattis and hard-boiled eggs, served with salt and fiery jackfruit pickle. What she called 'cutlets' were similar to 'veggie-burgers'. Glucose biscuits. More sweets – *jalebi* this time that looked like pretzels and tasted of golden syrup. When everyone had washed and was ready, we walked back to the station.

It was late in the evening and people were already bedding down on the pavement. Coconut-sellers and *nimbu-pani-wallahs* were doing a brisk trade; there were a few *bhel poori* stands and men, with machines like chafe-cutters, selling sugar-cane water. The platform was jam packed. It was obvious that most of the people who'd planned to travel on the cancelled train were doing the same as we were and taking the Grand Trunk Express instead. The Grand Trunk Express runs between Madras and New Delhi, a distance of some 1,400 miles. We were travelling as far as Itarsi, that would take nearly twenty hours. Then Mrs Trivedi and I would change trains for Jabalpur. Dilip and Mohan were also taking that train but continuing on to Allahabad where they had to change again for Benares. The women's compartment where Mrs Trivedi had her berth was halfway down the train. It was decided that she would look after the bulk of the luggage. We made sure that she was comfortable and had everything she needed. Sharing the compartment were three elderly sisters, so alike that they might have been triplets. Mrs Trivedi pressed a parcel of food upon us before we left, in case any of us were hungry in the night. We left the women chatting away in Hindi, joking and giggling like old friends. I was always impressed by this spontaneous Indian capacity for friendship. It made me ashamed that so often, out of shyness, I was standoffish. The berth that the three of us had to share was much further down the train. On the way down the platform we passed two very scruffy backpackers, young German hippies with sprouting beards and pink faces. Mohan didn't like the look of them and became incensed when he found out that they were travelling third-class unreserved. 'They are pretending to be poor, that is all. I cannot understand why. Why do they let themselves get so dirty? Do they not know of dhobi-wallahs? It is my opinion that in their own country they are rejects. Is that so? Then why do they come here?' We found our berth. Mohan looked around and said, 'I think it is not so bad after all.' Dilip was looking miserable. I wasn't too happy about the idea of sitting up all night either. 'What I am saying is that I think I can sort something out, leave it to me,' said Mohan and went off to talk to the ticket inspector. Dilip smiled patiently, sighed and sat down. Mohan soon came back and announced triumphantly that we would each have a berth for the night as soon as we'd passed the first station outside Madras. He'd arranged everything. I asked if he'd had to pay baksheesh.

'Hush, hush,' he laughed, 'you must not make such accusations. As a matter of fact it would be illegal to offer.'

To celebrate, Dilip devoured the entire contents of the food parcel. Mohan and I talked for a while. He told me about his weight-lifting, how he'd been a weakling before he'd taken it up. He told me of this achievement with a great deal of pride, visibly swelling as he spoke. We moved on to politics. He had very strong opinions. He was, for instance, fiercely atheistic and saw religion as the main obstacle to India's progress. He loathed priests (though a member of the Brahmin caste himself) and blamed them for holding the country back. 'If we took away such nonsense there would be no stopping India. As it is, our great men leave the country. Other nations benefit from Indian brains, only stupidity and repression flourish here. We must move forward.' He sounded like a politician (and a fanatical one at that) but I couldn't question his sincerity. My own feeling was that the hindrance to progress was political corruption. I saw the need for a secular government, of course, but that was different from one that banned religion. Besides, it seemed to me that Hinduism was flexible and multifaceted enough to adapt infinitely without compromising any of its essential truths, and far less oppressive than either Islam or Christianity could be in many other nations.

I slept on the top berth, extremely well, waking just
after six-thirty. A legless man was trundling down the
aisle on a trolley. There was the usual dawn chorus of
men clearing their throats. I drank three cups of coffee,
it was such a weak brew that it took that many to get
my regular fix of caffeine. Mohan and Dilip were still
asleep on the two berths below me. I read *The Sunday
Times*. It was an airmail edition without a colour
supplement. Within about an hour they both woke up.
At nine o'clock Mohan and I walked along the train to
see Mrs Trivedi. It was a long train and it took at least
twenty minutes of fast walking to get to her carriage. It
was as though we were passing through a great series
of dormitories. There were lots of people washing,
cleaning their teeth[1], scraping their tongues with
U-shaped wires attached to their toothbrushes. The
colour and texture of one's tongue is a matter of daily
concern to the health-conscious Indian. There were
people sitting in prayer, silently mouthing mantras,
others practising yoga or eating breakfast. Most of the
men wore lungis, having changed out of their trousers
before retiring to their berths, but some wore kurtas,
usually white or cream, sometimes in a light-brown
brindled *khaddi* or, very occasionally, striped like
Western pyjamas. I looked out for other Europeans and
saw just two, an exhausted-looking couple. Along the
train, in the first-class compartments, there would
have been several. Mrs Trivedi and the three sisters
were up and nattering merrily. The sisters were very
interested to know what I thought of Indian life. Was
the food too spicy for me? 'For him?' exclaimed Mrs
Trivedi. 'You should see him eating green chillies! My
husband says that in a past life he must have been
Indian.' Would the Trivedis find me an Indian bride? If
not, they would look out for a pretty Madrassi girl.
They clapped their hands and laughed. Before we left,
the sisters gave Mohan and me three little parcels
wrapped in newspaper. Inside the newspaper were

parcels of leaves and inside these parcels, curd rice flavoured with tamarind. On our way back down the train we passed a strange scene, a group of people sobbing loudly. They seemed to be a family, all huddled together and wailing. I asked Mohan if they were mourners. 'They are showing off,' he replied intolerantly. 'I have no time for such displays.' I still wanted to know why they were crying. There had to be a reason for it. Mohan could not understand my curiosity. 'Ignore them,' he said. 'Any interest will encourage them.' The exhausted European couple were in the same carriage as this noisily doleful group. They looked fed up and bewildered, as though the unexplained racket had been going on throughout the night. As we approached our carriage, I said, 'I expect a relative of theirs has died. They probably came down to Madras to be at the deathbed. Now they're returning North.' I was really thinking aloud but Mohan snapped at me. 'What does it matter, the reason? All I know is that they are acting without dignity. How long have you been in India that still such behaviour impresses you?' I said that I wasn't impressed, I was just looking for an explanation. Mohan apologized for being cross. 'Often in Benares I see Europeans photographing beggars and cripples, inadequate housing. Why are you people so interested in our weakness? Always we have our weaknesses pointed out. Is that what you find colourful?'

All day the train moved northward and the country that we saw through the windows changed gradually and subtly into a moist watercolour landscape of flooded paddies and dramatic skies. It grew colder as well. I finished the newspapers and decided to pass them on to the German backpackers so I made my way down to the third-class carriages. There the berths were slatted like park benches and most of the pass-engers appeared to be locals carrying produce a few stops along the line. Some I recognized as fruit-sellers who'd come through my carriage. It was easy enough to find the Germans. They were sprawled out, smoking *bidis*, and all around them was strewn litter – biscuit wrappers, banana skins, empty Bisleri bottles. I introduced myself and offered the papers, which they took without thanking me. In fact, they seemed wary of me. I tried to start a conversation but it soon became clear that I wasn't enough of a 'freak' for them to associate with. I was fairly pleased to get away from them. They had high whining voices and the narrow-minded arrogance of late adolescence.

I listened to Bismillah Khan on my Walkman. I'd bought a selection of cassettes in a music shop in Bangalore, various *ustads* and *pandits* (the Muslim and Hindu equivalents of maestro) on a range of different instruments. I found Indian 'classical' music perfect for long train journeys; time passed so slowly that one entered a sort of trance and then the music unfurled like a sequence of short vivid dreams. There was a similarity to the serious jazz of John Coltrane, the same transcendent quality and the feeling of going over and over a melody as if trying to break free some divine message encoded in the notes. Also, as in jazz generally, the instruments seemed to speak or sing as extensions of the human voice. It was as if the landscapes that I could see through the bars of the windows (the glistening paddies, green plains, nullahs stirring back to life with the rains) were being described by the music. That's exactly right, I kept thinking.

Late in the evening we came to Itarsi. It was drizzling. Cows ambled along the platform. We clustered next to a stand selling omelettes. If I'd been on my own I'd have bought one but Mrs Trivedi had made it clear that anything other than fresh fruit was dicing with dysentery. 'Even we ourselves must be careful.' She'd told me a cautionary tale about an aged uncle of hers who had actually died after eating an illicit samosa. Mohan and Dilip were quiet and tired. I was looking forward to sleeping on the next stage of the journey. We were informed by a fellow passenger that the train to Jabalpur was running late. 'How late?' Mrs Trivedi asked a platform manager. 'Who can say?' he shrugged. 'Maybe one hour, maybe five?' I was aghast at this vagueness. Why didn't they know? There are telegraphs, surely? I'd seen computers. 'Those are just tools,' said Mrs Trivedi calmly, 'Somebody must operate them.' She seemed to accept the situation. But surely it's the driver's responsibility to inform the station managers if the train's running late? 'Do you realize how many people use this railway system every day? That it runs as efficiently as it does is a miracle enough, we say. The occasional inconvenience we must bear, that is all.'

We decided to relax in the waiting-room, if possible to sleep. There was a separate waiting-room for women travellers, cleaner and more comfortable, where Mrs Trivedi stayed. The general waiting-room was packed out. People were lying on the floor. It seemed the best thing to do. A man came in with an ancient and short-sighted dog. He lay down and the old dog crouched beside him, awake all the time and growling at the slightest noise. I might have fallen asleep if it hadn't been for the flies that kept settling on my face and arms, tickling me back into wakefulness the moment I nodded off. So I gave up the idea. On either side of me both Mohan and Dilip were sleeping soundly. At about three o'clock Mrs Trivedi came in, announcing loudly that the train would arrive within ten minutes. Nearly everyone in the waiting-room had been asleep and her news caused a stir. Mohan and Dilip woke up, then after a short discussion, decided to sleep on and travel on a later train after breakfast. I said goodbye to them. Mohan had given me his address in Benares and I'd arranged to visit him when I went there. I followed Mrs Trivedi down the platform. I bought us both some tea from a *chai* stall. 'Quickly,

quickly,' she warned me, 'soon the train comes.'

Within minutes it arrived. Mrs Trivedi found our berths. The ticket inspector was an old friend. His name was Mr Paul and he had served in her father's regiment. 'Since madam was a girl I have known her,' he told me. They talked for some time. As he moved down the train she turned to me and smiled. 'An army station is like a small village. That is how we live in Jabalpur.' I was feeling very tired by this time. However, our berths ran alongside the windows and were much shorter than the ones that ran across the carriage and Mrs Trivedi insisted that I keep all my luggage beside me and not under the berth so I found myself curled into a space of about four feet; the window was jammed and rain seeped in and I found it impossible to sleep at all.

We reached Jabalpur at seven. I had to wake Mrs Trivedi up. It was raining quite heavily. Outside the railway station we hailed two cycle-rickshaws. Travelling along the slick roads, through the quiet streets of the cantonment to her father-in-law's house, we seemed to glide, the rickshaws listing like Chinese junks. The house stood in a compound, with a cluster of outbuildings and a pretty, overgrown garden. It was a proper bungalow with a shady verandah and a *porte-cochère*, a Victorian building.

Colonel Trivedi came to the door and his daughter-in-law stooped to touch his feet. He was a tall old man, light-skinned and with the same flaring nostrils as his son, but broader in build, altogether larger than the Major. He wore kurta pyjamas of fine white cambric and chappals. He was quite bald, about seventy-five years old. His wife, who appeared behind him, looked very like Major Trivedi. She had an intellectual and serious manner. She wore a sari of *khaddi* silk that must have been blue once but had faded to a subtle mauve. They were very friendly and welcoming but, as I was introduced, I felt uncomfortably rumpled, dirty and unshaven. The room that we entered, the living-room, had the highest ceiling I'd ever seen, cut off halfway up the wall by a transparent gauze. The walls were unpainted but an attractive buff colour and decorated with family photographs and regimental memorabilia. I noticed the photograph of Major Trivedi and General Kapur. There was some fine old rosewood furniture. The older Mrs Trivedi said, 'Here you should feel at home for it is an English house. In one hundred and fifty years we are the only Indian family to live here.' It occurred to me that British domestic architecture in India was unlike any vernacular archi-tecture in Britain. A bungalow is an adaptation of a Bengali cottage – a Bengali cottage is a stationary tent. The climate demanded certain features, as did the presence of numerous household servants. The kitchen was normally a separate building connected to the house by a covered walkway. In the case of the Trivedis' house this walkway had been turned into a corridor. Colonel Trivedi had moved into the house in 1945 after it was vacated by a retiring English officer. A few years ago he'd been able to buy the house from the Army.

I would have preferred to go straight to my room to change and wash but the older Mrs Trivedi had prepared breakfast. There was a good strong coffee to drink and a great bowl of *upma* (similar to semolina). It was all brought from the kitchen by a Gurkha bearer. The Colonel was fasting. He fasted one day a week, a practice he'd adopted in the Army, apparently for mental alertness. So he stood and talked while we ate. He had the same interest in history as his son and we were soon discussing the holding of the Uri-Poonch Bulge. Mrs Trivedi asked about the weather. The Colonel banged on the screen. 'This year there has been too much rain already. The Narmada[2] is about to flood. Marble Rocks will not be safe. You see, it is no water or too much water, in between there is nothing.' My bedroom was formerly Major Trivedi's grandfather's room. The old man, who had only recently died, had lived to be a hundred years old. A distinguished Sanskrit scholar, he had published a book the year before his death. The room was musty and lined with books. The younger Mrs Trivedi warned me to keep my case locked because she believed that the Gurkha was a thief. 'It is best not to tempt him,' she said. I found this strange as, at breakfast, the Colonel had mentioned that the man had been his bearer for over thirty years. Later, the Gurkha knocked on my door saying, '*Pani garum, Baba.*' The bathroom was cold and dark but the *pani garum* warmed me and it was marvellous to wash and put on fresh clothes. I lay down on my bed to read and fell fast asleep until lunch-time.

In one of the outbuildings lived the older Mrs Trivedi's sister, Mrs Ramachandram, with her husband, her grown-up daughter and a small mongrel dog called Hamlet. I went to their house for tea. Mrs Ramachandram was the headmistress of a private school for girls. I had been informed that Mr Ramachandram was an invalid though he seemed to get about quite well. Mr Ramachandram had a nervous twitch. He was a thin aristocratic-looking man. (His hobby was whittling. 'Beautiful spoons he makes!' exclaimed the younger Mrs Trivedi.) It was a tiny house. Instead of furniture there were tea chests and piles of books; a board placed on top of four piles made a table. Hamlet wouldn't stop barking at me. Mr Ramachandram, who was making the tea, was more concerned about Hamlet's inhospitality than I was. 'Oh, please forgive him. You are the first Westerner he has seen.' He spoke softly and his English was precise and orthodox without sounding like an imitation of a British accent. Having grown used to the inflections and inversions of Indian English, it sounded strange.

Mrs Ramachandram sat very still. She was younger and rather better looking than her sister and there was something regal in her manner. 'My nephew wrote and told me that you are a great reader. Then we have much in common for English literature is my passion,' she told me. I thought she had one of the most beautiful voices I'd ever heard; it was more Indian than her husband's, with exquisite modulation, like a tune played on a flute. Mr Ramachandram took Hamlet outside and chained him up on the verandah. 'Now we will have some peace,' he said and I noticed that his hands were shaking.

'Don't you love Jane Austen, coming from Bath?' asked Mrs Ramachandram. 'And there is Sheridan too, of course.' I said that I believed Edward Lear[3] had come to Jabalpur, then usually spelled Jubbulpore which sounded like a place in one of his poems. Mrs Ramachandram clapped her hands. 'It is true! He was here. There is a book here somewhere of his life. There is a poem even, filled with Hindi words, all wrongly used, that is so funny. Indeed I learnt it to amuse the girls.'

'Can you still remember it?'

'Oh yes, yes,' said Mrs Ramachandram and, without a hint of self-consciousness, she began:

> 'She sat upon her Dobie,
> To watch the Evening Star,
> And all the Punkahs as they passed
> Cried, "My! how fair you are!"
> Around her bower, with quivering leaves,
> The tall Kamsamahs grew,
> And Kitmutgars in wild festoons
> Hung down from Tchokis blue . . .
> Beware, ye Fair! Ye Fair, beware!
> Nor sit out late at night, –
> Lest horrid Cummerbunds should come,
> And swollow you outright.
>
> Below her home the river rolled
> With soft meloobious sound,

Where golden-finned Chuprassies swam,
In myriads circling round.
Above, on tallest trees remote
Green Ayahs perched alone,
And all night long the Mussak moan'd
Its melancholy tone,

And where the purple Nullahs threw
Their branches far and wide, –
And silvery Goreewallahs flew
In silence side by side, –
The little Bheesties twittering cry
Rose on the flagrant air,
And oft the angry Jampan howled
Deep in his hateful lair.

She sat upon her Dobie, –
She heard the Nimmak hum, –
When all at once a cry arose, –
The Cummerbund is come!
In vain she fled: – with open jaws
The angry monster followed,
And so, (before assistance came,)
That Lady Fair was swollowed.

They sought in vain for even a bone
Respectfully to bury, –
They said, – "Hers was a dreadful fate!"
(And Echo answered "Very.")
They nailed her Dobie to the wall,
Where last her form was seen,
And underneath they wrote these words,
In yellow, blue and green: –

Beware, ye Fair! Ye Fair, beware!
Nor sit out late at night, –
Lest horrid cummerbunds should come,
And swollow you outright.'

Mr Ramachandram and I clapped, which set Hamlet barking on the verandah. I noticed that Mr Ramachandram was silently crying with amusement. It was an amusing poem, to be sure, but I was more struck by the fact that Mrs Ramachandram could recite the whole thing from memory. Her nephew, Major Trivedi, had often amazed me with his memory for poetry; it was clearly an inherited talent. Mr Ramachandram wiped his eyes and said, between quiet heaves of laughter, 'What's so funny, you see, is that all those words are just the words that a visitor to India, in those days, would've learned right away. In fact,' he started to shake, 'he mightn't have learnt any others. That's the joke.' He broke down again and had to blow his nose. I said that I'd never come across the poem before. It was very like 'Jabberwocky'. 'Then I will write it down for you before you leave. "Jabberwocky", by the way, is Lewis Carroll, but I do see the resemblance. I myself prefer it to "Jabberwocky" because, for us in India, it better illustrates nonsense in poetry.' I didn't understand. 'Well, you see, my girls can enjoy the humour. With "Jabberwocky" they do not know what is a nonsense and what isn't. How should they know that a borogrove doesn't exist?' Mr Ramachandram, composed again, poured the tea. It was *masala chai*[4] with ginger. 'Here comes Saraswati.' (Mrs Trivedi had told me about Saraswati on the journey up. It was, apparently, a great family worry that they could not find a husband for her. 'She is a very clever girl, first-class honours. And pretty. But she turns everyone away.' How old was she? Mrs Trivedi shook her head despairingly. 'Already she is twenty-eight.' Perhaps she doesn't want to get married yet? Mrs Trivedi clucked at the suggestion. 'It is hardly up to her to make that choice.')

Saraswati came in, carrying Hamlet upside down in her arms like a baby. She also taught in her mother's school. She was plump in the way that Indian film stars are, comely rather than overweight, and had a dark complexion. Her eyes were an unusually light brown. She was bright and talkative. She told me that she was reading George Bernard Shaw. *Major Barbara*, did I know it? I said that I didn't but had read or seen other plays by Shaw. I asked her if her school ever put on plays? Sometimes, not every term. It depended upon the girls. It was a very small school.

Mrs Trivedi was visiting her parents in another part of town. She slept at her father-in-law's house but spent most of her days with her own family. It rained and rained and I had to stay indoors a lot of the time, reading and writing letters. Colonel Trivedi and his wife were talkative people and told me some interesting stories. The Colonel had been a great shikaree in his day. There were skulls mounted on the verandah. I asked if he'd ever shot a tiger. He had, near Pachmarhi, and he produced a photograph of himself with the slain beast. I had read a marvellous book by a man called Hugh Allen called *The Lonely Tiger* that was set in Madhya Pradesh. It turned out that Colonel Trivedi had known Allen. I told the Colonel that I'd enjoyed browsing through the shikar books in the library of the Ooty Club. Shikar writing interested me. It seemed to me to be the most vital literature to have come out of the British presence in India; almost unconsciously so, in that the great majority of its practitioners were amateurs without literary notions. I think that, because veracity was of the utmost importance, the style of prose had to be sparer and closer to speech than the contemporary literature. A good shikar story is like a story heard around a campfire, it has a primitive quality. Accuracy of detail, the hunter's respect for and knowledge of his quarry, the straightforward narrative, all these struck me as impressive. The Colonel agreed. 'I would even say that a writer like Corbett is a great Indian writer, full stop. Oh, people say he is not Indian. I ask, was he not born here? In fact, he was an old man before he even visited England

and he never lived there. No, no, no, let India claim him.'

The Madhya Pradesh Tourist Office was in the railway station and I went there to find out about visiting Khajuraho. In the station forecourt there was a great deal of commotion and chanting and it turned out that an old man (a hajji) was returning from his pilgrimage to Mecca. A band started playing and the old man was carried out of the station on a silk sheet. I watched all this from the tourist office. It seemed a very joyful and harmless celebration but the man in charge of the office grew very anxious, tugging at my arm and exhorting me not to look. 'Please, sir, please, come from the door. It might not be safe.'

I mentioned his concern to Colonel Trivedi who shook his head sadly. 'The problem is that Muslims feel threatened. There has been violence. Hindus are becoming intolerant. Goondas there are on both sides. What do the politicians do? They stir up the problem!' And he made the gesture of one stirring a cauldron.

The Trivedis had their own private cycle-rickshaw-wallah, who lived in another of the outbuildings. If anyone needed him he was on hand, otherwise he'd scout for fares down at the railway station. His bicycle was in very bad condition and the chain kept falling off. According to the younger Mrs Trivedi, he had a problem staying away from the arrack shops. Between showers I'd venture into Jabalpur, usually staying within the Civil Lines. This wasn't due to lack of curiosity, the rickshaw-wallah never managed to take me any further. I was surprised to see a number of Africans. I asked the rickshaw-wallah about them but he couldn't understand me. He knew that I was asking about the Africans though because he said *hubshees* in a derisive voice and spat. Mrs Ramachandram told me that they were students from East African countries. I noticed that a film called *Snake*

117

Woman was playing at the Empire Cinema. Closer scrutiny of the poster revealed that it was Ken Russell's *Lair of the White Worm,* renamed and marketed as pornography. I was interested in Bram Stoker and would like to have seen how Russell had modernized the plot. There were no dates on the poster so I asked the rickshaw-wallah to drive past the Empire Cinema. It was boarded up.

Arun Dandapani, Mrs Trivedi's old schoolfellow, whom I'd met at Atul's *bhel poori* party, came to see me one morning. He drove me around the old city, pointing out splendid buildings in the bazaar area, ornate temples and the houses of old merchant families. Arun and I had very similar taste in buildings. I found him extremely congenial and he seemed to know just what would interest me. With all the bustle and noise of the bazaar and its feeling of being untouched by any European influence, the old city was so different from the cantonment that it might have been another country. Arun was interested in Bath. 'I believe it is a famous spa. Perhaps it resembles Droitgate, am I right?' Droitgate? I was puzzled. 'You must know it. It's where Freddie Fitch-Fitch went to visit his uncle, Major-General Sir Aylmer Bastable. You must know *Romance at Droitgate Spa*, a wonderful story.' Arun was a Wodehouse buff, able to quote entire paragraphs and with a precise knowledge of every story. I must have disappointed him, knowing only a few of the stories and, for the most part, finding the humour enormously overrated; funny enough but not deserving the acclaim that serious critics lavish upon the books. 'You are the one, I am afraid, who is wrong,' Arun told me good-naturedly, 'for it is acknowledged that old Plum is a genius. He creates an entire world.' We met some friends of his at the Indian Coffee House. They were a bookish group, as informed and up-to-date as Giggles in Madras, and anxious to talk about the Rushdie affair.

On the way back to the Trivedis' house we drove past the railway station and, yet again, there was a crowd gathered in the forecourt. 'Acha,' smiled Arun, 'this you must see.' In the centre of the crowd were two snake-charmers and their huddled entourage, lean dark-skinned farouche men. 'Gond tribals[5],' explained Arun. He had been talking earlier about 'Adivasis' (the pre-Aryan aboriginals of Central India, of which the Gonds and the Santals are the largest tribes) and the furore caused by the Mandal Commission. I'd noticed that Arun's attitude was of complete detachment, the political stance of many Indian intellectuals. 'It is Naga Panchami, a very popular festival with tribals,' he said. 'You will see displays of the cobra-pipes all over the country this week.' The snake-charmers squatted on their hunkers playing pipes made of gourds and metal tubes. The melody that they played sounded vaguely Scottish to me. The cobras came arching out of the straw baskets. It was creepy and impressive and not in the least touristy. When the snakes had danced back into their baskets, one of the entourage picked up a smaller basket and started to make a speech. Arun translated for me. 'He says that in the basket is a wondrous beast, smaller than a cat but the most savage creature in the forest. It has come from the jungles of Rajasthan. It is the natural enemy of the cobra, braver than the mongoose.'

The man started to open the basket and the crowd stepped back.

He pulled out a small hedgehog that blinked and licked its lips.

'A porcupine,' said Arun.

'That's not a porcupine, that's a hedgehog,' I whispered.

'He is saying,' Arun whispered back firmly, 'that it is a vampire.'

The crowd recoiled further.

'He says that its cry resembles the sound of a frog. When the cobra approaches, it curls into a ball.' To illustrate this the man folded the hedgehog into that position.

'The cobra strikes but hurts its mouth on the quills. Then it is enraged. The cobra continues to strike until it is exhausted and faints. Then the creature uncurls and bites the cobra's neck, draining the snake of all its blood.'

There were gasps of horror and nobody dared touch the hedgehog.

'We have them at home,' I told Arun.

'Then it must be adders that they live on, am I right?'

One day I went to a bookshop that Arun had recommended. The proprietor had red hair and green eyes. (Later on I asked Mrs Trivedi, who knew the shop, if the man was Eurasian. 'He is Punjabi originally.'

'But he must have some European blood.'

'Why should he?'

'Because of his colouring.'

'I can show you many of that colouring in the North. Kashmiris, in particular. You see, the South Indians are so dark but up here we have the full range.')

It was a well-stocked bookshop but badly laid out so that it was impossible to browse. All the books were piled, spine down, behind the counter. You had to ask to look at a specific title and if you didn't want to buy it, the proprietor sighed and looked cross. I found a collection of short stories, so battered and dusty that I was sure it was second-hand – 'No, all are brand-new' – it included a Bram Stoker story, 'The Burial of the Rats,' so I bought it. Outside, on a wooden pole, were three loudspeakers, the old-fashioned kind that one associates with holiday camps. Intermittently, highly distorted film music would blast out. It was unbelievably loud, an awful screeching, all treble and no bass. I asked the green-eyed proprietor how he could stand it and he told me that it was an idea devised by the Chamber of Commerce (of which he was a member) to encourage shoppers. 'You see, all these songs are very high in the hit parade.'

The train to Satna passed through the town of Sleemanabad, named after Colonel William Henry Sleeman who, between 1828 and 1837, was responsible for stamping out the sinister cult of Thuggee[6]. The train journey wasn't very long. Near me sat a young man wearing a shirt with playing-cards printed on it. This fellow would engage the other passengers in a guessing-game, a mixture of 'I Spy' and charades. Many people joined in the game and there were shouted guesses and shrieks of laughter. He was a very good mime and with his elastic features and dark rolling eyes, he reminded me of Harpo Marx.

In Satna I stayed at a state-run tourist motel with a pleasant garden and I sat on the verandah for a while, reading and drinking coffee. Two young Sikh boys, their long hair knotted under white handkerchiefs, were knocking a ball around with hockey sticks. Unfortunately the rains had brought a plague of mosquitoes and, even wearing my 'jungle formula' repellent, I was driven back to my room.

The manager told me that the bus to Khajuraho stopped right in front of the motel and that it wouldn't be necessary to go to the bus station. At six the next morning I was waiting as instructed at the *chai* stall beside the banyan tree. The bus, I had been warned, was not marked in English so it would be necessary to ask the local people for assistance. A small crowd gathered around me as soon as I spoke and, as each bus pulled in, there was such a confusion of shaking heads and instructions that when I eventually boarded a bus that appeared at least to be heading in the right direction I was by no means confident of its destination. It was a very ramshackle bus with hard seats. It wasn't crowded but that seemed to emphasize its lack of suspension. We moved forward in jolts and judders, bumping around, sometimes thrown forwards and back again. I realized how bony my bottom had become. Beside the main road out of Satna lay a dead cow in a ditch. We could smell it in the bus as we approached and most of the passengers flocked to the windows to see the gruesome spectacle. There was a gash down its side through which the stomach protruded like a great white balloon.

After a while we were climbing into the Vindhyachala Mountains and the cultivated land gave way to jungle. Two musicians got on. One had a drum and the other had a long stringed instrument made from a gourd and a pole. They were tribals, I guessed Gonds but they could have been from one of a profusion of tribes in this area. They had elaborate marks painted on their foreheads. 'Snake worshippers, very bad,' whispered a man behind me.

'This is the festival of Naga Panchami,' I said coldly, without turning around. It didn't strike me as bad at all.

'Sir, I am a Jehovah's Witness,' whispered the man.

'Then you have discarded a perfectly valid and ancient religion for one that is spurious and ill-founded and you are certainly in no position to criticize the beliefs of others,' I whispered back, still without turning around. I felt ashamed of myself for being so rude though I'd meant what I said. The tribals were only on the bus for about half an hour. The bus stopped in the middle of nowhere, without so much as a house to indicate a village or any kind of settlement and they slipped away through the trees. The jungle, lush in the monsoon, was striking. We passed a splendid waterfall, crashing through the dark vegetation into a cloud of white steam.

And soon after that we came to Panna, a small dirty town where a crowd gathered to hear the results of a lottery. The amplified distorted voice growled and boomed as if an angry demon was raving from deep underground. Most of the passengers got off there and, for a ghastly moment, I wondered if I had taken the wrong bus. 'Khajuraho?' I asked the driver who wagged his head and grinned which I took to be affirmative. The bus rattled off again with only myself and a pathetic wheezing cripple aboard (whenever the juddering was really bad the cripple coughed and coughed and made a whimpering sound) but as we passed through jungle villages, more and more people got on and, by the time we pulled into Khajuraho, the bus was full again.

Khajuraho is one of India's major tourist attractions. A complex of twenty-two medieval temples, sufficiently out of the way to have avoided Muslim iconoclasm, they stood undisturbed and overgrown in the jungle until rediscovered, in 1838, by Captain Burt of the Asiatic Society. The temples were built by the Chandelas, a dynasty of Rajput kings who claimed descent from Hemvati, a priest's daughter who fell in love with Chandramas the moon god. They met while Hemvati was bathing in the river Rati. The child of this union was the first Chandela king, Chandravarman. For five centuries his descendants ruled the area until they were conquered by Muslim invaders. The temples are certainly beautiful but there are older and finer temples in the South (which, by and large, the Muslims left alone) and most of the Southern temples are still functional as places of worship rather than archæological sites. The great attraction of Khajuraho is partly its proximity to the other main tourist attractions of Northern India and, more than that, the famous bands of fine stonework, including some carvings of extreme eroticism, that embellish the temples. On every temple, besides the usual pantheon of Hindu deities, there are figures of *apsaras*, celestial dancing girls. If the girl is not dancing but performing some other function, carrying flowers or a water-pitcher, putting on make-up or gazing into a looking-glass, she is not an *apsara* but a *surasundari*. Whichever, they are the hand-maidens of the gods, beautiful, scantily clad or naked and sexy in a sweet uncomplicated way. One senses that the craftsmen who carved these figures worked zealously; sometimes one is amazed at the gynæcological accuracy. Smaller and less painstakingly carved are the *mithuna*, friezes of tiny figures engaged in every possible sexual activity. Compared to the *apsaras* and *surasundaris,* these represent a transition from soft to hard pornography. There are depictions of group sex, oral sex, anal sex, homosexuality, lesbianism, even someone buggering a horse. There are all sorts of theories for the existence of the *mithuna*. Some people believe that the carvings have a significance related to Tantra, which is certainly feasible. Some believe that they are instructional, like the Kama Sutra (but who would encourage horse buggery?). Others say that the figures are there to ward off evil spirits (they'd have to be pretty feeble evil spirits, in my opinion; I'd have thought the carvings more likely to attract them). And others still (including Mrs Trivedi) say that they were to prevent lightning from striking the temples. I think that they are just an example of bawdy medieval humour, the sort of thing that abounds in all the European arts of the same period. It struck me that a disproportionate significance has been given to the *mithuna*, firstly by outraged Victorians, then by sleazy entrepreneurs. There are friezes of processions, hunts and battles that are quite neglected by comparison. An entire industry has been created around the images of the *mithuna* and the souvenir shops sell very bad reproductions of the most salacious couplings. The assumption that all Westerners were priapic oafs annoyed me.

I was outside the largest temple, the Kandariya Mahadeva. I had a guidebook and had been managing well without hiring a guide. Most of the guides who'd approached me had been less than confidence-inspiring, with vulpine looks and poor English, promising 'more sexy carving, I show you' for one hundred rupees. It was hot and muggy. I'd chosen an expensive hotel because it had a swimming-pool, an indulgence that I was looking forward to. I was also, to be honest, slightly bored; finding the temples too similar to one another and the atmosphere of the whole complex lacking the craziness and colour that I loved about India. Maybe I was in the wrong mood.

I sat on a step next to an old man dressed like a Congress Party politician. In fact he looked very like Pandit Nehru and even wore a white forage cap. He was writing something in a notebook. As soon as he noticed me he put the notebook away and introduced himself as Mr Deepak Rahul, Bachelor of Arts, poet and philosopher. He asked me what I thought of Khajuraho and, when I told him that I wasn't thrilled, he scratched his neck and looked quizzically at me. 'Then I am wondering if you recognize the true achievement of the architecture?'

I replied that I had read the guidebook but Mr Rahul was dismissive. 'The real magnificence of these temples is not mentioned in that book. I am in the process of composing the first philosophical guide to Khajuraho.'

'Philosophical in what sense?' I asked.

Mr Rahul beamed at me. 'Philosophical, mathematical, geometrical, cosmological. All will be aspects of my book,' he promised. 'You must be bearing in mind that since archæological discovery, 1838, these temples have attracted scandalizations. Now, the Indian people, my friend, have no desire for scandalizations. They stay away. My wish is for them to see that Khajuraho is more than perversity. Let them see that these temples can teach us of God's universe and our place in it. Tell me, what do you know of our Vedic religion?'

I said that I didn't know much at all; the names of a few gods; terms like *karma, dharma* and *prana*; a few concepts and a handful of myths.

'You must be knowing about Brahmanda,' said Mr Rahul.

I guessed from the 'Brahma' part that it meant creation. 'You are almost right, my friend. It is the Sanskrit word for the cosmos. Now, tell me, what is the form of the cosmos?'

Surely it would be formless, infinite?

'Oh no, it has the form of an egg! You see, Brahma plus Anda, Brahmanda. Anda means egg,' he said. 'Now, am I not right to say that an egg is not a circle?'

I nodded.

Mr Rahul smiled. 'Then I put it to you that every Hindu temple is a model of the cosmos.'

Here I was lost, I couldn't see that the temples were egg-shaped at all. Mr Rahul was adamant. 'The point is that a temple can fit inside an egg.'

I felt like pointing out that anything could if the egg was big enough.

Mr Rahul went on. 'Not just a temple is a cosmic model. Oh no, my friend, you and I and all human beings are cosmic models. And not just human beings but every living creature is a model of the cosmos!'

I was starting to wonder if Mr Rahul belonged to some peculiar religious sect. Flecks of spit appeared on his lips. 'The object of all prayer, is it not, is to remove the boundary of self, you will agree? That is, for the cosmos within to join the greater cosmos?'

Mr Rahul's theories leaped about too much for me. He gave me no time to gather the threads.

'You are perhaps aware of fractals?'

I was, vaguely. I knew that they were a recent mathematical concept, a type of advanced geometry, put forward by a Frenchman called Mandelbrot. Put very simply, a fractal remains just as complex in composition whether it is enlarged or reduced. Illustrated by computer, they are strikingly beautiful, swirling psychedelic patterns; each section is a reflection of the broader pattern.

'Do not fractals appear anyway in nature?' asked Mr

Rahul. 'Is not the little brook a version of the mighty river? Is not the twig at the end of a branch a version of the branch? And is not the branch a version of the tree? Or take the humble *gobi* or cauliflower, eh? Each section of *gobi*, a miniature of the whole vegetable, no?'

I could see what he meant though I wasn't convinced that any of these examples really qualified as fractals. But Mr Rahul was off and running. 'So, my friend, look at these temples. If you can imagine that you were to break off a part of the masonry, then that part, it could be any part, would be the shape of the whole structure! And the shape of the whole structure is the shape of the cosmos, no? That, I can assure you, is so! My friend, this proves that fractals were known in India almost one thousand years ago.'

What I could see, at Khajuraho and most of the older temples that I'd visited, was a style of architecture that seemed almost organic, jagged forms repeating themselves vertically from base to spire and, in friezes and edges, horizontally. Columns were created from piles of plates, or trays or flattened stars, not necessarily circles; the edge of one plate followed by a smaller version and so on and so on, finally resembling spines or tree trunks and seeming to possess an intricate, almost shimmering vibrancy. This I took to be Mr Rahul's point. I wished him good luck with his book and walked to the village, pestered on the way by money-changers and touts for handicraft emporia.

There was a large party of Belgians in the lobby of the hotel, some of the women wearing *salwar-kamiz* outfits. They were on a three-week tour of Northern India and Nepal. The tour operator was arranging for a doctor to visit the hotel as several of his clients were suffering from diarrhoea.

It was hot when I got to the pool. Because there was no sunshine, just glare, the garden was deserted. The sky was like white perspex and the plants and flowers

127

seemed to be artificially scented, almost stifling, as if someone had sprayed an air freshener about to disguise an unpleasant smell. The water was warm and chlorinated and I swam a few lengths, then floated on my back with my eyes closed. I could hear crows and insects and, not far off, a herd of goats.

The following morning I woke up early and read a fascinating article about General Stroessner, the dictator of Paraguay. Then I got up and went swimming again. In the pool were hundreds of little red frogs; those that hadn't drowned in the night were struggling to get back to solid ground. So I spent some time gathering the survivors and placing them on the lawn. A mali (gardener) watched me and shook his head in disbelief. The Belgians were already leaving the hotel for the airport. In the restaurant were the remains of a breakfast buffet, a lot of uncleared plates and brimming ashtrays. A scowling waiter came to my table. I asked him if breakfast was still available (it was, after all, only eight o'clock). 'Yes, sir,' he grunted. I think he was disheartened at the prospect of clearing up the mess the Belgians had left. Would it be easier for him if I ate in my room?

'Sir, please take breakfast here in the restaurant.'

I ordered *ekoori* (scrambled eggs with chillies, onion and coriander) from the printed menu. 'It would be impossible,' said the waiter. I asked why – were there no eggs left? 'There are many eggs.' So what was the problem? 'Sir, *ekoori* takes an hour to prepare.' I could see that there was little point in pursuing 60-minute scrambled eggs so I asked what I could have. 'Here is plenty,' he waved, indicating the depleted buffet. All that I managed to find was half a cooked tomato and a hard shiny roll, something like a bagel. Nevertheless I was charged for a full breakfast – considerably more than I would have paid for *ekoori*. I read for a while and retrieved my clothes from the dhobi-wallah and sent some postcards of *mithuna* scenes to friends. I checked out at twelve o'clock exactly. The bus back to

Satna wasn't until half-past three but I wouldn't have put it past the hotel to charge me for remaining on the premises. I walked to the gates and summoned a cycle-rickshaw to take me into Khajuraho. The rickshaw-wallah was a wiry man with an extra thumb on each hand, smooth and hook-shaped with very sharp nails; they looked as if they'd be handy in a fight.

At a café run by a woman who had lived in Alberta, Canada, I ordered lunch. Canada has a large Indian population, usually clustered in the larger cities. This woman seemed to have stepped out of an 'Old West' pageant, she looked like a fan attending the annual country music festival at Wembley. She was an agile old creature, dressed in a rhinestone cowgirl outfit, an elaborate fringed rodeo shirt and jeans. Her hair was hennaed and she chain-smoked Charminars.

Two French girls were arguing with a man who was pointing a super-8 film camera at them. They moved to my table and introduced themselves as Annie and Corinne. They seemed agitated. 'The camera is not even loaded,' said Corinne. 'He is an imbecile.'

The cameraman, an earnest and chinless man of about my age, was hovering around as we talked so I stood up and asked him what he was doing. He was quite indignant. 'I would prefer it that you ignore me.' I said that we found his behaviour hard to ignore. 'My friend,' he said. 'I have already explained myself to the ladies. I am soon to make a documentary film on the subject of tourism. Now I am merely practising a widely accepted *cinéma-vérité* technique. The fly is on the wall.' I asked the fly to buzz off.

Annie and Corinne were architecture students from Paris. They were serious girls with pensive expressions. India presented a series of brain-teasers, logistic problems. Sometimes, like members of a quiz team, they would withdraw and quietly confer before reaching a solution. Annie came forward and said, 'You are travelling to Benares. Well, if you please, we propose that we travel with you.' As two girls travelling alone they had found themselves attracting too much unwelcome attention. Overnight train journeys were particularly fraught. I was perfectly happy to travel with them (and flattered to be cast in this chivalrous role) and they went off to pack. I was finishing my *thali* (and thinking to myself that I must exude 'the right stuff') when the proprietor of the café moseyed over and told me off for preventing the would-be director from practising. 'Put it this way, buddy, would you tell a sitar-player to quit playing his sitar?'

'Of course not,' I replied.

'All right already. If I want to encourage the arts in my café, it's my say-so, understand?' I paid for my lunch and left, feeling rather deflated.

At just after three we were waiting at the bus stand. A suave young pharmacist presented us with his card and, out of the blue, started to explain the fundamental principles of the Jain religion to us. The French girls, at least, were fascinated. Two young mothers were also waiting for the Satna bus. Their feet and ankles were stained with bright pink *mandi*, applied with a stencil, so that it looked as if they were wearing pretty lace socks.

Then the clouds burst and the dusty forecourt of the bus stand turned into a bubbling red pool. The bus back to Satna was just as decrepit as the one that had brought me to Khajuraho, but considerably more crowded. The three of us had to squeeze on to a seat designed for two, with our luggage crammed into the foot space, instead of up on the roof rack, because of the rain. 'It's only for a few hours,' I said cheerfully. Before long the aisle was filled with people and crates and sacks of produce. The roof leaked. The driver would start the engine and stop it again to let even more people and cargo aboard. A whole section of window and window frame caved in. This caused a certain amount of uproar. An old woman started to wail but was calmed by her son. A lot of rain was coming in. We rattled off. Passing through villages and small towns, I thought how much more pathetic and desperate poverty looked in the rain; roofs patched with soggy cardboard, sewage ditches that turned into foaming rapids. Once the bus was held up for a moment and I thought that I saw a ghost – a fair-haired European girl, aged about six and wearing a blue Edwardian dress with a pink sash, was throwing stones into a puddle. But when she turned towards me I saw that she was an albino with blood-red eyes.

We reached Satna, an hour later than scheduled, at half-past eight. The train for Benares left at nine and neither of the French girls had tickets. We got off the bus and realized that we were a long way from the railway station. We flagged two rickshaws down and Annie and Corinne set off in the first one while I followed with the luggage in the second. '*Jaldi, jaldi,*' I told the driver who shook with laughter. 'I mean it,' I insisted. In fact, as the rickshaw-wallah had calmly insisted, there was nothing to worry about. The train to Benares was late. Annie and Corinne managed to get berths right next to mine. We drank *chai* from little clay pots and dined on omelette sandwiches and Horlicks biscuits.

We got to Benares at four in the morning. It was still dark and pouring with rain. We crept through quiet streets, past ragged figures crouching in doorways and somnolent cattle, towards the cantonment and a cheap hotel that a guidebook had recommended. It was a vile place. Annie and Corinne got the last decent room. My room was a windowless cell, cold and damp. There was no bedding on the urine-stained mattress. The lavatory was full of reeking ordure and there was no running water until eight o'clock. I'd arranged to meet the girls again at noon. I was certain, however, that I wouldn't sleep so I decided to go down to the Ganges to watch the pilgrims bathing at dawn.

The rain had eased into drizzle now and I had got used to wearing damp clothes. I found an auto-rickshaw but the driver demanded three hundred rupees to take me to the ghats. That was almost ten pounds sterling, an absurd price. I brought him down to thirty rupees (even that seemed quite high but I wasn't sure how far the ghats were) and we set off for the old city.

It was a strange, other-worldly place. Of course, it is the holiest of holy sites in India, the most important of the seven sacred cities (the others are Ayodhya, Mathura, Hardwar, Kanchi, Ujjain and Dwarka). Benares is also known as Kashi, the City of Light; as Varanasi, the place between the rivers Varuna and Assi; as Avimukta, the Never-Forsaken (or Never-To-Be-Left); as Anandavana, the Forest of Bliss; as Rudravasa, the City of Shiva; and as Mahashmashana, the Great Cremation Ground. In its own way it is as sacred to the Hindu as Mecca is to the Muslim – for to die in Benares is to achieve moksa, liberation from the cycle of rebirth. To die in one of the other holy cities is to be reborn in Benares. I'd read about it but reading hadn't prepared me for the crowds, the clamouring, the lunatic intensity of it all. Whatever I thought that I understood of Hinduism flew from me. All the colour and noise that I loved about India were concentrated here into an experience that was weird and alarming. No frame of reference to cling to, nothing familiar, I was out of my depth in a great flood of people. There were sannyasi clad in washed-out orange, with their staffs and coconut-shell water-bowls; frail widows in white saris, who'd made the barefoot pilgrimage and would stay here for the rest of their lives. All kinds of cripples and invalids, barely alive, just creeping in at the eleventh hour. Even the Europeans fitted into the picture, adding more colours and human variety; their clothes took on a strangeness; their cameras and money belts became the emblems of a weird pallid sect; unclean and untouchable, they are condemned to observe but not participate in the purifying rituals. There were several hippies, most of whom seemed to be in the final throes of chronic dysentery. Had they come here to die? There was an assortment of sadhus, some with matted dreadlocks, some carrying tridents, some almost naked with the genitals covered by knotted handkerchiefs.

I looked out for *Aghoris*, the ghoulish Tantric sadhus, who choose an existence of demonic perversity the quicker to achieve the great liberation. They turn traditional Hindu values upside down. Their name actually means 'not terrible' (as if the infamous Tsar had introduced himself as Ivan the Not As Bad As People Make Out) but, from all that I'd read and been told, nobody is fooled. They come to Benares to hang around the cremation grounds. Often drunk, they collect food and alms in bowls that they fashion from human skulls. They cook meat on the embers of funeral pyres and, when times are hard, can survive on their own excrement. Perhaps this last practice, more than anything, vouchsafes their scarcity. I never saw one of these radicals.

I did see a man with lacerated feet and ankles, leaving bloody footprints in his wake.

Everyone was chanting '*Ram, Ram*' and other prayers, or perhaps just shouting for the hell of it, and the din was awesome. I paid the rickshaw-wallah his thirty rupees. 'Three hundred rupees,' he said, smiling hopefully, but I just walked away through the crowd, heading towards the Dasaswamedh ghat, and stopped at a *chai* stall.

A man who looked like Dustin Hoffman approached me. He wore a college scarf over a kurta and dhoti and plastic galoshes that had been moulded to resemble penny loafers. Would I like to hire a boat? He was somewhat evasive when I asked how much. We walked down to the ghat through a bazaar. Stalls were set out under great cloth umbrellas; barbers were shaving heads; there were little boats for sale, made of leaves and flowers, with candles to light. Priests bellowed prayers. I could hear somebody blowing what sounded like a hunting horn – it would have been a conch shell. The river was sludgy, the colour of coffee. I saw a party of Germans crowding into a long narrow boat. Sixteen of them, paying eighty rupees each. I wanted a boat to myself. I wanted to drift up and down and take photographs. I didn't want a guide, I'd wait until I came down with Annie and Corinne for that. 'Boat for one person, two hundred rupees,' Dustin reckoned. I weighed this up against what the Germans were paying for their boat and it seemed reasonable. What I didn't realize, until later, was that we were all being outrageously fleeced. The average cost of a boat for a couple of hours, regardless of the number of passengers, is twenty-five rupees. Benares is, more than anywhere else in India, a city of con men. All Westerners, probably all visiting Indians, are fair game. Cheats and swindlers abounded in the great places of Christian pilgrimage after all. Blissfully ignorant, indeed feeling that I'd struck a bargain, I boarded my private craft. All around me were tiny floating candle-boats and bathers, pilgrims entering the churned-up monsoon river.

The Ganges is, to the Hindu, more than a great river, she is a great goddess, no less than the earthly reflection of the Milky Way. Long ago, a king called Bhagiratha prayed to Brahma for her descent. Sixty thousand of his ancestors had been burned to ash by his enemy and only the celestial Ganges could raise them up again to dwell in heaven. Brahma sent her down and she fell into the Himalayas, at a place known as Gangotri, where Lord Shiva caught her in his hair. Bhagiratha was waiting for her and she followed him, down from the mountains and across the great arid plains, which she fertilized, all the way to the sea at a place called Ganga Sagara, where she slipped away to enter the netherworld and restore the king's ancestors. Thus she is said to flow in three worlds – in heaven, on earth and in the netherworld. The entire course of the river is sacred (and indeed the other great rivers of India, the Cauvery and the Godavari, though geographically quite separate, are seen as honorary tributaries of the Ganges) but nowhere is she more sacred than in Benares. For, as Kashi, the City of Light, the city was there before the river flowed through it, and even then it was a place of pilgrimage, a place of many *tirthas*. *Tirtha* literally means a ford or a crossing – and often is such a place – but also means a spot where the gods appeared on earth or where a miracle happened. So the Ganges passing through added her powers to this existing power and guaranteed the bestowal of moksa. Her powers are enormous and fundamental – the salvation of the dead and the purification of the living. Furthermore, she is the liquid manifestation of *Shakti*. *Shakti* means energy and although this emanates from Shiva, *Shakti* is a feminine force. So the Ganges is often represented as one of Shiva's consorts, the other being Parvati. The Ganges is Shiva's most effective means of moving through and working in this world – otherwise he is invisible, unknowable, indescribable. But, just as the sacred river bursts her banks on the earth, so in the world of the gods she swells beyond a single designated role. She is the only goddess to be claimed as a consort by all three Gods of the Hindu Triumvirate. With Brahma, she travels in a special brass pot. Alongside Lakshmi, the goddess of wealth, and Saraswati, the goddess of learning, the Ganges is the consort of Vishnu.

Devout Hindus make what is called the Panchatirthi (Five *Tirthas*) Pilgrimage. This means bathing at five holy ghats along the three-mile riverfront. The names of these ghats are Assi, Dasaswamedh (which is where I was – because of the main road and parking, the principal 'tourist' ghat), Panchaganga, Adi Keshava and Manikarnika. Each ghat has its own specific heavenly influence. Scholarly Brahmin pilgrims recite a statement of intention (called a *sankalpa*) at each

135

ghat but ordinary pilgrims hear the statement read by an attendant priest (*pandya*). The men were bathing in loincloths or white underpants, the women fully clothed. Some might just have been in a public bathroom. They were using soap and shampoo, lathering up. Some of them cleaned their teeth, scraped their tongues, gargled with and actually drank the water, an idea that appalled me – but that was only because I couldn't grasp the supreme cleanliness of this river whose very essence was purity, both physical and spiritual. It was the old people who most impressed me. Thin and frail, they entered the cold swirling waters meekly, muttering prayers, their faces twitching with humility and devotion. If submersion in the Thames was a central part of the Anglican faith, would British pensioners take such risks?

'*Chalo, chalo*,' I asked the boatmen to row off. They signalled back to wait a moment. A man was wading towards the boat. He was as fat and as shiny as a seal; indeed he seemed to be covered in a film of grease, like a channel swimmer. He clambered aboard and pressed his palms together in salutation, making a squishing sound as he did so. There was a glint of such depravity in his eyes that, at first, I thought he might be an *Aghori* inviting me to breakfast. 'I'm afraid we're just off,' I told him. 'Master, I am Ravi, your guide.'

'I don't want a guide. I just want to drift along quietly and watch.'

'Master, I am a Brahmin. Supreme caste.' He pulled up his wet stained kurta to show a grubby grey thread across his chest. His stomach was enormous and covered in flea bites. 'Look, I'm sorry but I don't want a guide. You'll have to get off.' The Brahmin ignored me and told the boatmen that we were ready to leave. This I thought a hell of a cheek. 'Master, Master. Have I asked you for money? I am your friend.' He smiled unctuously. I was stuck with him. 'Well then, just don't say anything. If I have any questions I'll ask you.'

'Then there is not a problem.'

Benares from the river was stunning. A three-mile-long cliff of massive and dilapidated masonry. Platforms, temples, staircases and passageways, vast decaying palaces rising in layers from the filthy water. It was like a monstrous Venice, a vision to thrill Piranesi, the fever-dream of a Gothic novelist, the opium hallucination of a doomed French Symbolist. The sun, through the damp mist, was a great yellow beam. Ravi leered at me. 'Master, single man? You'd like to meet Benares girl, true virgin?' I ignored him. 'Master prefer strong Indian boy, maybe?'

'You said you wouldn't talk to me.'

'This is not guide business, Master. This is your friend's business. How would you like hashish? Hash boat just over there.' We were passing a ragged hulk, a most unriverworthy vessel. A ginger-haired hippy with light-green skin (like the pre-Raphaelite painting of Chatterton) staggered about on its deck. 'Good hashish, Master,' Ravi grinned and shouted his greetings across to the hippy who stumbled around in a loose circle before lying down, coughing horribly. 'Very good friend,' Ravi assured me, 'from Dusseldorf. I take him to the hash boat, all night he stays there, good price.'

We were drifting towards the Harischandra ghat[7], one of the two famous burning grounds (the other being the Manikarnika). I could see a smouldering pyre and a great mound of soot and ashes being swept into the river and birds hovering for solid remains. But that was all that I saw because, suddenly, it started to pour with rain. The boatmen rowed for the shore. 'River tour finished,' Ravi explained, 'cancelled, due to inclement weather.' It had lasted less than twenty minutes. We sheltered together in a little shrine. I watched the boat move off and felt marooned. 'Now you like to shop,' announced Ravi.

'I have no intention of shopping.'

'We get a drink of *thandai*, Master?'

'What's *thandai*?'

'*Bhang lassi*, Master. Make you feel high, high, high!'

'Certainly not,' I replied though, to be honest, I was rather intrigued.

'Then you like to see a temple? Special Benares temple?' That sounded all right. We set off up some damp mossy steps and up a muddy alley. We stopped at what was plainly a private house. 'This is not a temple,' I said.

'Yes, Master, special temple.'

'Look, I know a temple when I see one and this is somebody's house.'

'Acha, Master. It is the house of a great, great Swami. Wherever Swami resides it is revered as a temple.' I followed him inside. It was a squalid and depressing place, like a derelict house that dossers sleep in. The floor was carpeted with old newspapers, stained with gobs of betel-spit, as if somebody was house-training an animal. Flies swarmed around a pile of orange peel and banana skins. I could see nothing to suggest religion of any kind. A bald old man was resting on a charpoy, making disgusting gurgling sounds in his throat. I could smell *bidis*, garlic and drains. He blinked at us. Ravi muttered something to the old man who smiled blearily. He had the bland expression of a baby and bright-red toothless gums. 'Give him mother's name, father's name, date of your birthday.' I told Ravi that I wasn't interested. 'Master, Master, it is puja.' I said that I also knew puja when I saw it. 'This is special puja for non-Hindu.' The old man, still lying down, was chanting. '*Hawan*,' said Ravi, 'very holy.' The chanting lasted about as long as the Lord's Prayer. 'Now you have Swami's blessing. Your future is most auspicious.' The old man closed his eyes and burped. 'Give him offering,' urged Ravi, 'two hundred rupees.'

'You've got to be joking!'

'One hundred and seventy-five, special-offer offering.' I left the house. Ravi called after me. 'Master, I am your best friend!' I wandered along in the rain, down narrow corridors, poky little streets. People stared at me through barred windows. I met alley cats, cows and great slimy buffaloes, goats and pi-dogs, chickens that had been dyed in pastel shades (to identify their owners). Sometimes I heard sitar music or the wail of a *shehnai* and I could tell that it was real and not a tape. Underfoot, the ground was squelchy with river mud, rotten vegetables, every kind of dung. A rubble of stones, broken pots, bones, scraps of cloth. I went into a barber's shop for a shave and a haircut. The barber scratched my head with the tips of his fingers and massaged my neck and shoulders. When I came out, to my great annoyance, I found Ravi waiting for me.

'Master, Baba, my friend, why you leave me?' He seemed genuinely surprised. 'You like this as a present, no charge?' He offered me a lump of hashish. I told him to clear off. 'OK, OK, Master. You give me small baksheesh, maybe? What you like?'

'I'll give you a black eye.'

'Oh, Master! Master!' he implored.

But when I shook my fist he slipped away, a greasy and amorphous shadow.

At eight o'clock I took an auto-rickshaw back to the hotel. I was further away than I'd thought and the journey took nearly three-quarters of an hour. I longed to wash. There was still no water in my bathroom. I was told that I'd missed it. 'You want bath, eight o'clock,' the receptionist explained, 'no bath, eight fifty.' I ate a dish of *khichri*, the very basic ancestor of kedgeree. I'd had it before and had enjoyed it but this was a tasteless pabulum. I made up my mind to move to the fine old hotel that Mohan had recommended. It was near by and I could afford it. The point is, I told myself, that no hotel is going to offer 'the real India'. Backpackers confuse crummy hotels with authenticity. I'd sooner be comfortable than wasting my energy quibbling over water.

Just before noon, when I was feeling clean and re-
freshed, reception called me to say that my hired car
was waiting. The driver's name was Barkhu. He looked
about sixteen but was, in fact, in his late thirties. He
was dressed in a track suit with 'Abilene Christian
College' on the back but he wasn't a Christian, he'd
been given it as a present. He was an interesting,
informative man. Until he was fifteen years old he
had tended buffaloes in a rural village. Then he'd
come to Benares, looking for work, and had been
taken on by the hotel as an assistant handyman. He'd
learned enough English working in the hotel to
become a waiter. He discovered that he had a talent
for languages and was soon able to speak French,
German and Italian as well. After ten years he'd saved
enough money to buy himself a taxi. He'd established
a reputation for honesty and reliability in a city full of
rogues and cheats and his business had flourished.
The top hotels recommended him, even travel agencies.
Such was Barkhu's charm and straightforwardness
that he could tell me all this without sounding in-
sincere or in the least boastful. Just as I'd instinctively
disliked Ravi, so I instinctively trusted and liked
Barkhu.

We picked up Annie and Corinne, who'd been asleep
all the time. Barkhu drove us down to the ghats where
we hired a boat for just twenty-five rupees. He got in
with us as our guide. We floated up and down for over
two hours. The rain had stopped, it was quieter than it
had been in the morning, there weren't as many
bathers. We spent a long time near the Manikarnika
ghat, discreetly floating some distance offshore. At
Manikarnika there is a sacred fire which has been
burning since time immemorial. It is tended by the
Doms, the hereditary cremators, members of an
untouchable caste. The Doms live by selling the wood
that is used for the pyres, collecting a tax for each

corpse and keeping any valuables, rings or gold teeth, that remain among the ashes.

We watched a cremation rite (called *antyeshti*) from start to finish, with Barkhu explaining what was going on. The French girls were full of questions. A funeral party brought a body (*shava*) to the ghat; it was on a stretcher made of bamboo, all wrapped in red silk and decked with flowers. Then most of the mourners appeared to leave. Barkhu told us that widows are strictly barred from the burning ghats, in case the tempation to throw themselves on to their husbands' pyres proves too great. Corinne wanted to know more about *sati*, the infamous ritual of a widow burning herself to death on her husband's funeral pyre. Barkhu told her that although it is illegal it still goes on in rural areas. There was an incident of *sati* in his own village a few years ago. Anyway, it seemed to me that just a handful of immediate relatives stuck around.

The Doms were in charge from that point. I had presumed up until then that Dom was just another word for a sweeper in general but Barkhu explained that a Dom is a particular type of sweeper who can handle cadavers. They were an irreverent bunch, almost like English dustmen. Their appearance and attitude was somehow clownish. They removed the flowers, chatting and smoking all the time, then carried the body, on its stretcher, down to the river for a final dunk. They sawed the handles off the stretcher and placed it on a bonfire made up of driftwood, chair backs, bits of crate, stretcher handles, certainly nothing as expensive or exotic as sandalwood. They covered the body with more lumber so that it was, in effect, inside the bonfire, not on top like a gruesome Guy. Then the chief mourner (usually the eldest son) took some twigs which he lit in the eternal fire, and torched the pyre. Hopeful pi-dogs watched intently, lest a tasty charred foot or hand should drop their way unnoticed, but a grinning Dom was always there to poke the protruding limbs back into the flames. When the body was almost completely burned, the same chief mourner took a stick and smashed it down on the skull, so as to release the spirit. This ritual is called *kapalakriya*. After a good sift, the Doms swept the ashes into the water. For a while the ashes floated like an oil slick, then seemed to mix with the current and disappear.

Barkhu told us that certain people (he mentioned priests, pregnant women, small children, sufferers of skin diseases – there may be others) are traditionally not cremated. Instead their shrouds are weighted and they are dropped, from a boat, into the river – like a funeral at sea. But the shrouds, he told us, eventually decay and the bodies float to the surface. A few moments later we witnessed one of these macabre emergences. A small corpse, as white as milk, shot up to the surface in a froth of gaseous bubbles. It was impossible to tell its age or its sex but it was less than five feet long. The instant it surfaced some kites descended to pluck off what they could and Barkhu, sensitive to our feelings, told the boatmen to pull away.

We were moving steadily along when one of the boatmen, putting his oar down, pointed to the middle of the river hissing '*susu, susu*' excitedly. We looked where he was pointing but could only see a series of ripples. '*Susu, susu*,' he kept repeating. I asked Barkhu what the excitement was. His answer was most unexpected, the boatman had seen a dolphin. I knew that river dolphins existed in the Amazon but found it hard to believe that they could survive in this foul swirling torrent. But they certainly did exist. The Ganges Dolphin (*platanista gangetica*) is about six foot long with a slender beak and such tiny eyes that it has to hunt for its food (such as catfish) by echolocation. I read that in a book called *Dolphins of the World* but at the time I simply nodded and thought that I was having my leg pulled.

We floated past the Chaumsathi ghat. There was a
home for widows. From every window there hung
a drying white sari, like a sheet used in an attempt to
escape or a flag of surrender. Barkhu explained that
many of the buildings had been the palaces of wealthy
maharajahs but had since become hostels for pilgrims
from those rulers' erstwhile kingdoms. A herd of
buffaloes sploshed about at the foot of the next ghat.
They were the colour of India rubber with a weird
prehistoric appearance. A black-and-white dog, like a
bull terrier, barked at them. A sadhu with the longest
dreadlocks that I'd ever seen came down the steps and
stood at the water's edge. Barkhu told us that the man
was well known for the length of his hair and that
when he entered the water he often put his locks, as fat
as ropes, on a tray that floated beside him. I was
beginning to feel exhausted. I'd only slept for a couple
of hours on the train and all the strangeness and
spectacle was taking its toll.

Barkhu drove us to various temples around the city.
There was a modern temple called Bharat Mata
(Mother India) that was opened by Mahatma Gandhi.
Covering the floor is a large relief map of India, with all
its mountains and rivers and sacred *tirthas* marked. A
smaller eighteenth-century temple was dedicated to
Durga[8]. It was built by a Bengali maharanee and it is
stained blood-red with ochre, a suitable colour as
Durga is considered a 'terrible' deity to whom, at
certain festivals, goats are sacrificed. The temple
stands next to a large stagnant tank. The goddess
Durga, who wears a red sari, is often depicted carrying
a sword and riding on a tiger. Non-Hindus are not
allowed into the sanctum of the temple but there is a
walkway from which one can look down at the
worshippers. Apparently, inside the sanctum, there is
a silver mask and underneath it a red cloth. It is said to
have appeared magically, of its own accord, rather

than to have been placed there by the maharanee or any other benefactor of the temple. Many Westerners know the Durga temple as 'the monkey temple' because of its large population of verminous monkeys. I found the monkeys repulsive. One was suffering from an awful glandular disease and had grown monstrously fat, swaddling about like a balloon filled with water. He looked very ill and stank horribly.

Next to the temple there was a fair going on. There were all sorts of rickety-looking rides and stalls selling sweets and ears of corn and cheap toys, wooden flutes, yo-yos. There was even a travelling zoo but Corinne and Annie were adamantly against going in. I could see a very shabby pelican in a cage near the entrance.

Later that afternoon we visited a silk emporium. Benares is famous for fine brocade, the most luxuriant wedding saris come from the city. Real gold and silver threads are woven into the cloth. I wanted to see 'cloth of gold' but it is now very rare. Once upon a time maharajahs wore coats made of the stuff. First we looked around the workshop. It was like a firework display. Bright naked light-bulbs shining through webs of the most colourful silk thread. Apprentices worked the looms. Their eyesight has to be perfect and the work is so meticulous that a certain amount of eye strain is inevitable. A single sari can take as long as six weeks to produce. We went into a showroom where we were offered *chai*. We sat on the floor on a futon. The salesman was a young Muslim. He had a strong American accent, not the Americanized Indian accent that Atul and his friends used but the real thing. I asked him where he'd lived in the States and was surprised when he told me that he'd lived his entire life in Benares. He was a very skilled salesman. He took great piles of brocade shawls and flicked them out on the futon, each one more fabulous than the last as they spilled open. The French girls were most impressed and we managed to haggle the prices right down. Next he showed us lengths of raw silk. After a certain amount of conference Annie and Corinne bought two lengths, enough for each to have a skirt and blouse made. He showed us some ties and they were a disappointment, the patterns were dull and the cut unfashionably narrow. When I told him that I found them boring he clicked his fingers and a peon brought in another box. 'OK, OK. These you'll like. These are wedding ties, a whole different story.' And he opened the box to reveal the most bizarre ties that I'd ever seen. Ties of red silk overlaid with silver tinsel. Yellow ties with sequins and pearls stitched on to them. Each one weighed at least a pound. I asked if it was possible to have a tie made from 'cloth of gold'. He scoffed. 'You and your cloth of gold. Forget it, it's not even made any more.' He produced a series of ties that had semi-precious stones woven into them. 'From Sri Lanka,' he told us. The French girls laughed and insisted that I buy one. I would have but they were very expensive, even after haggling, and I couldn't imagine myself ever wearing a jewelled tie. In fact, the only person I could ever imagine wearing one would have been Dr Lal.

Barkhu told us about his wife and children. He had two sons at school in Benares. In the school holidays they stayed with their grandparents in the village. The French girls wanted to know if his marriage had been arranged. 'Of course.'

'But how would you know if you loved her?'

'To love her is my duty.'

'But you had not met her!'

'I had not even seen her until the ceremony was over.'

'What if you did not find her attractive?'

'But I did.'

'But what if you hadn't?'

'It would never have been so. My parents choose

carefully.' It was surprising that they were so aghast at the concept of arranged marriage. I was interested that Barkhu only had two children. I had presumed that he was a Sudra from what he'd told me about his humble background. Small families were becoming the norm among educated Brahmins and Kshatriyas but the rural poor traditionally had large families. He acknowledged that this was unusual and said that some of his contemporaries had as many as eight. There was a reason. He told us that he knew an Italian couple, both doctors, who had visited Benares for two months annually over the last decade. He had promised them that he would only have two children and, in return, year after year, they promised to employ him and pay him what they would pay an Italian driver. This bargain has given his family some financial security.

When I got back to the hotel I tried to ring Mohan but the receptionist told me that all the lines to Benares Hindu University were closed. So I took an auto-rickshaw to Mohan's hall of residence. The campus was very spread out but the rickshaw-wallah knew the building. It was built around a quadrangle and there was a porter's office. The porter told me that Mohan had been moved to another hall. So off we set again, to the other side of the campus. I found Mohan's rooms this time and knocked on the metal door. A bald young man wearing a black woollen cap came to the door. Mohan was at the gym. I left my address and phone number, suggesting that he join me for dinner that evening as I was returning to Jabalpur shortly. As we made our way, through the bazaars, to my hotel, I noticed a lot of stalls selling tinsel bangles, some very elaborate. They looked like Christmas tree decorations. '*Rakhi, rakhi*,' explained the rickshaw-wallah.

The French girls joined me for dinner. We had a very good meal: *mutter paneer, dahi wada, channa dhal*, enormous *romali rotis* like great white handkerchiefs, and rice. A trio of musicians played on a dais. The harmonium player sang *ghazals*, sad courtly love poems, in a beautiful floating voice and, as he sang and played, he made graceful descriptive gestures with his free hand. Annie and Corinne had arranged to go to the river with Barkhu at dawn. I would join them to visit Sarnath in the afternoon.

Sarnath is about six miles away from Benares. It is a major Buddhist centre, the famous deer park where the Buddha gave his first sermon[9]. I didn't find the ruins very exciting. The *stupas* weren't much to look at. There was a good archaeological museum. A modern temple with Japanese murals and some large kitsch figures. A sad little deer park in a mango grove. It all seemed sterile after Benares. Perhaps if one was a devout Buddhist it would be thrilling.

There was another street fair. We bought soft drinks and some sweets that were like little cubes of shortbread. A group of very dark men were chanting and banging metal implements that looked like spanners. There were seven of them and they moved around in a circle and in the centre of the circle was a microphone; they took it in turns to shout into the microphone, like gospel singers 'testifying' while the others kept up the chanting and the rhythmic banging in the background. That was much more my cup of tea. I watched them for some time. Later, as we drove back into Benares, I asked Barkhu about the singers. I guessed that they were from Sikkim or Ladakh but they were not like the pictures that I'd seen of those people. In fact they were more like Dravidians. 'Acha,' said Barkhu, 'then they are new Buddhists.' What did he mean? 'I mean they are the followers of Dr Ambedkar[10].'

As soon as we got back to Benares, the rain came down. The streets were cleared of pedestrians. A thin horse clattered gloomily along the shining road and stopped to drink from a puddle. Men huddled around a pan stall; the female proprietor sat on the counter itself among the layered betel leaves. We stopped at a junction and there was a shop selling aluminium luggage: bright metallic trunks, all kinds of cases in piles; the largest at the bottom and rising up like a *gopura*, each would have fitted inside the one below. I said goodbye to the French girls as the next day I was going back to Jabalpur and we exchanged addresses.

That evening Mohan came to dinner. He was wearing a dark silk shirt with a paisley pattern and jeans. He was in a good mood, he'd been at the gym where he'd broken a personal record on the bench press. 'It is a good feeling to move up.' The musicians played in the dining-room again. Mohan said that the songs were well-known poems and translated some of them. They were very like stanzas from the *Rubáiyát of Omar Khayyám*. 'Well, of course,' said Mohan. Because he was in training he followed a dietary regime and he ordered for both of us. We had grilled chicken with lime pickle and *palak paneer* (spinach and curd cheese) and unbuttered *naan*. Then for pudding mango *kheer*, not as good as Mrs Trivedi's – it tasted like tinned rice pudding with mango juice stirred into it.

I'd asked the receptionist to get me a ticket for the train to Jabalpur but he'd insisted that it wasn't necessary. In the morning Barkhu arrived to take me to the station. He left me in the forecourt, having given me his card. I promised to tell visitors to Benares about him. When I entered the station it was pandemonium; queues that broke down into disorganized clusters of clamouring travellers. I couldn't work out which window to buy my ticket from. I asked a policeman. 'Where to?' Jabalpur. 'Acha, Jabalpur. Come!' The policeman pushed people away, brandishing his night-stick (*lathi*) and took me straight up to the window. There were resentful mutters. I was embarrassed, I'd have been quite willing to stand in line if I'd only been told which one. The policeman shouted 'VIP! VIP!' then spoke to the ticket-seller himself. He turned to me and said, 'Jabalpur, second class. One hundred and seventy rupees.' I gave him the money and slipped away to the platform. It was some time afterwards that I worked out that the privilege of VIP status had cost me at least an extra hundred rupees.

Two young white women were taking photographs. I couldn't work out what country they were from. They were both fair-haired, certainly not Mediterranean types and speaking a guttural lispy language that I didn't recognize. They turned out to be Israelis though neither looked remotely Jewish. They both spoke good English. We shared some biscuits. A beggarwoman with dangling naked breasts and a filthy brown sheet for a sari approached us; she had tight Afro curls and no teeth. One of the Israeli girls took a photograph. That enraged the beggarwoman; she screamed at us repeatedly, making a noise like a seagull. A man explained that 'this woman is unsound in the mind' but it didn't help matters. We had to move down the platform. The Israeli girls had been in India a month. They were fed up with the rain. They had avoided Indian food. I asked why and they said that it looked so unappetizing. They lived on biscuits and fruit and ice-cream. Indian men had been a nuisance. In Pushkar one of them had been approached by a student who'd confided that he had a lifelong ambition to make love to a white woman – would she grant his wish? They burst out laughing as they told this story.

It took fourteen hours to reach Jabalpur. A man on the top berth opposite was chewing bhang. He looked like a frog and as soon as the bhang took hold his eyeballs rolled upwards in their sockets. Then he went into a trance or he might have been asleep with his eyes open. On the upper berth that ran along the side of the aisle lay a very beautiful woman in a dove-grey sari with an orange choli and petticoat. Lord Leighton could have painted her. Below her were two arguing men with croaking voices, possibly her husband and his brother. The argument got fiercer and fiercer and sometimes other travellers stepped in to adjudicate. Flaming June would wake up, sigh loudly to express her displeasure, then close her eyes again. Late in the evening a drunkard got on. He could barely stand. He sat down beside me and collapsed with his head on my knee; it stayed there all the way to Jabalpur.

On the platform, waiting for me, was the Trivedis' rickshaw-wallah. It was raining and he wore a plastic cape that looked like Christmas wrapping-paper. He greeted me and reached out to take my bag. Quickly a policeman rushed over and was about to strike him. I stopped the policeman. 'He must do business outside!' the policeman barked.

'It's not business. He's come to collect me.'

'You do not live here!' the policeman barked back. I had to do a lot of explaining before I could leave the station. We got to Colonel Trivedi's bungalow some time after midnight. Two *chowkidars* (night-watchmen) were on the verandah; one sleeping, one guarding the house. The *chowkidars* had the key and let me in. The Gurkha was still awake, padding about. I went to my room and fell straight to sleep.

Colonel Trivedi was furious about the policeman in Benares Station. He wanted to ring up the Chief of Police in Benares and report the incident. 'It makes me so angry, this corruption.' The older Mrs Trivedi said, 'You are here, safe and sound. That is the main thing.' We were eating *parathas* for breakfast. The younger Mrs Trivedi was away visiting cousins. It had rained continuously since I'd left for Benares. 'Now it is serious. There are flooding reports. Villages and crops destroyed. So the cities fill up with incoming rurals and there is more unemployment.'

Arun telephoned to invite me to the Narmada Club.

We went there in the early evening and sat in the bar, eating hot peanuts fried with slivers of onion. It was an old building, rather desolate, much less preserved than the Ooty Club. Arun (who must have imagined himself at the Drones Club) was considered a great wit by the other members. One big empty hall had a high border of regimental shields; the various regiments that had been stationed at Jabalpur. Later I mentioned the shields to Colonel Trivedi who flared his nostrils. 'Don't speak to me of that club! It is five years now since I resigned as a member. Box-wallahs have come in and ruined it. Only Army and Civil Service in the old days could join. Nowadays a pan-wallah might if he has the money! Those shields should be returned to the officers' messes.'

I had bought my ticket for Bangalore, via Madras. Looking at a map of India it seemed to me that a straight line southward would almost connect the two cities but the journey would take me south-east then west. Colonel Trivedi said, 'Bangalore is a new place on the map. When the railways were built it had little significance, it was just a little town. Now things are different but we can't afford new railway lines.' Because of the rain it had been impossible to have any washing done. Electric driers didn't exist outside big hotels. I suggested that I washed my things in a bucket and let them drip dry. Mrs Trivedi, who'd returned from her cousins, said, 'In this weather, that would bring mould, that's all.' I was down to the shirt I was wearing and another for the journey. Somewhat inconveniently, the train south left in the middle of the night. I considered booking a retiring room but Colonel Trivedi insisted that I sleep at their house until it was time to leave for the station. The rickshaw-wallah would take me. So we had an early dinner and the Ramachandrams joined us. I gave Saraswati some paperbacks that I'd finished, including the *Granta* magazine. Mr Ramachandram apologized that he hadn't made me a spoon, 'I've really not felt up to much in this damp weather.' Mrs Ramachandram had written out the Edward Lear poem for me. I was sorry to leave them all. I thanked the Trivedis for all their kindness and hospitality then I went to bed. The Gurkha had been instructed to wake me in good time.

I was absolutely horrified to wake up at seven in the morning, certain that I'd missed the train. The older Mrs Trivedi put my mind at rest. 'Word came from the station that the train is indefinitely delayed. So we let you sleep on.' Colonel Trivedi laughed out loud. 'I bet you hit the roof when you woke up.'

The train finally reached Jabalpur at four in the afternoon. There were some Africans in my carriage and a Tibetan. The Tibetan's T-shirt had a rose on it and the calligraphic message: *Than in Amsterdam you were beautiful. Than in Barcelona, you lost your honour when you shot that Spanish dancer.* It was vaguely familiar (a lyric from a song by Cockney Rebel?) but the 'than' instead of 'then' annoyed me; my eye kept returning obsessively to it as if I could correct the misprint. My berth was the top one but it was occupied by a very old man with a large bundle that he was using as a pillow. His ankles were swollen as if in the early stages of elephantiasis. I asked another passenger to let him know that it was my berth and that, later on, I'd want to lie down. The passenger, taking the line that I was heartless and cruel, said, 'He gets off at Nagpur. He is sick. Please let him rest.' The Africans chain-smoked. They had red whites to their eyes and long yellow teeth. The old man got off at Nagpur and I climbed up to my berth. It was damp where his back had been sweating but I fell asleep immediately.

I woke up with a stiff neck and went to wash. I was feeling very run-down; I wasn't surprised to discover that I had a large boil on my bottom. I drank coffee and gazed out of the window. I had no idea where we were. I saw a procession passing through a village; two enormous brightly coloured puppets held up on poles and a troop of very serious marchers. The train kept stopping in the middle of nowhere. A man with leukoderma, albino patches on his face and arms, sat and asked questions about political life in England. 'And Pamella, ha, ha? Is she to bring down the Thatcher government?'

At ten in the evening we got to Madras. The smell of the city was noticeable long before we arrived. The mail train to Bangalore was pulling out just as we pulled in. I was filthy and exhausted. I went to enquire about retiring-rooms. 'Not possible.' I sat on my bag and thought for a while. I decided to go to the Connemara, using my credit card. They'd wash my clothes for me and when they were ready I'd travel on. I wasn't sure that such a grand hotel would admit such a scruffy guest but it was worth a try. Within an hour I was clean again, sitting up in bed watching *The Witches of Eastwick*, my supper (a *masala dosa* and a fresh fruit salad) on a tray beside me. My laundry would be ready at eleven. I felt completely looked after, as if I was in hospital.

When I got to Bhagpur Extension there was nobody at home. I sat on my bag on the patio and the next-door ayah came out with a cup of tea for me. She kept smiling, a sexy half-mocking smile, standing like a ballet dancer with one foot thrust forward. She couldn't speak English so I smiled back at her and she stood and watched me while I drank; her eyes went from my mouth to my eyes and down to my mouth again. When I'd finished she took the cup and burst out laughing and, as she walked back to her door, she turned back coquettishly and grinned. Major Trivedi and Atul drove up, they'd been delivering a consignment of books to a school. It was good to see them both again. The Major told me that his parents had liked me; he'd spoken to them while I was in Benares. I said that

I'd liked them, and the Ramachandrams, enormously. It struck me how lucky I was to know the Trivedis.

The next day was the festival of Raksha Bandan[11] when women tie *rakhi* bracelets (the bracelets that I'd seen on sale in Benares) to the wrists of their brothers and protectors. In return the men give them presents. It's a fairly light-hearted affair, popular with teenagers. I asked Atul if it was similar to Valentine's Day. 'Well, not really. You see, if a girl gives you a *rakhi* it means that you will never marry her. A brother doesn't marry his sister.' Did Atul receive many *rakhis*? 'Too many!' Surely it's good to be so popular? 'Maybe! Do you know how many presents I must buy in return?' Everywhere I went I saw men wearing *rakhi* bracelets; rickshaw-wallahs, policemen, Mr Abishek at his Medical Hall. That afternoon Mrs Sen and Suchie arrived, with a white box full of sweets – *ladoos, jalebis, burfi, rasgullas* and *cham-chams* – which they arranged on a *thali*. Mrs Sen wanted to know all about my trip. 'And Saraswati? Has she found a husband?' Suchie emptied a packet of vermilion powder on to a saucer. She put three *rakhis* on top of the sweets. Later on a girl called Shalini arrived; rather pretty, a Bangalore Valley Girl. She came flopping through the door, saying, 'Hi, hi, Auntie!' Shalini put some *rakhis* on the *thali* as well. Atul and Ajay came in. Both were already wearing *rakhi* bracelets. Atul protested, 'Oh, no! This year I thought I'd escaped!' and pretended to turn back through the door. Suchie and Shalini started giggling so much that they couldn't speak. The girls took turns to dab the powder on to the boys' foreheads, then took a handful of sweets and shoved them into the boys' mouths, then they slipped a bracelet on to each boy's wrist. 'Oh, please no! I'm trying to reduce!' joked Atul as Suchie approached with the sweets. 'You don't need to reduce!' said Mrs Sen and Ajay took a photograph of Atul with his mouth full of *cham-chams*. Atul mumbled, 'That's it! I shall get you!' Ajay gave his sister a set of felt-tips and Shalini an American paper-back, *The World's Worst Polish Jokes*. Atul gave them both cassettes: Suchie, George Michael's *Faith* and Shalini, a compilation called *Lovers' Moods* that had the blue-tinted 'Anais' scent advertisement as a cover. Suchie said, 'Joe! Come on!' and Mrs Sen said, 'Yes, yes, you too!' I had my forehead smeared with vermilion and my mouth stuffed with *ladoos*. I hadn't expected to be included so I had to go to my room and choose each girl a cassette. I gave Suchie the first Soul II Soul album and Shalini the second one. Major Trivedi came back and said, 'Now it is your duty to protect these young girls.' That evening he told me that there were various ways to celebrate Raksha Bandan; most years he sent *rakhi* bracelets to his childhood friends. 'Only Brahmins do that. It comes from priests having protectors.' Orthodox Brahmins annually change their sacred threads on the same day as Raksha Bandan; a ritual called Sravani that's quite separate. And a third ritual falls on the same day: Narali Purnima ('Coconut Full Moon') when coconuts are cast into the sea as an offering to Varuna, the Hindu Neptune. 'This is a time of year full of festivals. You see, the rains are over.' But it was still very grey outside.

The grey weather started to get me down. I felt depressed and the boil wasn't healing at all. I had lost a stone since my arrival. One morning I woke up with an aching back. I didn't want to mention it to the stoic Major Trivedi. It was agony to bend and almost as bad to straighten up. I crept about with a stoop. 'You are a bit stiff this morning,' commented the Major. I said it was nothing.

Saddam Hussein had invaded Kuwait. The Major was very excited and came up with a string of relevant prophesies from Nostradamus. 'With fire and weapons, not far from the Black Sea, he will come from Persia to occupy Trebizond. Pharos and Mytilene tremble. The sun is bright. The Adriatic Sea, covered with Arab blood.' Iran is Persia, not Iraq, I pointed out churlishly. The Major said that maps change, borders shift; the general theatre of the war was correct. 'We shall see,' he announced, 'if this is truly the end of the world. Not for a while, maybe, but today's events will set the ball rolling.' He studied the *Deccan Herald* again, then, folding it, proclaimed, 'When the dark ferocious one has exercised his bloody hand through fire, the sword, the drawn bow, all the nations will be so terrified to see the great ones hanging by their feet and neck.' As the day wore on the backache got considerably worse until I wanted to shout. I went to the Medical Hall and asked for some painkillers. I was given some great big pills like pony nuts. I've no idea what they were but they were incredibly strong; they made me as high as a kite (but still miserable) and unable to feel my teeth.

Asunta was still not engaged. I teased her about ending up 'on the shelf'. The expression made her laugh. She translated it for Anasuya who laughed as well then said something to Asunta who responded with a cluck of the tongue. 'Anasuya says it is better to be sitting on a shelf than living with a drunken husband.' Trying to lighten things, I suggested to Asunta that Dr Lal was available. 'Doctor-Sahib is not available! He is not RC. And he is divorced.' She translated all this for Anasuya, who had gone into the kitchen. When she came out she muttered again to Asunta. Asunta covered her mouth in shock and her eyes widened. I asked what Anasuya had said – it was obviously something outrageous – but Asunta gulped and refused to tell me. 'Just that Doctor-Sahib would not make a good husband.' But whatever had been said caused giggles and whoops of laughter for at least an hour afterwards.

Alan Davidson had sent me some queries about Indian fruit and vegetables in connection with the *Oxford*

Companion To Food. I'd been able to find out a lot simply by asking people but needed botanical names and more specific information. I'd been told of a place in Mysore called the Central Food Technological Research Institute. I wrote to the director on Saturday morning, asking permission to use their library; on Wednesday the permission came and I made plans to go to Mysore. I rang up the Metropole Hotel and booked a room.

On Thursday morning I caught the early train. I still felt low. If I didn't take the painkillers, my back ached from the neck to the coccyx; if I did, the pain ceased but an unpleasant disembodied numbness overcame me, a weary cafard, a drifting floating blues. I felt like a ghost. I listened to mournful sarangi music all the way to Mysore, like rainclouds being sawn in half. At Maddur I bought some *idlis* from a vendor. Just as I was biting into the first one, I looked out of the train window and on the platform there was a pi-dog with a length of tapeworm hanging from its anus; I was so put off that I threw the *idlis* to the poor creature, who devoured them with one gulp. An old blind man came down the aisle playing a penny whistle. He was led by a girl who held out a cloth sack for coins. It seemed a Dickensian arrangement.

In front of Mysore Station I stood in line for a rickshaw. A man in red-and-yellow-checked Oxford bags (Rupert Bear's trousers, but baggier) came out of the station and waved to me. He walked over, it seemed that he knew me. But I couldn't place him. 'My good friend, hello! How fine it is to see you!' I wondered if he was from Bhagpur Extension. 'At the precise moment I leave the station my eyes land on you! I think, truly, this is auspicious.' Where had we met before? 'Ah, a philosophical question. But who can describe the previous life cycle? Perhaps we were brothers? But is not the world one family? Are we also not brothers in this life?' So he didn't know me at all? I waited for it. 'Like you I have just arrived in Mysore. My home is Channapatna. A terrible fire has destroyed my dwelling-place . . .'

My room at the Metropole was fine, pretty much what I had expected, a tall narrow wedge shape, a single bed under a mosquito net, rosewood furniture. The bathroom was actually bigger than the bedroom and there was a proper bath in it. I tried the taps. Hot water, bliss. So I had a bath there and then. And afterwards I sat on the red-tiled upper loggia where green bamboo tatties could be rolled down for shade.

The same unctuous *maître d'hôtel* presided over the dining-room, wringing his hands and speaking in a tiny childish voice, but there were more guests this time: a Sikh family – mother, father and three grown-up daughters; two businessmen, drinking lager and talking loudly and, sitting alone, an old European woman, possibly German, with a powdered white face and a headscarf of black silk net like a veil pulled back, drinking mineral water and swallowing tablets. Another European came in as I was finishing the last *poori*; a little man with brillo-pad hair and the face of a ventriloquist's dummy. He was wearing a grey safari outfit; I'd never seen a white man in one before. He spoke to the noisy businessmen in a broad Belfast accent; it seemed that he was a jockey or a racehorse trainer. There was a race meeting in Mysore the next day.

The Central Food Technological Reseach Institute was near the hotel, further up Jhansi Lakshmi Bai Road. It was a great Edwardian mansion with cream stucco columns. I was shown to the library and I found some useful reference books. I worked there for the rest of the afternoon, undisturbed, until the institute closed at five. I walked back to the hotel, with my back starting to ache again, and had another bath and a couple of the pink tablets.

I ordered a pot of coffee and tried to read *News from Nowhere*. I could hear moaning from the room next door; a woman's voice repeating, 'Lilian, oh, Lilian, Lilian,' then a series of wordless cries. It was creepy. When I left my room to go for a stroll I told the receptionist about the moaning and he said, 'That is Mrs Kupfer. Don't worry, a doctor has been sent for.' Mrs Kupfer was obviously the woman with the black headscarf. 'What's wrong with her?'

'I am not the doctor, sir. Nor am I a specialist in mental aberrations.' I told the receptionist that Mrs Kupfer was calling for someone called Lilian. 'That is her daughter, Mrs Ramprakash, she is on her way from Bombay.'

I walked down Dhanvantri Road towards Sayaji Rao Road. It was a pleasant evening. Mysore is a smaller city than Bangalore; it looks to the recent past where Bangalore looks to the future. Both were developed in the 1930s, when the Wodeyar dynasty ruled the princely state of Mysore; Bangalore was chosen as the administrative centre and Mysore, as the capital city, was the cultural centre. There was a strong smell of sandalwood and joss-sticks. The bazaar was busy. Lottery tickets, plaster images of Ganesh, bracelets, unconvincing plastic flowers. A Friesian bull bellowed angrily and barged through the throng.

Next to a Punjabi *dhaba* I found a bookstall with a spinner of second-hand paperbacks and, as I was looking at a collection of shikar stories, two young English girls and an English boy (carrying a wooden flute) came around the corner. The boy spoke to me. 'Excuse me, what's this Punjabi place like, do you know?' I said I hadn't been there but that, as a rule, Punjabi food was heavier and oilier than South Indian food; closer to the food in English curry-houses. Punjabi *dhabas* are the transport cafés of India. 'So it's not vegetarian, then?' asked one of the girls (a bush-baby – fair and frail with enormous eyes) and I replied that it probably

159

served both. The other girl, almost as frail but darker and with smaller eyes, said that she'd just have coffee while the other two ate. They invited me to join them but like the darker girl – whose name was Miffy – I just had coffee. The bush-baby was called Helen and the boy with the flute, Neil. Miffy (short for Myfwany) and Helen were studying psychology at London University. They'd arrived in Bombay and headed straight for Goa but hadn't taken the monsoon into consideration. Now they were heading for Kovalam Beach in Southern Kerala, where the monsoon had ended. 'Sunshine! Yeah!' They'd met Neil, equally disgruntled by the rainclouds over Colva, at Margao Station. Neil was travelling for a few months before going to Cambridge to read Modern History and was planning to meet a schoolfriend in Nepal at the beginning of September. They had another travelling companion called Steve whom they'd met in Goa. Steve kept buying arrack and fenny and getting drunk ('it's brilliant') and, when he was sober, he had a predilection for fortune-tellers. They'd just left him having his palm read.

The *dhaba* was like an old-fashioned seaside café; orange formica, a huge panoramic photograph of the Himalayas, even a jukebox. The proprietor was a giant, at least six foot seven and as wide as a door. Neil and Helen ordered vegetable curry and rice. I asked Neil if he could play the flute. He hadn't tried yet, he'd just bought it. 'Go on,' urged Helen. 'Not in a café,' he said. Miffy asked if I'd seen a leper on a trolley begging. 'It was really awful. I gave him twenty rupees. Do you think I should have?' I said I always gave lepers money. Neil said that he'd met a man in Goa, a hippy who'd been in India for five years, who told him to hug lepers.

'Eergh! Yucko!' said Helen.

Neil reddened. 'No. You can't catch leprosy like that. But it makes them feel loved.'

Miffy said that pieces might drop off if you hugged them too hard and Helen cackled.

Neil said, 'Yeah, well, that's what this guy said he did. I don't think I would.'

The food came and they fell on it. 'Not bad,' declared Neil with his mouth full – but the coffee wasn't up to much. 'Have you been to the Devaraja market? It's right here, behind this building.' I was going in the morning, it'd be closing down now.

I asked about Goa and Helen said it was very Portuguese, lots of old churches, people wearing Western clothes. She and Miffy had been to a party where 'all these guys got drunk and wanted to dance with us, they were really sweet.' But one man had fallen in love with Miffy. 'He seriously wanted me to marry him. I thought he was joking but he was serious. Can you believe it? Then he came over the next day and said he was going to kill himself.'

'You told him you would marry him!' laughed Helen.

'Anyone could see I was joking!'

'Well, he couldn't.'

So what happened? 'I don't know. We left. He probably did kill himself though.' Miffy seemed quite matter-of-fact about the possibility.

Out on Dhanvantri Road we met Steve. He was older than the others, in his late twenties, wearing a white T-shirt and track-suit bottoms, big padded trainers. A cockney accent. 'So what was the palmist like?' asked Neil.

'Oh, what? He fucked my head! Spot on, man! Spot on!'

'Well, what'd he say?'

'Oh, man. It was fucking uncanny. He had my past spot on!'

'What about the future?'

'I tell you, I don't know what it is he's got, right? But what he told me I could handle. Don't know how he did it, right?' Miffy wanted more specific prophesies. 'Are you going to be rich?'

'Well, he didn't say I was going to be a millionaire or

161

nothing cause that's so corny, right? I mean he said I'd be comfortably off and that, didn't lay it on too thick or nothing. But all the stuff about the past, about my dad and mum and my brother, right? I mean how would he know it? It fucked my head!'

'That's it, I'm going tomorrow,' declared Miffy.

'What are you doing tomorrow?' asked Helen. The next day, after an early visit to Devaraja market, I was going to finish my research at C.F.T.R.I. But on Saturday I'd decided to visit Brindavan Gardens and I asked if they'd like to share my taxi. They arranged to meet me at the Metropole on Saturday morning.

I had dinner back at the hotel. I was feeling much happier, the backache was subsiding. The Irish jockey was holding court at one end of the dining-room beneath the Maharajah's portrait. An English couple in their early forties sat at the next table, Henry and June. We talked about Madras, Bangalore and Mysore. They were going to Ooty next and were planning to stay at the Fernhill. I told them what had happened to me. 'Thanks for the warning. Well, we'll scrap the Fernhill idea.' The service was remarkably slow that evening. It took an hour for one's order to arrive. Henry was amused by my description of Steve and the expression 'it fucked my head.'

June said, 'Our guidebook recommends the food here. Try the pepper steak, it says. It ought to say: try getting the pepper steak!'

A stunningly beautiful woman came in, like Greta Garbo but on finer lines. She was tall with honey-coloured hair and pale skin and brown eyes and wearing a bottle-green silk *salwar-kamiz*. The whole room fell silent as she found her table, she was so glamorous. 'Gosh,' whispered June, 'I bet she's a model, don't you?'

'That would be Mrs Ramprakash,' I told them quietly. 'Her mother's staying here. She's in the room next to mine, she's ill.'

'What's the matter with her?'

'I don't know, she moans a lot. The receptionist implied that it was psychological.'

'Golly,' said June, and Henry said that he wouldn't want to crack up out here. Mrs Ramprakash was joined by a majestic and very broad-shouldered Indian in jeans and a white button-down shirt, lots of gold at the wrist and neck.

I had breakfast at the Punjabi *dhaba*. A group of Tibetan monks in maroon robes were drinking tea and eating slices of white bread (double-roti). I had an omelette and toast and the monks stared at me while I ate. I was charged for two omelettes. The Punjabi giant loomed over me when I pointed the mistake out. 'It is not a mistake,' he said coldly, a growl of menace in the statement. 'Ask the monks,' I suggested. 'My friend, how many eggs in your omelette, please? Tell me.'

'Two, I'd guess.'

'Menu prices per egg. Single. Fried, half-fried, poached, omelette. Any style. Single egg price only.'

The market was extraordinary, much bigger than I'd imagined, hundreds of stalls selling flowers, fruit and vegetables, incense and joss-sticks, puja powders. There were different rows for each category of produce so that you walked past the herb-sellers (I recognized fenugreek, coriander leaves, chives, curry leaves) and turned a corner and there were tomatoes stacked into pyramids stretching all the way to more pyramids of red onions and garlic and countless other vegetables. The displays were splendid: red roses set out on a blue cloth; thick ropes of marigold garlands; writhing snake gourds and perfect, almost waxen aubergines, hardly like real vegetables at all. Dazzling mounds of vermilion powders (*kum-kum*) and other pigments like sculptures by Anish Kapoor. In an alley of banana-merchants a swarm of beggar children surrounded me so I gave one of the stall-holders ten rupees, enough to fill them all up. Cows wandered around eating damaged fruit or stealing from the stalls. I saw one snatch a mouthful from a woman's basket and she banged its forehead with the side of her fist. Some of the stall-holders wore silver chains around their necks with what looked like silver-plated bean-pods on them. I came out on Sayaji Rao Road and had my hair cut at the 'American' barber shop. There was a poster of Samantha Fox. 'From your country,' the barber informed me.

I finished my research in the library just after four and walked down to New Statue Circle. I passed a shop selling great bundles (not tidy bales) of fluorescent chicken-wire: lime green, hot pink and vivid orange clouds spilling out on to the pavement. A procession came by wheeling a temple deity, that I took to be Krishna, on a wagon. It was a lively affair, happy chanting and clapping and the wagon was loaded with flowers and little clay pots of yoghurt and some of the worshippers darted about smearing vermilion on passers-by. New Statue Circle was full of stalls selling Ganesh images – Ganesh Chaturthi was coming up – and fruit stalls selling red apples from Himachal Pradesh, lovely to look at but completely tasteless, like the apples in American supermarkets.

Henry and June had left for Ooty. Mrs Ramprakash was dining alone, wearing a black raw-silk *salwar-kamiz* with an almost metallic Benares brocade shawl. She was one of the few white women I'd seen who looked perfectly natural and elegant in Indian dress. Having said that, her *salwar-kamiz* was informed by Western notions of chic and line and could have been shown by a Milan couturier. The whole outfit was more 'on an Indian theme' than Indian. Even her sandals looked sculptural and expensive, far from mundane chappals. She ordered some food to be sent up on a tray to Mrs Kupfer. Later that evening I saw

Mrs Kupfer. She was out on the loggia, wearing a madras dressing-gown clasped at the neck with an emerald brooch and the black net scarf was drawn right down over her face. She paced from the door of her room to the balustrade, backwards and forwards, muttering in a low guttural voice.

At ten the next morning Neil, Steve and Miffy were waiting in reception. Helen had been sick earlier on and was lying down; they were all catching a night bus to Trivandrum so she was resting. We drove off towards the Brindavan Gardens discussing stomach problems. Steve was forthright. 'You don't get a holiday in India. You get an endurance test. You've got to have a good system. That's what I've got, you see. I haven't been ill.'

'Well, I haven't been ill,' said Neil. 'Stands to reason that people do, though, doesn't it? I mean, it's not on, gobbing everywhere, crapping in the open.' Miffy asked if I'd noticed all the men squatting next to the railway line; she thought it was hilarious. 'I've taken a photo! I had to, a whole row of bare bums! One man saw me and he shouted.'

'Do you think it's a tradition or something? Like all the men getting together in a pub except they go down to the tracks for a crap?' asked Neil, and Miffy laughed until she started coughing. Neil said, 'Don't *you* be sick!'

The Brindavan Gardens were a disappointment; laid out below the Krishnarajasagar Dam in a very municipal and unimaginative way, not worth the 20-kilometre drive out of town. I'd been expecting something like the great Kashmiri gardens. The driver told us we should have gone at night when the gardens are illuminated and there's a musical fountain. 'Big deal,' sneered Steve.

Neil and Miffy went off to find a restaurant called 'R.R.R.'. 'It's meant to be good,' said Neil. 'Aargh! Aargh! Aargh!' Miffy groaned, pretending to be doubled over in pain. Neil laughed. 'No, it's run by farmers. Arr, arr, arr.'

'You're both nutters,' said Steve. I had some lunch at the Punjabi *dhaba*: *sarson-ka-saag* and *macchi-ki-roti* which reminded me of soul food – collard greens and cornbread. Steve watched me eat with an expression of horror on his face. He stuck to vanilla ice-cream. I was going to the Maharajah's Palace; Steve said he'd come as well. As we walked along he told me about Sikh gangs in Southall and around Heathrow. 'They're real violent bastards, I tell you. People come here and think all Indians are into fucking peace and love. But it's bollocks, I can tell you. They're hard cases, plenty of them. They'll use the old machetes, given half a chance. Oh yes, mate, I can tell you!' A beggarwoman sidled over to us. 'Oy, just clear off!' Steve shouted. He said, 'I tell you, I'm under no illusions with these people, no illusions.' We got to the palace gates and went into the grounds, then up to the ticket office where it was necessary to leave one's shoes and camera. Steve said, 'Fuck that!'

'I'm sure they'll be safe.'

'No chance, mate, no chance,' he shook his head at my gullibility and turned back.

The Amba Vilas Palace is the third palace to be built on the site. The first dated from the fourteenth century but was knocked down and rebuilt at the very end of the eighteenth century when Krishnaraja Wodeyar III came to the throne after Tipu Sultan's defeat. This palace was largely destroyed by fire in 1897 and Sir Henry Irwin (the architect of Simla's Viceregal Lodge) was called in to design a replacement.

Irwin's building took fifteen years to complete. It is eclectic to the point of lunacy; a confusion of Indo-Saracenic, Rajput, European classical and British Victorian architectural styles. It's such a weird muddle, all on the wrong scale for a city like Mysore. A fantastic ornamental mess, domed and pinnacled;

sometimes, during festivals, its edges are picked out with 50,000 light bulbs, like Harrods. The Maharajah at the time of the palace's construction was Krishnaraja Wodeyar IV.

The interior was just as extreme. Plaster elephants' heads with real ivory tusks loomed from the wall. One chamber was decorated on three sides with a multi-panelled mural of a Dussehra procession in the late 1930s. Every face in the crowd was a portrait – one was of Sabu the Elephant Boy[12]. The octagonal Peacock Pavilion, where marriages took place, had iron pillars supporting a dome and a stained-glass ceiling. The pillars and the ceiling were shipped over from Glasgow. We filed through the Durbar Hall, a blazing Tiffany lamp transformed into a room. Sinuous pillars, a ceiling of teak and stained glass; the walls inlaid with amber, lapis lazuli, jasper, jacinth and carnelian. A golden throne – said to have belonged to the Pandava kings described in the *Mahabharat* – silver-plated doors . . . There was a temple inside the palace grounds but a money-grubbing priest soliciting at the door put me off entering. The temple was much older than the palace and probably pre-dated the burnt palace as well.

There was a fascinating museum in a surviving section of the burnt palace. Viennese chandeliers and a glass sofa. Portraits of the Wodeyar family. Krishnaraja IV's robes, his hairbrushes, his hunting clothes and boots (strangely loose-fitting like leather Wellingtons). The son of the last Maharajah (the grandson of Krishnaraja) still lived in an apartment above the museum.

That evening, about six, I went back to the Metropole and there was a commotion on the loggia. Cleaners were moving the furniture out of Mrs Kupfer's room. I could smell paint. 'What's happened?' Nobody could tell me. They shook their heads and grinned. The receptionist came up the stairs and said there'd been a small fire, nothing serious; most of the damage was to the paintwork. Was Mrs Kupfer all right? The receptionist scowled. 'Physically, Mrs Kupfer is unharmed. She has been given a sedative and is at the clinic. Mrs Ramprakash will come all the way back from Bombay to collect her. Only this morning Mrs Ramprakash flew away from Mysore. Now she must return.'

Did Mrs Kupfer start the fire? 'Between you and me, this lady is a risk. What mental state she is in, who knows? It is better that she damages her family properties, not hotels. That is between you and me and my opinion alone, sir.'

The television in my room was not connected to a central video player. I turned it on and watched a broadcast programme of film clips, mostly songs. Watching the programme, watching Hindi movies generally, made me feel an absolute outsider. The films went against all my Western notions of taste. I could appreciate Indian 'art films' like Satyajit Ray's films or *Salaam Bombay*. I could enjoy the weekly *Mahabharat* on television. But these commercial films seemed vulgar and idiotic. Perhaps my attitude was wrong, my expectations too high. Try as I might (and I really did try) I couldn't enjoy the songs. The melodies were weak and the male and female voices in the duets generally mismatched. Often a song that might have stood a chance was ruined by overblown orchestration – violins in swooping glissades or trumpets that punched the air for emphasis. Having said that, *very* occasionally a song was so kitsch that it transcended mere banality to become something fascinatingly strange: a percussion break played on car horns or a sampled passage from 'Duelling Banjos'.

The stars, because they weren't stars to me, just looked absurd. The heroines were pretty enough in a dimply way but the leading men were flabby creatures with blue jaws and kohl-rimmed eyes. They went in for tight white slacks and blousy shirts, open to the waist, revealing not hairy chests but white cotton singlets. The dancing wasn't dancing at all but the sort of high-speed 'wacky' editing that Richard Lester used in the Beatles films. I suppose this was because most of the heroes were too stout to dance convincingly. The heroines spent a lot of time fleeing from these portly figures who seemed anxious to kiss them. To run around a tree was a popular dodge. From time to time a heroine would confront her pursuer and then their two faces would fill the screen, their lips drawing closer and closer – at the last possible moment, she would turn away and resume her avian trilling. Then the frustrated hero, presumably for relief, would jerk his pelvis, dog-like, against a tree trunk or lie stomach-down on the grass with his great bottom bobbing up and down suggestively.

When I told Major Trivedi about Mrs Kupfer's blaze, he pondered a while. 'This affair is a very sad one. A cry, I would say, for help. If this old lady suffers it is for her family to comfort her. But they leave her in an hotel. This has become the way of the world today.' Mrs Trivedi had returned from Jabalpur that morning. She was extremely tired. Nevertheless the story of Mrs Kupfer was told to her (by her husband) and at dinner, out of the blue, she gave me her opinion. 'You see, this Mrs Ramprakash, she is very beautiful and probably Mr Ramprakash is a big Bombay business-wallah. The old mother is perhaps only a simple woman. Perhaps she does not fit Mr Ramprakash's notion. Not even in Bombay they will have her so she is sent to Mysore. The poor old lady is heart-broken and tries to kill herself. It is a terrible story.' It had struck a chord and, looked at from their angle, the story had a melodram-atic pathos – a beautiful daughter's rejection of her mother – but I don't think it was as simple as that.

The Trivedis had another visit from Nagaraja Naidu. I was out when he arrived. I came back to the flat and found the Cobra King ensconced in the Major's rosewood chair, a cup of coffee and a plate of glucose biscuits set before him on the low table. The Trivedis stood. Nagaraja Naidu looked worse than ever and was breathing heavily. There were jet-black bags under his eyes and he seemed to be sweating tiny beads of a dark oily substance. I said hallo but he chose to ignore me. 'Uncle, you have all you need?' asked Atul solicitously. The Cobra King gestured his satisfaction with a wave of dismissal. Atul disappeared into his room. 'He is a good boy,' explained Mrs Trivedi lest Nagaraja Naidu think her son rude, 'always studying.'

'These modern subjects,' Major Trivedi joined in, 'I call it cramming but so much they must retain for any expertise.'

'Students!' growled the Cobra King. 'What of this self-immolation? Is it nonsense?'

'What a tragedy! The young men of India setting themselves alight!' Mrs Trivedi wrung her hands.

'Because? Because?' Nagaraja Naidu jabbed the question, surprisingly, at me.

'I think it's because of the Mandal Commission.'

'Mandal is the half of it. Many problems. Corruption, the biggest obstacle. What can they expect of our country now? And the world. These are bad bad times. Gulf crisis is symptomatic, that is all. Not just India suffers! India, in fact, is healthier than most. What did General Kapur say of Gandhiji?'

'Ah, Gandhiji,' sighed the Major.

'I don't know.'

'Mahatma Gandhi is the spokesman of the troubled conscience of mankind.'

'Of Bapuji this is true!' Mrs Trivedi was inclined to speak of Gandhi as a beloved grandfather.

'We are Gandhiji's children, are we not?' The Cobra King put the question roughly as if inviting me to challenge him. 'We must pay attention to these students.'

'I thought they were protesting about reserved places at universities for backward—'

Nagaraja Naidu cut me mid-sentence. 'What the politicians and press-wallahs say is not necessarily truth. When such tragedies occur, not once but accumulatively, then we must look to Gandhiji's teachings and see that it is time for . . .'

We all waited. The Cobra King paused. He scratched his head by inserting one finger beneath the nylon wig. 'Time for . . .' He put his cup down and placed his great gnarled hands on his knees. 'Satyagraha!'

'Satyagraha!' The Major echoed in agreement, then asked me if I knew this concept. I thought it meant non-violence. 'No, that is *ahimsa*. Satyagraha is the force of the truth. Action or pressure motivated by truth or love.'

'It is as if these students cannot help it, what is happening is happening naturally. I say they are a warning. A warning to the whole world,' growled Nagaraja Naidu and he wiped his forehead with a white handkerchief. His sweat was just like sump oil. As he was talking, Mr Prakash the *darzi* came to the screen door, smiling and wagging his head. Upon seeing the Trivedis' visitor, his smile faded and he looked genuinely frightened; he turned and skulked quickly away.

'Were Bapu alive today!' lamented Mrs Trivedi, coming from the kitchen with more glucose biscuits. I couldn't think of a less likely follower of the Mahatma than the Cobra King. There was nothing passive or humble about him. He had a swaggering, bullying manner; menacing the Trivedis who *were* meek and gentle and kind. 'Bapu's teachings live,' growled Nagaraja Naidu.

The Trivedis spoke Hindi and English, often mixing the languages together. Atul's Kannada was just about fluent, certainly stronger than his parents'. I had noticed that Mrs Trivedi spoke to Anasuya in Hindi. Wouldn't it have been easier to use Kannada? I was surprised to find out that Anasuya didn't speak

Kannada. I knew that she was local and presumed the local language to be Kannada but Anasuya, it turned out, spoke Tamil. There were many Tamil-speakers in Bangalore, it was so close to the border of Tamil Nadu. 'It isn't good Tamil, it's broken,' said Mrs Trivedi. She told me that Dr Lal could speak all the Southern Indian languages, most of the Northern languages, Spanish, German, Italian, Japanese and Swahili. She spoke proudly of her neighbour. Because I trusted Mrs Trivedi completely and knew her to be the very soul of tact, I told her that I thought Dr Lal spoke a good deal of nonsense. She clapped her hands and laughed. 'That is the doctor-sahib's humour! Such a funny man! Humour is the truest sign of a very great mind!'

Dr Lal had produced a photograph of himself in a smart navy blue achcan coat with white jodhpurs, holding a glass of champagne. The photograph was slightly marred by the effect of the flash – the doctor had bright red eyes. 'This was a gala dinner in Los Angeles. Nancy Reagan was there.'

'Also Bill Murray,' Atul told me. He knew all about the gala.

'Yes, he was there too,' said Dr Lal. 'In real life not a wisecracking fellow.'

'It is well known,' said Major Trivedi, 'that many clowns hold sadness in their hearts.'

'What, after all, is fame?' asked Mrs Trivedi; just the sort of question she liked to ask.

I was going to Commercial Street to buy some *khaddi*. I was pleased with the shirts that Mr Prakash had made me. Dr Lal said he'd come too. Would I wait ten minutes? He came back wearing a fuchsia and egg-yolk yellow Hawaiian shirt. 'Oh my, my,' clucked the Major.

As we went along our conversation turned from *khaddi* to Gandhi. I mentioned that the Trivedis' friend, Nagaraja Naidu, was an admirer of Gandhi. Dr

Lal spat on the road. 'That is what this fellow says. He is involved in politics. Politicians bandy the name of Gandhi around because it lends them integrity. What could such a fellow understand of Bapuji's teachings. Everything he has gained by bribery and intimidation. Gandhi, ha!' Which was more or less what I'd been thinking.

The auto-rickshaw dropped us outside a *kulfi* and *lassi* shop. The doctor asked if I liked *lassi*. 'Very much,' I answered and ordered us two *masala lassis*. The *lassi* was creamy with tiny flakes of ice in it and the *masala*, as far as I could tell, was just salt and pepper. '*Lassi*,' proclaimed the doctor, 'is most medicinal. For the relief of impotence and the increase of virility.' Then he laughed and said that he was fired up. The doctor's rolling walk made me think of Yogi Bear. He sang Hindi film songs as he went along. I felt sorry for him; he'd become the archetypal middle-aged swinger. Perhaps it was the *lassi*. Commercial Street is always full of teenagers, particularly in the early evening when the schools and colleges are out. The boys form groups and the girls form groups and they wander from shop to shop, like Italians taking their *passeggiata*, looking at clothes and the latest cassettes. Dr Lal was tantalized by the girls. He walked close behind them, singing hits from the film *Dil*; it wasn't a particularly effective approach. I liked Commercial Street; it was how I imagined Hong Kong would be. You didn't find great bargains – most of the goods were shoddy, often badly pirated fakes – the atmosphere was fun. There were cheaper places to buy handloom cottons but I knew a shop, run by the Khan family, that carried a good range. Dr Lal seemed to have gone mad. Outside a cassette shop he was miming to the broadcast music; a grotesque gyrating dance like a drunk imitating Elvis. A crowd stood around him spellbound by the exhibition. Among the spectators I noticed Dr Stickney, in a pink sari and choli that emphasized her bony puppet-like arms. She was watching Dr Lal

173

intently. I felt rather embarrassed and decided to escape down a sidestreet. I went over to M.G. Road and browsed in Gangaram's for a while, then headed back to Bhagpur Extension.

Bhadra

The temple at Bhagpur Extension had a gaudy entrance, with coloured figures that resembled fairground carvings, but was otherwise a plain building. I assumed that it was the equivalent of a low church, there was little to draw one's attention to it. One day, however, a terrific noise flooded the neighbourhood and I was surprised to find that it was coming from the temple. A recording of a woman's voice chanting. I asked Atul what she was singing. He said it was a recording of a famous Carnatic singer (he couldn't remember her name — 'my father would know') chanting the thousand names of God. There was a priest who stood in, every now and then, when the resident priest was away, who liked to play the tape. It went on a long time; hours and hours and hours. 'It's a loop,' explained Atul. 'It goes round and round until everyone has heard it.'

'It will be hot, hot,' warned Mrs Trivedi when I set off for Pondicherry. I didn't mind, I was looking forward to sunshine. French India intrigued me. And for some reason, I'm not sure why, the name Pondicherry made me think of Wallace Stevens. I travelled on a bus full of nuns; jet-black Tamil nuns in light-brown and light-blue habits, sitting very quietly, hardly speaking to one another at all. Across the highway stretched an arch to indicate that we were leaving Karnataka and entering Tamil Nadu. At Hosur, I noticed a leprosy hospital and a man with live snakes in a glass tank on a trolley. At Krishnagiri we stopped for lunch: I had a *dosa*, a bowl of *sambar* and a bottle of Thums-Up. A wall covered in layers of torn movie posters resembled a modernist collage. I took a photograph of it, then a gang of urchins wanted to be photographed; some pulled faces, some saluted. The nuns got off at Tiruvanna-malai, a town with over a hundred temples, where the twentieth-century Tamil saint Sri Ramana had lived. Ramana, who from the age of eleven had renounced worldly goods and moved to the top of Arunachala Hill, passed his days in prayer and fasting and the teaching of a simple lucid wisdom that secured the de-votion of many followers and the admiration of Carl Gustav Jung. Just beyond Tiruvannamalai I saw the ruins of Gingee, a Vijayanagar fort, high on a bluff.

Pondicherry, at least the part that's called Ville Blanche, was laid out exactly like a small French town; the street signs were in French and the buildings were more ver-nacular French than colonial. The remaining British buildings to be found in cities like Bangalore would certainly look strange in England – a distinct colonial style had developed very early on in domestic architec-ture and even the offices and government buildings were different in scale and material – whereas the French buildings of Pondicherry seemed practically identical to buildings in France. It was a strikingly clean city, I didn't see any cows or pi-dogs. The cycle-rickshaw-wallahs wore straw hats like Vietnamese. There were a few elderly French people, obviously residents, sitting outside, their little dogs, also elderly, poodles or dachshunds, on leads. Tree-lined squares, benches under shade trees. Along the Rue de la Caserne to the sea front. An expanse of beach, a long pier; out on the horizon, big white tankers. I went to the Integral Guest House at the end of Avenue Goubert, opposite the Alliance Française where a painted board advertised a season of classic French films and language courses at different levels. The guest house belonged to the Sri Aurobindo Ashram but anyone could stay there. My room overlooked the beach.

There was a balcony and a good breeze, away from which it was baking. There was a portrait of Sri Aurobindo[1] on the wall; he looked like an Old Testament prophet. I walked down to the refectory, a room that was built right onto the sea wall. A languid woman in a white smock served me, she had stepped out of a Gauguin painting. The other guests were mostly Europeans, lots of French people; quite a few were followers of Aurobindo, wearing white Indian clothes, bourgeois couples who'd been young in the 1960s, one or two children. A black American wearing crimson and orange clothes, a follower of Sri Bhagwan Rajneesh, was chatting in English with a Nordic couple, both flaxen-haired and pinkly sunburned. The Nordic man had a crewcut and one thick rope, a single yellow dreadlock like a battered corn-dolly, growing at the back. The American had a singsong voice. I heard him saying, 'You take in all the protein you need from pulses, let the cows be.' It was like the dining-room of a school and the menu was a blend of Southern Indian and European wholemeal. The coffee was good, no doubt due to the French influence. On every table, next to the salt and pepper, was a quotation from either the Mother or Aurobindo. I was reminded of Kahlil Gibran, Alan Watts, the Desiderata: that same quasi-mystical high-faluting tone and the tang, however faint, of charlatanry. Or perhaps it was my reaction, not quite cynicism but a wariness that sprang up like an electronic fence whenever I felt that the great infathomable mysteries (that are *meant*, after all, to take a lifetime to solve) were being brushed off with a set of platitudes. If you can tell a man by his friends, you can tell a prophet by his followers; I didn't get the impression from the devotees in the refectory that much intellectual vigour was required nor any adjustment of lifestyle. Whatever makes them happy, I thought, let them get on with it; they think they've got the answers, I'm still confused.

I left the Integral Guest House and walked along the

promenade – past shipping agents' offices and Joan of Arc Square, shoe-shine boys and slow bicyclists, men gazing at the white ships on the horizon or just at the horizon – to the Gandhi Memorial. The Mahatma strode forward as if he'd waded in from the sea. Near by was a war memorial, '*Aux Combattants Des Indes Françaises Morts Pour La Patrie 1914-1918*'. I tried to remember if I'd ever been aware of Indians in Paris but I couldn't recall any. Vietnamese, other South-East Asians, all the different North African races, West Indians. Perhaps I hadn't been looking for Indians. Then, jumping about, as one does with memory, I thought of Catania in Sicily with its community of Mauritians of Indian (almost certainly Dravidian) descent.

Agastya[2], the great rishi, who befriended the exiled Rama and gave him Vishnu's bow, came to Pondicherry, then known as Vedapuri. Agastya is an important figure in Tamil literature. He is supposed to have brought the Hindu religion south, to have converted the Dravidian tribes. Archæologists have discovered that a Vidhyasthana or Sanskrit University existed in the area. Pondicherry was a trading port known to the Greeks and Romans as Poduca. It's mentioned by the anonymous author of *The Periplus of the Erythraen Sea* in the first century AD; the effect of the north-east monsoon upon certain oceanic tides allowed relatively easy sailing from the classical Red Sea to the Bay of Bengal. Excavations around Arika-medu on the outskirts of Pondicherry have unearthed Roman remains, what might have been a warehouse. A Roman sword is displayed in the town museum. The Pallavas and later the Cholas ruled the area through the Middle Ages. By the time the Portuguese arrived in the early sixteenth century, the Nayak of Gingee was in charge of that part of the coast. The Nayaks were originally from the Vijayanagar empire and they held a position similar to the governor of a colony but eventually they asserted their independence and broke away to become autonomous rulers. The Nayak didn't take to the Portuguese and invited a group of Danes to set up a trading post at Tranquebar (where a ruined castle still stands). The Danes were driven off by the French. The French had already set up trading centres in India but throughout the last quarter of the seventeenth century, under the supervision of François Martin, Pondicherry gradually took over as their principal foothold. Fabrics, precious stones, indigo, rosewood and spices were exported to France through Pondicherry. It was by no means easy. Continual conflicts with first the Dutch, then the British, kept Pondicherry in a state of siege. When Martin died in 1706, the town was in ruins and had changed hands, between the Dutch, British and French, nine times. The French East India Company eventually established undisputed rights to the port in 1720. In 1742 Joseph François Dupleix became Governor. Dupleix, who'd served in India for thirty years, had married a Eurasian widow who understood the intrigues and rivalries that festered in the courts of the local Nawabs and Rajahs. Madame Dupleix encouraged her husband to exploit these weaknesses and to establish a French empire in Southern India. Dupleix started out successfully with a series of local victories. The city of Pondicherry was rebuilt to reflect this glory.

Soon, however, it became clear that he'd bitten off more than he could chew and he found himself confronting the British. And, to make things worse, the French government was unwilling to finance these prolonged and expensive wars. Dupleix was recalled to France where he faced financial ruin. The French withdrew to Pondicherry and the conquering British, as a result, found themselves more powerful in India than ever. The idea of an Indian empire was never revived by the French. They kept Pondicherry and their other territories (Yanam, up the coast in Andhra Pradesh, and Mahe, across the Deccan on the Malabar coast) as tiny enclaves of France in India, right up until 1954, pulling out of India seven years later than the British. For some reason, guidebooks insist that the French atmosphere in Pondicherry is less engrained than it is. Everywhere I went I heard slow clear French spoken.

In the early evening I sat on the garden wall of the guest house and looked down at the beach which had become a pleasure ground. The fishermen had finished work and families sat beneath the pier to eat picnic dinners in the twilight. Young men performed multiple cartwheels across the sand; children splashed about in the surf; girls walked in single file along the water's edge, only their toes getting wet, and their saris glowed against the grey-blue waves. Sometimes children called up to me, '*Bon soir, Oncle.*' Behind me on the lawn were a very old man in a wheelchair and his attendant playing catch with a soft blue ball. An Indian woman in her early thirties sat on the wall beside me but faced the other way, her back to the sea. She wore a red silk *salwar-kamiz* and gold bracelets; she was very pale-skinned and pretty in a woozy underwater way. Big liquid eyes, a soft red mouth. She said, 'I'm not a bit happy. In fact, I want to die.' It was such an unlikely thing to announce to a stranger that I presumed she was talking to someone else. 'It's all right for you, you can leave.' She had a similar accent to the members of the Ooty Club; perfectly correct but somewhat old-fashioned English. I asked her if she was talking to me. 'Who else is here?' She gave me an angry look. I said I was sorry that she was unhappy. She seemed to want to argue but was too exhausted to muster the energy. She sighed loudly. 'Don't start talking about philosophy, please.' I didn't intend to. 'Good,' she sighed again. 'Because there's a lot more to life. You think it's so jolly simple.'

'I've never thought life was simple. I sometimes wish it was.'

'Let me put you straight on one thing. Aurobindo knew nothing about life.'

'I've never read anything by him, except the quotations on the tables. I'm just staying here.'

'Don't tell me . . . you're in India to discover the truth.'

'Why should I be?'

She smiled ruefully and her voice dropped. 'There's no truth here. I hate it, hate it, hate it.' Whether she meant the Aurobindo Ashram, Pondicherry or India as a whole, I never discovered because she got off the wall and went indoors without saying another word. I wondered if she was loopy. I noticed how dark it had become.

I walked along looking in shop windows. I found a French bookshop and a shop selling Catholic paraphernalia. The bazaar was as full of T-shirts and towels as a Mediterranean resort. Stalls selling plaster models of Ganesh. I passed a noisy temple; there were shouted prayers and somebody was banging a drum and it struck me that all that wacky exuberance was closer to the heart of Hinduism than the lofty platitudes of spiritual philosophers.

I had dinner at the Aristo Hotel, seafood curry and *naan* bread, sitting out on the roof terrace. A man, at the next table, in a white uniform (I think he was a male nurse) stared at me – I expected him to start talking but he just stared. When I'd finished my meal he spoke at last, scolding me. '*Les fruits de mer ont une tellement mauvaise reputation, c'était vraiment imprudent d'en commander pour votre repas.*' I felt this was rather interfering but he continued. '*Toute la côte Coromandel est polluée, monsieur, toute la côte.*'

As I walked back towards the guest house I passed the woman from the garden wall travelling into town in a cycle-rickshaw. She had changed into a luscious brocade sari. She could have been a very reluctant bride. Her eyes were closed and she was sitting up straight, wobbling slighty, as if she felt seasick.

*   *   *

The next morning I sat in the refectory and read while I drank my coffee. The sun had just risen over the lilac sea. The American Rajneeshi (he'd have called himself a sannyasi) was looking for someone to buttonhole so I pretended to be absorbed in my book. It was absorbing, in fact (*Vathek* by William Beckford), but I knitted my brow in exaggerated concentration, just in case. The Gauguin woman stretched and peeled herself an orange. Two old men, both in white shirts and lilac lungis to match the sea, walked along the beach, hand in hand. I watched a man carrying a crippled girl down to the sea – her pelvis was twisted and her legs were spindly and wasted. She sat in the surf and smiled at her father and he smiled back with a touching gentleness. I thought how lucky the girl was to be loved and looked after when so many similarly afflicted children are forced to beg.

The museum was chaotic and charming, like a junk shop. There were reconstructions of typically French rooms ... furnished with what the colonists hadn't considered worth shipping home. The *pièce de résistance* was Dupleix's own bed. The Pallava and Chola exhibits were more convincing but it was all a happy muddle. I saw the Roman sword. I stayed in there for a long time. It was much hotter in Pondicherry than anywhere I'd been and walking about was tiring. Later on I went for a swim. There was a strong northerly drift to the tide and, despite the male nurse's warnings, the water seemed perfectly clean. I lay on my towel and a young French woman came down from the guest house and asked me to watch her things while she swam. She came out again quite quickly and we talked. Her name was Clothilde and Pondicherry was the only part of India she'd visited so far. She asked if I'd seen a film called *India Song* by Marguerite Duras that was set in Pondicherry. I had, as it happened, years ago, when I was still at school. I wasn't so sure that it was set in Pondicherry though, I seemed to recall Calcutta. Anyway, the whole story takes place inside a house and was filmed in France; India is evoked by the dialogue and sound effects. Clothilde shrugged, what does it matter, Pondicherry or Calcutta? She herself had not seen the film but Marguerite Duras, she assured me, was the greatest living writer in any language. Then we talked about Nathalie Sarraute whom she also admired. In Britain, we'd considered such writers to be somewhat avant-garde, certainly at the time. Clothilde said everyone in France read those kinds of novels, there was no problem. There was a string of loud booms that sounded like explosions. Clothilde said she'd heard them before, she'd been told that fishermen were using dynamite. Then it was quiet again. Clothilde left the beach and I stayed for a while sunbathing. I closed my eyes and when, a few minutes later, I opened them again, I found myself surrounded by fishermen. They were staring at me like medical students and doctors around a hospital bed. When I sat up, they smiled and moved off politely.

I read *Vathek* for a bit and an Indian boy of about eighteen came and sat next to me on the sand. His name was Guddu and he was a Madrassi. 'Slowly I am heading south. What is the hurry? I will go right down to Kanniyakumari, then up into Kerala. That way I see maximum country, minimum distance from Madras. Should my family need me, quite easy it would be to return.'

'Are you going to Kerala for any particular reason?'

'No special reason. I am telling my mother it is a pilgrimage but really it is to enlarge my circle of friends. Believe me, I need all the friends I can get.' That sounded ominous but I think it was a phrase that he'd heard or read and had misapplied – it was said with a happy-go-lucky wag of the head.

Before he could say anything else, there were another three booms. 'Are they dynamiting fish?' I asked Guddu. He laughed. 'Oh, no, no, no. Why would they blow up the little fishes? That is a temple, just down the beach, past the fishermen's huts. Famous fire temple.' I wondered why I'd not read of this temple. Tamil Nadu is full of temples, of course, but even so, fire temples are comparatively rare and one would expect any guidebook to Pondicherry to mention it.

Guddu asked me if I had been to the Live Aid concert in 1985. I said that I'd watched parts of it on television. Guddu was disappointed. 'You should have gone. I can't believe that you didn't.' Bob Geldof was his hero. Guddu himself was a writer of protest songs. He smiled. 'Also, by my friends, I am considered to be Pankra Karish.' I didn't know what that meant. 'You must know Punk Rock? My nickname is Punk Rocker.' Ah, punk-rockerish. But Guddu didn't look remotely punk to me. He was wearing a white shirt and shiny blue terylene trousers.

'I am Indian punk. Madras style.'

'But lots of people in Madras dress just like you.' Guddu patiently explained that, 'It is not so much to do with clothes but my attitude. My attitude is considered that of a punk rocker.'

'What is your attitude?'

'Well, I am very non-conformist. My father is a doctor but I will not study medicine. Do you know Dave Edmunds? "Hold On Tight To Your Dreams", that is my outlook.'

'Then what are your dreams?'

'Do you know John Lennon? The song "Imagine"? What John Lennon dreamed, I also dream.'

'So what's punk about that?'

'You can't see?' Guddu was less patient now, I was asking too many questions. He blew his nose on to the sand. 'If you can't see the connection, then, in the words of Madonna's protest song, "you are living in the material world and you are a material fellow!"'

'I'm sorry to disillusion you but I don't think "Material Girl" is meant to be a protest song.'

'Disillusion? Me? You are living in the world of illusion, not me!'

So I steered the conversation away from Guddu's dreams. He told me that he had sent songs to film studios in Bombay and Madras. 'So far I have been ignored. Perhaps the authorities are afraid that my songs would promote a youthquake. I can tell you, honestly, they are hot potatoes!' Three more booms. From the fire temple.

On the garden wall sat the sad girl, wearing a green *salwar-kamiz* this time, reading. As I walked by she caught my eye and I smiled and asked her if she was happier now. She said, 'I am never happy, but I can be distracted,' and gave me an inviting smile. Her lipstick was smudged. I asked her what she was reading. 'An anthology of poetry. Do you like poetry?' Some poetry, I answered. I was afraid that she was going to start reciting her own work but instead she gave me a scrutinizing look; it was as if she doubted that I was capable of appreciating anything that required so much sensitivity. 'Do you know what an anthology is?' Of course, a collection of poems. 'Well then, you are wrong. It means, literally, a gathering of flowers, like a garland or a bouquet. This was my grandmother's choice, she had this book printed. My grandmother loved poetry.' She told me that her grandmother was a poet in her own right and related to the Maharajah of Travancore, then she read aloud:

> 'Who is this? and what is here?
> And in the lighted palace near
> Died the sound of royal cheer;
> And they cross'd themselves for fear,
>   All the knights at Camelot:
> But Lancelot mused a little space;
> He said, "She has a lovely face;
> God in his mercy lend her grace,
>   The Lady of Shalott."'

She read it well. It struck me as a strange, quite

romantic, somehow appropriate choice and the sad girl intrigued me. She looked at me condescendingly. 'Do you like Lord Tennyson?' I had to confess that I hadn't read very much and I felt like Pip around Estella. Rather crossly, she declared that, 'Tennyson is the most wonderful poet and don't say he's old fashioned,' and she sighed and turned back to the book. I felt that I'd disappointed her and went up to my room to get dressed. I guessed that the sad girl (I didn't know what else to call her) was staying at the guest house with relatives (perhaps followers of Aurobindo) but it was unusual that she was so often alone.

I wanted to visit the fire temple so I went back to the beach and headed south. I passed the pier and came to the fishing village. Small fish like sardines were laid out in patches to dry. Children begged to be photographed. I asked where the temple was but they just answered 'Pondicherry' and pointed back towards the town. A man who could speak English told me that there wasn't a temple, that I was mistaken. When I asked about the booms, he burst out laughing. Behind him, under a canopy, some men were gathered around a cauldron – a happy little group like Australians around a keg. 'Special buttermilk,' said the man. 'For you?' A ladle went into the cauldron and a glass was filled. 'Please drink.' It was thick and sour and there were chopped herbs in it. The men were delighted – they even cheered – and offered me another glass but one was enough. They shook my hand and patted my back. I couldn't think why they were so thrilled but I thanked them and turned back. 'Please, stay here,' I was entreated but I wanted to go.

As I was making my way along the beach it occurred to me that it could have been *bhang lassi*; that would explain the enthusiasm for a drink that had tasted pretty ordinary. It couldn't do me much harm and if I found myself incapacitated I had a bed to lie down on. Perhaps it'd be enjoyable. I felt quite excited as I reached the pier. But if it was *bhang lassi* its effects were negligible. I put a cassette of Ravi Shankar on my Walkman and sat out on my balcony and waited and waited for *le paradis artificiel*. I hoped for a sky full of dancing gods, at the very least some new insight into sitar music. Nothing happened. It must just have been plain old buttermilk after all, with a few herbs added for flavour.

The Rajneeshi sat on the garden wall practising Rajneeshi Yoga. It involved blowing very hard through his nostrils, spluttering and blinking as he did so and he looked very strange and silly, like a kettle coming to the boil. Several children watched him from the beach below, clapping their hands and giggling. I think they were interested in him because a black man was a rarity to them; a black man about to explode was even better. I had dinner at a restaurant on the promenade. Clothilde and another French girl were having an earnest discussion. The night sky was very dramatic: heat lightning illuminated great sweeping vistas of stars and clouds like black-and-white engravings of John Martin's paintings; one expected it to rain but nothing happened. 'Rain will be coming in one week or two weeks or three weeks,' said the waiter, hedging his bets meteorologically. When I got back to the guest house I sat out on my balcony to go on watching the sky. The sad girl was down on the lawn and called up to me. 'I say, you don't know Italian, do you?' When I said I didn't she called back rudely, 'You're quite useless. I don't know why I bother with you.'

Villupuram, Kiranur, Veppur, Ranjangudi, then mountains of piled boulders to the west of us as we passed through Padalur and approached Trichy. Viralimalai, Valanadu, Tovarankurichi, then the foothills of the Palanis, Melur, at last Madurai. A teeming temple town, cows and bicycles and huge film posters. Narrow streets, paan stalls, money-changers, sadhus.

Fly-blown sweet stalls, fruit and vegetables. Downtown was an enormous bazaar, peeling pale-blue paint, unfinished advertisements on the sides of buildings; all the chaos that was missing in Pondicherry. I saw the vast *gopuras* of the Sri Meenakshi temple, writhing with thousands of carvings. A cycle-rickshaw took me into what I presume had been the cantonment to a government-run hotel.

As we approached the gates there was a naked man face-down on the ground, twitching and jerking, having some kind of fit. I told the rickshaw-wallah to stop, I wanted to make sure the man was all right. He laughed at me. 'No, no, sir. He is a liar.'

As I was checking in, a coach drew up. The receptionist said, 'Please you will excuse me one moment,' and notified the manager; then he signed me in and gave me the keys. The manager of the hotel came into the lobby to greet the coach party; taciturn elderly Spaniards, bad-tempered, hot, bored by temples and palaces, longing for familiar surroundings and decent food. 'Welcome, one and all,' he said – trembling like a whippet – but the Spaniards ignored him. They were followed by their courier, a Junoesque woman in a tight blue uniform, aviator sunglasses pushed up like a hairband, small green irritated eyes. She barked some instructions in Spanish. Everyone's nerves, it was clear, were frayed. When the last of her charges had been led along the corridor, she slumped on to one of the sofas and lit a cigarette. The manager quivered.

'Gabriella, how sweet to see you again.' His eyes flashed from her cross puffy face to her knees.

'Yeah, yeah, yeah,' grunted Gabriella who spoke English with an American inflection.

'You will dine with me tonight? It will be my pleasure?'

'Let me see how I feel, OK? Don't hassle me, Nilesh.'

'You misunderstand me . . .'

'I will wash and rest, then let you know, OK? Calm down.'

Nilesh (still a-quiver) walked over to a mirrored panel and combed his hair with his fingers. In a soft voice, he spoke to the courier's reflection. 'Eight months since I have seen you. Eight months I have waited.'

It was a clean anonymous room. It could have been anywhere in the world. I watched the end of a 1970s British comedy called *The Magnificent Seven Deadly Sins* on the in-house television. A sketch for each sin; poor stuff, a reasonable cast floundering with indifferent material, old comedians at the end of their careers. Then, after a shower, I turned the television on again and watched part of a Laurel and Hardy film made in the 1950s, when they too were old and winding things up. Both films depressed me so I turned the television off and started reading a biography of Edgar Allan Poe.

The Spaniards occupied two long tables. They had ordered Western food which seemed to disappoint them. They ate gloomily and drank Indian lager. I sat in a corner next to an American couple. I assumed at first that they were tourists but, listening to their conversation, worked out that they were missionaries. They weren't as crass as the missionaries I'd overheard in the Connemara Hotel, they seemed more assimilated to Indian life. The man was very pale and thin with a ginger crewcut and a close beard that was much darker than the hair on his head. The woman was obese with short mousy hair and oversized glasses that gave her a cartoonish appearance, she looked like Garfield. She wore a *salwar-kamiz* that didn't conceal the enormity of her bottom. They were discussing a convention to be held in Madras. They were planning to attend and to take a party of teenagers. 'I ask myself if they're ready. Most of them haven't been away from home before. It's easy to forget how immature these kids are. You've got to take their parents into consideration. Screw up this one time and that's that.' Arnold had a pleading voice. 'Lindy, lighten up, why don't you?'

'I'm sorry, Arnold. It's just, oh I dunno, kids like Vikram. I mean, he's a pain in the butt. None of this is serious for him, he's got no responsibility.'

'Hey, Lindy. Just breathe out slowly. Relax. He's just a dumb kid. You're doing fine. Just breathe out slowly.'

'Sure, Arnold. You don't see how obnoxious he can be sometimes. You know why they come at all?'

'They hear the true word and that's what I believe with all my heart, Lindy.'

'Some of them maybe, but Vikram and, well, I gotta say, Apu, they're not listening, Arnold. I ask them questions and they haven't been listening.'

'Lindy, come on. You mustn't think that way. That's Satan talking to you. Relax now, won't you? Hey, you've done real good.' Tears were rolling down Lindy's cheeks and welling up where her glasses rested on her cheeks. 'I'm sorry. I'm sorry, Arnold. I just get so uptight. I just wanna, I just wanna . . .' She made a funny growling noise that caused some of the Spaniards to turn around. 'Baby, relax, relax,' cooed Arnold soothingly.

I ordered *palak paneer* and *naan*. For some reason the *naan*, when it arrived, was soaking wet. My guess was that it had been cooked earlier in the day and the water was to revive it before heating it under a grill – the waiter had picked it up before it had been reheated. '*Naan*, sir.'

'I know it's *naan* but it's all wet.'

'Sir, I get you rice instead.'

'Could you get me another *naan* please?'

'Two *naan*, acha, sir.'

'No, just one, please.'

'This is one *naan*, sir.' Another victory for the Indian catering industry. 'OK, I'll have some rice.'

Two well-dressed Indian businessmen came into the dining-room. Arnold stood up (he was very short) and greeted them in fluent Tamil. He pressed his palms together in salutation and even wagged his head when he answered their questions. For some reason, no doubt jealousy, I found his linguistic skill intensely annoying. The head-wagging was a particularly silly affectation. He sat down again and said, 'There you are, Lindy, you know who that was? Apu's father.' I found it strange that the father was so friendly to a man attempting to steer his son away from his ancestral beliefs. Maybe the arrangement wasn't as simple as I suspected, perhaps they hadn't let on that they were missionaries – that seemed unlikely – maybe they weren't missionaries, just born-again types. I certainly didn't intend to ask. The rice arrived long after I'd finished the *palak paneer* so I ate it on its own. Just as I was finishing it, Nilesh and Gabriella entered the dining-room. Nilesh was wearing a dress shirt made out of satin chintz and high-waisted slacks. He was in a very excited state. Gabriella was very drunk. She was still wearing her blue uniform but it was unbuttoned at the front, revealing considerable cleavage and a lacy black bra. She could have been an air-hostess strip-o-gram. Her charges, who'd finished eating by now, stared at one another solemnly, then filed out of the room. Nilesh helped Gabriella, who could barely stand, to a table. As soon as she sat down, she kicked her shoes off and lit a cigarette. Lindy was horrified. 'Arnold, do you think that woman has a chemical dependency problem?'

'Sssh, now, sssh.' His tone was emollient. 'She'll find her Higher Power.' Apu's father and his friend were riveted. Gabriella was ordering whisky. Nilesh was trembling so much that he could hardly hold a glass to his lips. He made a sudden furtive darting movement, his hand shooting up Gabriella's skirt. She removed the thin little hand and shouted at him. '*No quiero*. Understand? I don't want it. Understand? Tell me you understand. Say it, OK?' Nilesh grovelled. 'Please, please, forgive me. I remember last time.'

'That was now, this is then, I mean, that was then . . .'

Lindy hissed frantically, 'You gotta do something, Arnold, that lady's heading for a date-rape situation.'

'Oh, Lindy, you can't make such allegations.'

'Arnold!' Arnold walked over to their table and, pressing his palms together, addressed Nilesh, quietly and politely, in Tamil. Nilesh, bristling, stood up and declared that he was a native of Calcutta. 'Tamil is not a language I speak. Why not, pray, English?'

'My colleague and I are concerned for the lady's welfare.'

'You will find, I think, that she is a Roman Catholic. She does not seek conversion.'

Lindy waddled over. 'I'll take you to your room. Come on, honey, tell me the number.' Gabriella took Lindy's arm and stood up, retrieved her shoes with some difficulty, grabbed her drink and downed it in one gulp before leaving the dining-room with the two Americans. I heard Lindy saying, 'Turn, honey, turn to the Lord,' and Gabriella muttering back in Spanish.

I had breakfast in my room then set off towards the town. As I passed through the lobby the Spaniards were gathering for the next leg of their journey. There was Gabriella, smoking, grey-faced behind the mirrored glasses. I felt sorry for her. I told the cycle-rickshaw-wallah to take me to the temple.

It was already hot. Madurai had more holy cows than any city I'd been to. Madurai was the capital of the Pandya kings from the end of the sixth century until the fourteenth when it was raided by Malik Kafur and became the headquarters of a small Muslim state. In the middle of the fourteenth century the Muslim state was overtaken by the rising Vijayanagar empire. A Nayak was appointed as governor. By the middle of the sixteenth century it was virtually independent. A prominent seventeenth-century Nayak called Tirumala was responsible for the construction of the great

Meenakshi Sundareshvara temple, though previous temples had stood on the site. Meenakshi ('the fish-eyed') is a local goddess. She was the daughter of a Pandyan king and was born with three breasts. Meenakshi was told that, when she met her true love, the third breast would disappear. At Mount Kailasa[3] in the Himalayas, she glimpsed Shiva and the extra breast vanished. Shiva became Sundareshvara ('The Lord of Beauty') and, eight days later, back in Madurai, the wedding took place. The whole enormous complex commemorates this romance with temples to both deities and an annual festival where the god and goddess are brought out of the temples and remarried.

I got down from the rickshaw in a street near the temple walls; stalls were selling devotional prints – Ganesh, Shiva, Saraswati. Men sold popcorn, peculiarly heavy-looking and as unappetizing as pulled teeth. I noticed a barber shop where a bare-chested priest was having his armpits shaved. An elephant came swaying out of an alley, led by its keeper, heading for the temple. None of the merchants or shoppers paid it any more attention than they would have paid a delivery van.

I was taking a photograph of the elephant crossing the street when somebody touched my arm. A young man was asking me for money; he was clean and able-bodied. I couldn't see that there was any reason for him to beg so I ignored him. To my astonishment, he fell to the ground and grabbed one of my legs. I shook myself free and the man rolled onto his back; he was sobbing with such overwhelming grief that his eyes streamed and his nose bubbled. The outburst had come on so suddenly that I felt sure it was an act. All the same I gave him a rupee. A middle-aged man stepped out of a nearby *dhaba*, took the rupee from him, which he handed back to me, grabbed the young man (wailing now) by the ear and hoisted him onto his feet. Still holding his ear, he led the young man into the *dhaba*.

I entered the temple through the Porch of the Eight Goddesses. I was surrounded by guides offering their services but I wanted to wander about alone. It was a huge place, more like a walled city than a temple. There was a doorway with carved figures of Ganesh and Subramanya leading into a great columned hall. Inside the hall were shops and stalls, begging sadhus, the temple elephant blessing people on the forehead with his trunk. All the columns were carved into representations of gods or monsters – it reminded me of an illustration in a book from my childhood where the tree trunks in a forest had faces. At the far end of the hall was another doorway surrounded by flickering oil-lamps. It was dark and crowded, vast scented corridors full of worshippers. I didn't know which way to go. Perhaps I should have hired a guide but I'd found that ignorance and surprise often intensified the experience. There were lots of small shrines with worshippers queuing to make puja. A frail sannyasi was singing prayers in a sweet crackling voice like an old worn gramophone record. I came to a door leading outside and there was a courtyard and a large rectangular tank with steps leading down to the water. In the middle of the tank was a brass lamp-column. I sat on the steps for a while and looked at the *gopuras*. Plaster figures of gods, animals, monsters, grotesque faces, rising nearly two hundred feet in diminishing layers. It seemed to me that there were moving figures – I was surely hallucinating – I worked out that each storey had a hollow chamber inside and people were walking about inside them. But everywhere one looked there *was* the suggestion of masonry bursting into animate life. Suddenly, within seconds and without warning, I felt nauseous. I was sweating and the sweat was turning cold and my hair was itching. I couldn't understand it. One moment I was happy, completely absorbed in the temple, the next I was about to throw up. It was very worrying. To throw up in the temple would be sacrilegious. I lay on the step breathing in great gulps of air. The weirdness of the masonry, its wriggling, pulsing Max Ernst forms made my head swim even more. How would I find my way out again? I doubted that I could retrace my steps. There were beads of sweat on my wrists and the backs of my hands. Standing up, I found I was unsteady on my feet. I leant against a column. It was a crazy situation. All I could think of was getting outside. I knew the name of the porch where I'd left my shoes. I staggered through the *mandapa* trying to find someone who spoke English to direct me. A tiny old man with a handlebar moustache and an orange lungi came to my assistance. 'Need some help, old boy?'

'Yes please. I'm not feeling very well. I'm trying to find the Porch of the Eight Goddesses.'

'Oh, that's perfectly straightforward. It's not far at all. Just follow me, what?' I followed the man, who seemed to be a temple official, along the corridor. 'I expect you're not used to our food, old boy, that's all. Often gives you chaps a run for your money. Won't last long though, if that's any consolation. You'll be right as rain again in no time.' He carried on in this implausibly gung-ho manner (it occurred to me that he was putting it on to tease me) all the way to the porch. I couldn't really make much conversation because I was concentrating on not being sick. The elephant swung its trunk towards me as I passed. 'Here you are, then, that's where you left your shoes. Chin up, eh? Come back when you're feeling better, what? Always welcome. Toodle-oo.' I thanked him for his kindness, collected my shoes and vomited in the middle of the street. The young beggar stood outside the *dhaba* and watched me admiringly – it was a more dramatic performance than his own had been. I wiped my mouth and looked for a rickshaw to take me back to the hotel.

As far as I could make out, it was a virus. I was repeatedly sick over several hours. I spent most of the day lying down reading the Poe biography. It was a second-hand American paperback and several pages were missing. Late in the afternoon I felt better but still quite dizzy. I decided to go back to the temple. I didn't think I'd be sick again and there wasn't any point in staying indoors longer than was absolutely necessary. I arrived at a different entrance this time and found myself in a covered market that was part of the temple complex though outside the actual walls. All kinds of stalls – *darzis*, toyshops, bookstalls, florists, devotional print-sellers. I made my way back inside the main temple and soon found the tank. There were lots of people, including one or two Europeans, sitting on the steps, passing the time. The sun was going down and the oil-lamps burned and children sold oniony *wadas* and paper cones of monkey-nuts. It was peaceful and happy. Women wore chains of marigolds in their hair. Religious music drifted from another part of the temple, incense floated on the air.

A young teacher sat near me and talked. He loved his work, making the children think. I always assume that teaching is a thankless and difficult job, probably because I was such an obstinate pupil myself. 'I like to employ riddles and brain-teasers. That is, after all, the key to algebra.' I remarked that, while I saw the applications of geometry, algebra struck me as completely irrelevant to adult life. 'No! It is central to experience!' His tone was of disbelief. 'Perhaps it is wrong to include it in mathematics – it is logical enquiry expressed in mathematical form.' I felt terribly dim. Logical enquiry didn't figure much in my daily life. 'I will give you an example. It is a puzzle invented by Professor Smullyan.' He clearly imagined that I was familiar with the name. 'There is a pet shop selling parrots, large and small. Large parrots cost twice as much as small parrots. A woman comes into the shop and buys eight parrots: five large, three small. Now, had she bought three large parrots and five small ones she would have spent twenty dollars less. So, how much do the parrots cost, large and small?' 'I'm hopeless at that sort of thing.' 'No! It is easy. Eight year olds can answer it. Take your time.' A boy tried to sell us some nuts. 'Let me ask him,' suggested the teacher. The boy listened, grinning, as the teacher translated the puzzle into Tamil. I got into such a muddle that I soon gave up but the boy came up with the answer in no time. 'That's right! You see, it's simple. Twenty dollars a large parrot, ten dollars a small parrot. Each large parrot is worth twice as much as a small parrot, therefore five large parrots are worth ten small parrots. Three large parrots and five small parrots are therefore worth eleven small parrots. So the difference between buying five large parrots and three small parrots and buying three large parrots and five small parrots is the difference between thirteen small parrots and eleven small parrots: in other words two small parrots. Now you know the difference is twenty dollars. So each small parrot costs ten dollars and large parrots twenty dollars. Think about it.' I nodded feebly but I'd been lost from the start and the explanation went over my head as well. The teacher refused to believe that I could be so stupid and went through it all again. Eventually I caught on. But I couldn't say that it proved his point about the practical application of algebra. I wouldn't buy a parrot anyway. And certainly not from a man who didn't know the price of each bird, only that the big ones were twice as expensive as the small ones.

Early the next morning, having the night before paid my bill, I left the hotel. I was going to Rameshwaram. I hailed a cycle-rickshaw to take me to the bus. The cycle-rickshaw pulled up in front of Madurai Railway Station. 'Station,' said the boy. 'Bus station,' I said and the boy repeated 'station'. To my alarm, I realized that I should have said 'bus stand'. We sped, if speeding is possible in a cycle-rickshaw, across town to the bus stand, just as the Rameshwaram bus was pulling out. The boy jumped off the cycle and ran to the driver's window. The bus stopped and the boy helped me aboard. I gave him a hundred-rupee note in gratitude – it would have been entirely my own fault if I'd missed it. Because I got on at the back of the bus most of the passengers turned to stare at me and some continued to stare for at least half an hour. A man with a stubbly jutting chin, sitting just in front of me, was one of the last to turn away. Such close scrutiny is disconcerting. Soon we had left Madurai, bumping through the parched countryside, past cracked brown fields and stony nullahs; the landscape of polymorphous rocks and poles that forms the backdrop of Krazy Kat cartoons. There were several pilgrims with powder-smeared foreheads: Rameshwaram is where Rama, helped by the engineering skills of the monkey army (led by Sugriva and Hanuman[4]), crossed the sea to Sri Lanka and where, returning victorious, having slain the demon-king Ravana and rescued Sita, he gave thanks to the lingam of Lord Shiva. Rameshwaram, as a result, is a place of great holiness, almost a Southern Benares. It is an island in the Gulf of Mannar, joined to the mainland by a bridge across the Pamban Channel; the nearest part of India to Sri Lanka. A ferry used to run between the two countries but the recent troubles have stalled it. All along the dusty highway that led to the bridge were military gun-posts. Even the gun-posts, the stacked sandbags, had a funky Philip Guston quality in keeping with the Krazy Kat scenery. I listened to the Rockabilly cassette. Desperate Dan turned and asked if he could listen so I passed him the headphones. He smiled and clapped to the rhythm. 'Oh yes, it is happy, happy music.' Other people wanted to listen and the general reaction to the happy, happy music was smiling and clapping. All the way from Memphis.

Desperate Dan asked me where I would stay in Rameshwaram. Hotel Tamil Nadu, I said. He shook his head. 'How will you get there?' Auto-rickshaw, I supposed, I hadn't given it a thought. The man shook his head again. 'Auto to hotel, one hundred rupees.' 'That's much too expensive,' I said. I'd seen a map and the hotel was less than half a mile away from the main temple. 'You understand, Rameshwaram, many, many visitors. You are European, charge more. What is money to you?' I told him I was prepared to walk.

'Please, my friend. Do not walk. I find you auto to hotel, seventy-five rupees.' That was still far more than I was used to paying. 'All are paying such an amount.' Desperate Dan's concern about my transport arrangements was, I decided, probably well intended but very boring. 'I'll cross that bridge when I come to it,' I told him – which threw him into a frenzy of transparent greed. 'Sir, don't cross the bridge in auto. Taxi, seven hundred rupees.' He'd given himself away. Then, as it happened, we came to the Indira Gandhi Bridge (which apparently took as long as fourteen years to build). The sea was as calm as a pool; the surface of the water was light blue, a reflection of the sky, and underneath were green-brown clouds of weed. Rickety abandoned boats drifted nonchalantly on either side of us. There was a funny smell, like a musty bedroom, old socks and sheets, that one wouldn't have expected out at sea. We reached the island which was even drier and dustier than the mainland, as if sacks of cement powder had been emptied from an aeroplane. The bus stand was some way out of town. Desperate Dan urged me to follow him (it was too hot to argue) as he commandeered an auto-rickshaw. He dismissed the driver who didn't seem at all put out and got into the front seat. 'Twenty-five rupees only,' I said. 'This is my brother's auto,' he explained. 'He would have charged you one hundred, one hundred and twenty-five rupees. I charge you seventy-five.'

'You are taking advantage of the fact that I'm a foreigner and trying to mislead me.'

'Fifty. What is money to you?'

'More than you'd think. I'm perfectly happy to walk,' and off I set towards the town. Desperate Dan stepped out of the rickshaw and his brother laughed and got back in. He trundled up beside me and agreed to take me to the Hotel Tamil Nadu for twenty-five rupees. I wondered if I was being petty-minded to haggle over such minimal amounts but it was the lying, the attempted confidence-trick, that had irritated me.

My first impressions of Rameshwaram were bizarre: all the dusty streets led to the temple whose looming *gopuras*, similar, but smaller, to those at Madurai, could always be seen. Amplified, weirdly distorted, religious music boomed out of them, like Deep Southern Soul – but the place was as deserted as a ghost town. The only visible inhabitants were two tawny dogs wearing scraps of orange ribbon around their necks (canine sannyasi?) who trotted beside us. It was the hottest time of day, I presumed people were sheltering indoors. The wheel part of a small ferris wheel was propped against a wall, as if it had broken loose and rolled through the streets; the dogs jumped into one of the lower seats and lay down. We circled the temple and trundled down a street that led to the sea and along a track to the hotel. It was a run-down modern building. I noticed that they accepted Mastercard, which was handy as I didn't have a lot of cash with me. There was black gravel all over the floor of my bedroom. The room was hot and airless and, when I opened the smeared sliding window, the same dirty laundry smell that I'd noticed on the bridge seeped in from the sea. It also reminded me of, as a child, passing the Smith's Crisp factory outside Bristol – except that was a nicer smell. Bougainvillaea crawled over an untended garden, right over a small concrete wall to the edge of the sand. Crows hopped about like gigantic bluebottles and the temple music thundered in the distance. I had a shower, using some soap from the hotel in Madurai as shampoo, and realized that I was showering in sea water. When my hair dried again it formed matted clumps. I lay on the bed. The sheets were coated in a grainy white powder that I guessed was starch.

When I woke up there was a crow perched on the bedside table, staring at me suspiciously. As soon as I moved it hopped out of the window. A bearer knocked on my door with a message from the kitchen that if I would like fish curry for dinner I should tell the chef now; the majority of the guests were strict vegetarians but the chef would get some fish for me. How considerate, I thought, and told the bearer that I would like fish curry very much. I walked towards the booming temple and noticed that the town had come to life. A kiosk sold cigarettes and *bidis* and cartons of Frooti. In front of the temple was a bathing ghat, steps leading down to the sea and pilgrims entering the water like penguins. Some had inflated inner tubes around their middle, not, it seemed, for fun but for safety's sake. I sat and watched and considered going in myself but didn't feel right about secular bathing in such a place. The small brown floating objects (pine-cones, I thought, then realized that there were no pine trees around) further dissuaded me. Along one side of the temple was a street where about a hundred sannyasi sat begging in the dust; all terrifically old and gnarled, *kum-kum* powder pressed between the creases on their foreheads, faded orange clothes, bowls made from split coconut shells. One enterprising sannyasi would change a single rupee into a pile of tiny coins which could be distributed along the line. '*Sita Ram*' was the murmur of thanks.

The fish curry was a disappointment, consisting of a solitary sardine in a clear orange sauce – it didn't even taste like a sardine, just muddy and salty. But the chapattis were good. The chef, a rotund man with a slicked ducktail, who could have passed for a Mexican, stood by the table while I ate, proudly watching each mouthful. There were three mouthfuls altogether. When I'd finished he took the plate away, saying, 'Fish,' in case there'd been any doubt. That night I was sick again. The stomach bug hadn't cleared up yet.

The temple started grumbling at half-past four in the morning but it was possible to get used to the noise and sleep on. At seven a bearer brought a metal jug of thin white coffee and a tin mug. Bougainvillaea petals covered the floor like confetti. I decided to swim but, remembering the floating turds around the bathing ghat, thought it wise to walk in the other direction and find a clean stretch of water. Primitive fishing boats were darting out to sea. It was bright and comfortably warm as I left the track and made my way along the gritty beach. Small black goats picking around a ruin and old bare-breasted women in pale loosely tied saris and younger, fully covered women carrying water-pitchers imparted an almost classical atmosphere – a poet with a lyre wouldn't have looked out of place. I came to some fishermen's huts, the outskirts of a village. A huge dog, a sort of husky, with pale yellow eyes and bright yellow fangs and raw mangy patches all over its back, barked and snarled at me, preventing me from going any further. I turned back and found a pleasant enough spot and, arranging my towel, took off my shirt and shoes and headed towards the water. The sand stuck to my feet. The water was luke warm, completely waveless. I noticed a curious black band that I took to be shingle a few yards out. As soon as my feet touched this band, which felt like tar, great bubbles, like jellyfish, rose to the surface and burst, giving off a ghastly sewerish methane stench. I waded back with this grisly substance all over my feet and ankles and even more sand stuck to me. Despite that, I felt much better than I had the night before. I washed my feet in the shallower tide.

Outside the temple barbers were shaving heads. I negotiated a trim and a shave and sat on the ground surrounded by shorn black locks. The barber used neither soap nor water. I'd got used to being shaved by now but even so I wondered if I was taking a risk. There was no need to worry, he performed with the precise movements of a surgeon. I went into a *dhaba* and ordered a *parotta* (like a circle of puff-pastry) and a cup of tea. A boy came to my table begging so I ordered a meal for him as well though the proprietor wouldn't allow him to eat on the premises. I was surprised to see several Sikh families walking about. I can only imagine that they were tourists like me.

The Ramalingeshvara temple is a seventeenth-century building and, like the Sri Meenakshi temple at Madurai, it was built by a local Nayak ruler on the site of an existing temple. It is a rectangular complex of shrines and temples, behind high walls, three of the four entrances being *gopuras*. There is the Gandhamadana temple, a side chapel, named after a monkey general, killed by Ravana but brought back to life by Hanuman (who administered special medicinal herbs from Mount Kailasa). There is the main Ramalinga shrine and a smaller secondary shrine to Parvati. I wasn't allowed into any of the sanctums. Corridors run around the inside walls, carved colonnades. Along the north and south sides the corridors stretch to nearly seven hundred feet long; an effect like a mirror reflecting another mirror, receding as far as the eye can see. There is a tank – apparently filled with water from the Ganges, though nobody could tell me how it was brought there – attended by a man with a bucket on a rope who is paid to splash the pilgrims, a curiously slapstick arrangement. I sat between two columns and listened to a drummer practising in a side chamber. The music that played all day was recorded – I wondered when the live musicians performed.

On my way back to the hotel I passed a small procession. A young man was being carried on the shoulders of a happy group. Other men were circling him and clapping and chanting. 'Hello, American friend. How are you? What is your name?' the hero, delirious with happiness, shouted down at me. 'Hell-o! How are you!' became the chant. Five syllables, quite without meaning.

There was a problem when I went to pay my bill. Although there were signs stating that the hotel accepted Mastercard, the fact that mine was called an Access card confused the receptionist. I pointed out that it was a Mastercard but he was convinced that it wasn't the genuine article. 'Mastercard only.' I showed him the hologram with the Mastercard symbol on it. 'Sir,' he said, 'Mastercard only. No good Access and Mastercard. Only Mastercard.'

Whatever was wrong with me returned with a vengeance as the bus approached Madurai. This time it felt like a fever, I didn't want to vomit but I was hot and giddy and my head ached. My approach to illness, so far, had been to regard it as a minor inconvenience and to press on. There was an overnight bus from Madurai to Bangalore but I didn't fancy a sleepless night. I'd wait and travel the next day. So I went back to the hotel where I'd stayed before and there, on the pavement, was the twitching face-down beggar. Nilesh himself signed me in. He was curt and looked drawn, his eyes were filmy and he had terrible halitosis, a reek that attacked one from ten paces. I hadn't noticed his bad breath before; not that it was necessarily a permanent condition. I had the same room that I'd had before. It was as if I'd never been to Rameshwaram. I lay on the bed with my head spinning.

A long headachey journey home: Chinnalapatti, Dindigul, Karur, Namakkal, Mallur, up through the Shevaroy Hills, Salem, Krishnagiri, Hosur, back beneath the arch to Karnataka, then Bangalore, through the wide modern streets to the main bus stand. Back at Bhagpur Extension it turned out that both

Atul and Mrs Trivedi had had gastric flu: high temperatures and vomiting. Mrs Trivedi had almost recovered. Atul was still ill. 'The only cure is bed rest,' said Major Trivedi. He asked what I'd thought of Pondicherry, 'Isn't it unlike India?' I told him about the strange unhappy girl at the Integral Guest House. 'Alfred, Lord Tennyson, acha! Then this was no ordinary lady, for what do most younger generation people know of such a poet? My aunt in Jabalpur, Tennyson is her favourite also!' And, straightening his back, he recited:

'The woods decay, the woods decay and fall,
The vapours weep their burthen to their ground,
Man comes and tills the field and lies beneath,
And after many a summer dies the swan.'

I was half-expecting Major Trivedi to tell me that Tennyson had predicted the Gulf Crisis.

For two days I stayed in the house. Anasuya would bring me coffee and biscuits, looking at me scornfully, to imply, I felt, that I was a weakling, if not a downright faker. A neighbourhood cat had come into season and crept about with an eerie wail, a wretched 'h-h-hello, h-h-hello' that often woke me from my feverish slumbers. Atul heard it too and was amused. 'This is an Indian cat. Not hello she says but chalo.' Major Trivedi was keen to raise morale. 'There. Now you must write to *The Times* of London about talking cats in Bangalore.'

Later on Atul was playing a Led Zeppelin album and there was a track that featured slide guitar. I was sitting in the other room. 'Acha, Hawaiian style,' commented the Major, which surprised me. He told me that he'd had a teacher once, an Englishman, who'd played the Hawaiian guitar and 'what is it called, like a miniature guitar?'

'The ukulele,' I said, 'apparently that means "Jumping Flea" in Hawaiian.'

'Ukulele. That's it. Mr Andrews was his name. At the end of term he'd sing to us, a great treat.' A far-away look came into his eyes and in a very quavering voice he sang what sounded like a novelty song from the 1920s. The quavering voice was exactly right (I don't know if it was intentional, I'd never heard Major Trivedi sing before) and I could just see Mr Andrews performing in front of a classroom of beaming boys:

'There's nothing else to do
in Malakamokaloo
but love . . .
All you do is spoon
under the tropic moon above . . .
It's just a happy playground of love and romance.
All you do is lay around,
you play by day and then
at night you play again.
The wicky wacky woo
in Malakamokaloo
is grand.
The lovely way it's done,
only the natives understand.
I'd like to live alone forever
and make that little island mine.
You have to keep the dream
for all the time you're thinking of . . .
There's nothing else to do
in Malakamokaloo
but love.'

It made me laugh. 'What do you suppose the wicky wacky woo is?'

'It's the Hawaiian language. I'm afraid I don't speak it,' shrugged the Major.

* * *

The festival of Ganesh Chaturthi[5], the birthday celebration of Lord Ganesh, was under way, it had been going on for three days. When I felt better I went for a stroll and beside the temple there was an enormous pink Ganesh on a wagon. It was beautifully made from sun-baked clay and surrounded by a triple halo of coloured light bulbs. Small Ganesh figures were sold from stalls but the Trivedis didn't buy one; they had a permanent soapstone representation of the deity, among a host of others, in their shrine alcove. Major Trivedi told me that Ganesh Chaturthi had been popularized as a national festival by Balwantrao Gangadhar Tilak, the leading cultural nationalist before Gandhi, who believed that Ganesh, as a symbol, united all the different strands of Hinduism. 'Everybody loves Ganapati,' explained the Major, 'so Tilak saw that he could bring the people together and develop cultural awareness.' Before Tilak, Ganesh Chaturthi had been celebrated regionally, more fervently in Western India (and particularly Maharashtra, Tilak's home state) than elsewhere. The Major himself considered it somewhat debased as a national celebration; it had, in his opinion, lost spiritual significance – 'it is like Christmas in America' – but it struck me as very jolly. Late in the evening we could hear music and drumming from the temple forecourt. All the men in the neighbourhood were heading towards the temple. I said I'd like to go along. 'There will be many drunkards and ruffians,' warned Mrs Trivedi. 'Don't take your camera.'

It was certainly crowded. There was a bonfire beside the illuminated statue. A marching band in red toytown uniforms was packing up, leaving to play elsewhere. A ragged group of local musicians remained, three drummers and two pipers, standing close to the flames. The sweet chemical smell of arrack floated by like gas and, through the boozy heat, the statue seemed to wobble. The drummers started drumming, not in unison, but three separate rhythms that met and overlapped in unexpected patterns, as if they were covering a blank page with dotted lines and dashes, each starting from his own point and carrying on towards his destination, ignoring the others in his staccato progression. The pipers worked together more, scything across the drum patterns, cutting the dotted page into smaller squares. A man started to dance, an odd arhythmic jerking-backwards like a fit or a tarantella; he collided with one of the drummers and lurched within inches of the fire. Another man started dancing; lifting his feet as if he was stepping on hot tarmac, painful abrupt leaps, casting his arms in wide circles and clacking his teeth. And another man rushed forward in little charging movements, shaking his hair like a mop, his arms straight out behind him, as if he wanted to throw himself into the flames but invisible ropes tied to his wrists prevented him from doing so. When he lifted his head I saw that this seemingly possessed dancer was Mr Prakash the *darzi*. A young man performed an imitation of Michael Jackson's Moon Walk, to shouted applause, but it seemed tame, without frenzy or spontaneity. Soon there were fifty or more dancers (all men, though there were a few women watching) young and old, each following a separate beat or no beat at all; swooping, hopping, stamping, eyes rolling, heads thrown back and twitching spasmically; leaping through the fire, crashing into one another clumsily or deliberately for the purpose of frottage. There was a definite under-current of violence – and homosexuality, though that might have been simply the absence of women dancers. Out of the temple came Nagaraja Naidu. The crowd cleared around him. I said hallo to him but, grumpy as ever, he just scowled at me. He glared at the crazed dancers, plainly disdainful of such carrying-on, and crept away towards the airport road. I couldn't help noticing that he smelt bad; he exuded a sickly odour, like Parmesan cheese. All coherence had left the music now, which was faster and madder. I kept thinking of poison flour and entire medieval towns afflicted by convulsive dancing. A large middle-aged man fell flat on his back and lay like a beetle with his limbs thrashing. I recognized him by his moustache – Mr Shekhar the barber.

'Whatever you do, don't look at the moon,' said a familiar voice. I turned around to see Dr Lal arm in arm with Dr Stickney. Dr Lal was at his most elegant, wearing his achcan coat and drenched in Old Spice. Dr Stickney, as wooden and angular as ever, was wrapped in a pale-green sari, held in place with safety pins, presumably because she didn't know how to tie it. 'May I introduce you to Dr Beryl Stickney of Providence, Rhode Island. Mr Joe Roberts from England.'

'It's a pleasure to meet you,' said Dr Stickney who had the sort of American accent that almost sounds English and, for that very reason, particularly odd. I told her that I'd seen her in Gangaram's and she replied, 'Very likely.'

'I was telling Dr Stickney—'

'Please,' she checked Dr Lal and smiled at me (little unnaturally regular teeth), 'call me Beryl.'

'I was telling Beryl not to look at the moon. For to observe the moon at Ganesh Chaturthi means that you will be slandered in the coming year.'

'Oh Lordy!' shrilled Dr Stickney, raising both her hands in a Victorian gesture. She turned to me and said, 'Lal's a fund of wonderful information.' I asked where'd they'd met. 'I know his work for United Nations. We had met briefly, some years ago, at a symposium at Tufts. But it was quite by chance I ran into him one evening on Commercial Street. "Aren't you Dr Lal?" I asked. "Yes," he said, "and you are Meryl Streep!" "Beryl Stickney," I said, "but what the heck."'

A man span towards us and was pushed away by Dr Lal. Within seconds he whirled back in our direction and this time Dr Lal grabbed him by the shoulders and held him still for a moment, then turned him around to walk away sensibly. 'Just high spirits,' he explained, 'please do not be alarmed.' I asked if she was writing a book on Father Bede. 'Lordy no! Whatever gave you that idea?' Mr Gangaram thought so. 'He did, oh my! No, I told him that a colleague of mine wrote a book on Father Bede.'

I asked Dr Stickney what she was doing in Bangalore and she explained but just as she started I found myself beside one of the pipers and unable to hear her soft New England tones. I picked out the odd phrase.

I heard *intermediate technology, appropriate, resources* and *infra-system;* then *appropriate* again and *existing methods.* All I could do was nod.

The statue was moving now, the wagon being pulled away from the temple. It rolled forward slowly.

'Where will they take him?'

'To Ulsoor Lake,' said Dr Lal.

'Will he come back?'

'No, no, no. The water of the lake dissolves him.'

'Shall we follow?'

'It's very slow,' said the doctor. We watched as a train formed around the great pink elephant, shaped like a tadpole, the manic dancers making a swishing tail.

Mrs Sen and Mrs Trivedi were drinking tea together. 'So last night you met Meryl Streep?'

'Beryl Stickney,' I said. 'Meryl Streep's an American film star.'

'Doctor-Sahib told us her name was Meryl Streep,' insisted Mrs Trivedi.

'This one hasn't the looks of a film star!' whistled Mrs Sen mischievously and both women chuckled. Mrs Trivedi wiped her eye with the back of her hand saying, 'Oh dear, oh dear.'

'I think Meryl Streep's the doctor's nickname for her; it's a similar name.'

'Always pulling the legs, Doctor-Sahib!'

'You must teach Dr Stickney to tie a sari.'

'That is how she chooses to wear it, how can I tell her it is wrong?'

I decided to have a suit made. Although Mr Prakash was perfectly competent at stitching shirts, I doubted that he'd be able to construct a suit. Major Trivedi agreed. 'For this you must find a pukka tailor.' I asked how much he thought I'd have to spend. 'Let us say seven, perhaps eight hundred rupees. Tell me, how much, round about, would that be in pounds sterling?' I reckoned £25. 'And how much, round about, would a tailor-made suit cost in London?' I'd never had a suit made but I was sure it would cost around £500. 'So this suit costs you one twentieth of the price!'

Dr Lal asked me if I wanted it made of silk. He could get it for me at a discount. I would have liked a silk suit but I just couldn't see when I'd ever wear it. What I had in mind was a light gaberdine suit so that I could wear the trousers, as 'chinos', separately. I saw myself, wearing this suit, looking lean and brown, at Heathrow Airport. Dr Lal recommended a Mr Pang on M.G. Road. Atul, who had been listening from the other room, called out, 'That fellow is expensive!' I pointed out that I was getting such a bargain anyway I could afford to go to the best tailor in town. Atul protested, 'Also he is square!'

Dr Lal laughed. 'Here speaks a boy of eighteen. What authority he has! Mr Pang is square, he tells us now.'

Mr Pang worked in a dusty little shed that leant against a shop called Academy Suitings and Shirtings. He was Chinese, very dignified and old. His manner was ambassadorial. He had the gravitas that I imagined a Savile Row tailor would have; I felt that I was in good hands. A small yellow bird hopped about, whistling furiously, in an elaborate pagoda-shaped cage. Mr Pang produced a catalogue. It had obviously been produced in America and was at least fifteen years old. Page after page of ludicrously wide lapels, burgeoning flares, high-buttoning waistcoats. Some of the models wore fedora hats and correspondent shoes as if some pastiche of the 1920s was intended – it was the era of the 'Gatsby Look'. I told Mr Pang that what I wanted was a straightforward casual cotton suit. 'Yes, sir, I understand. You will find suits like that further to the back of the book.' Eventually I came to the pages he meant. The suits were hopeless; *Saturday Night Fever* affairs. Atul had been right. Gently I ventured my opinion. 'Suits like these are rather old-fashioned now.'

'Sir, high fashion is not my concern.'

'Well, have you a photograph of a suit that you've made recently?'

'I have patterns for all the suits in that book.'

'But can you show me something that you've made in the last year?'

'This last year I've only made jackets, sir.'

'Do you think I could see one please?' Mr Pang went over to a rail and brought back a blazer, made of shiny light-brown material, with burgundy piping around the substantial lapels and a weird nautical embellishment at the cuff. On the breast pocket were the initials R.K. It looked like part of an air steward's uniform. 'Sports jacket, sir,' murmured Mr Pang and the little yellow bird shrieked with rage.

I told Dr Lal that Mr Pang had been a disappointment. 'Well, it must be about twenty years since I went to him.' I asked where he'd had his silk suit made. 'Always in New York I get my suits made these days. Morton and Fischbein, just off Times Square. That ventriloquist – what is his name? – Candice Bergen's father – he was their customer. Also Perry Como. I take the silk with me, of course.' Atul said I should try Blue Jean Junction. Again I stated that what I was after was a straightforward cotton suit. 'Yes, yes. I know what you want. You tell this fellow. He'll do exactly what you tell him.'

Blue Jean Junction reminded me of the sort of rag-trade boutique that flourished in London in the 1970s – the ersatz Americana and inaccurate references to the 1950s. REO Speedwagon throbbed over the sound system. I looked at the pleated snow-bleached jeans and rows of checked cheesecloth shirts with Budgie collars and the air-brushed poster of James Dean and was about to turn around when the stout bearded proprietor asked if he could help me. His name was Mr Haq. He had a high-pitched evenly modulated voice and a habit of rolling his Rs. A little tinkling laugh. His hands were as soft as marshmallows. Mr Haq listened as I described the suit I had in mind, then suggested we look at some pictures. I was prepared to be shown a selection of absurdities but Mr Haq returned with a pile of recent American *GQ* magazines.

'We'll sprrring ideas off each other. Rrralph Laurrren we'll begin with, OK?'

I waited at Bangalore Cantonment Station for the Trivandrum train. Because the flu had kept me in for a few days, my train ticket had been a last-minute affair. There'd been a lot of clucking and lip-pursing at Kamadhenu Travel. Did I realize that it was Onam? Of course, that was why I was going. Did I realize how many Malayalis were returning to Kerala from Kuwait? All the hotels would be full. I said I'd chance it. I'd been unable to reserve a second-class berth and first-class non-AC was full. Air-conditioned first-class was hardly cheaper than flying. So the only option left was second-class AC. This cost much the same as first-class non-AC and had the disadvantage of tinted-glass windows. Air-conditioning was unnecessary at this time of year, there were always breezes on the Deccan. Open windows and ceiling fans were enough. Begrudgingly, I'd gone ahead and made the reservation. A coolie found my carriage and berth for me. I'd been at quite the wrong end of the platform. The train was, just as the men at Kamadhenu Travel had told me it would be, packed with Malayalis returning to their families for the Onam celebrations.

Not all of the windows were tinted and, when I woke up in the morning, it was possible, after all, to see Kerala in its natural colours. The train moved down the coast and the country that I could see was a sparkling Douanier Rousseau landscape of palms and flowering trees and little red houses. Kerala is a long narrow state running along the Malabar Coast.

Its mythological origins are with the warrior god Parashurama, the sixth avatar of Vishnu, who, in one version of the legend, was persuaded by the other gods to stop fighting. Parashurama dropped his battle-axe and, as it fell from the heavens, it sliced down the side of the Western Ghats to form the sliver of land that's now Kerala.

The other version is that Parashurama had slain his own mother in a fit of rage. To expiate his sin he had to undergo a series of austerities and penances. Eventually the other gods decided that he'd suffered enough and should be rewarded for bearing his punishment with dignity. They let him reclaim some land from Varuna, the sea god. He was told to stand at Kanniyaku-mari, the southernmost tip of India, and to throw his axe. All the land within the distance of his throw would be his possession. Parashurama threw his axe over the Western Ghats as far as Gokarn, a small town just south of Karwar, near the present Goan border. Immediately there was land that stretched all down that coast between the mountains and the sea. Geologists have proved that this littoral strip of land is of comparatively recent emergence.

Historically, the Western Ghats have cut the region off from the rest of India. The Moguls, for instance, never conquered Kerala. It is a fertile place producing rubber, cashews, tea and a variety of spices, the most important being pepper. If the area was cut off from the rest of India by the mountains, the Arabian sea brought traders to its shores. In ancient times came Arabs, of course, but also Phoenicians and Romans and Chinese.

Saint Thomas, 'Doubting Thomas', established the first Christian colony in AD 52. He was followed by Syrian Christian settlers from Alexandria who built churches and cathedrals all over the region. The first Portuguese landing, in 1498, was on this coast. There were enormous profits to be made from pepper. In those days, before the introduction of root crops, all the northern European cattle had to be slaughtered at the beginning of winter. As the months passed the meat got unpleasantly high. Pepper was the answer. It had preservative properties but, above all, it disguised the taste. The Portuguese, inevitably, brought missionaries with them – who were somewhat taken aback to find Christianity already flourishing, albeit a Christianity that was ignorant of Rome. After the Portuguese came the French, then the Dutch, then the British who took over in 1795.

The modern state of Kerala was founded in 1956. The areas that were inhabited by speakers of the Malayalam language, basically the kingdoms of Cochin, Travancore and Malabar, became the state; just as Karnataka was made up of Kannada speakers and Tamil Nadu of Tamil speakers. The rulers of these kingdoms had been progressive, liberal monarchs and there'd never been the extremes of poverty that can exist in India. In 1957, the people of Kerala elected a Communist government, one of the few freely elected Communist governments. A weird governmental mixture of Marxist–Leninism and extreme religiosity still persists. Land ownership is more equitable than anywhere else in India; life expectancy is longer; there's a higher percentage of literacy than there is in Britain.

I hadn't decided where to stay in Trivandrum or Kovalam and was looking through the *Lonely Planet*. A very helpful and well-informed man, a medical supplies salesman who was travelling with his elderly aunt, recommended some places. I didn't want *grande luxe* but nor did I want squalor. I wanted something for around one hundred and fifty rupees. The salesman knew exactly the kind of places that would suit me. The elderly aunt had a box of delicious cake, a cross between flapjack and coconut ice, moist and sticky. She kept offering me pieces of it. When I asked her what this cake was called she just beamed and said, 'Slices.' Later I described the cake to Mrs Sen who said it was probably *beebeek.*

Onam is Kerala's harvest festival, the equivalent of the Punjab's Baisakhi or neighbouring Tamil Nadu's Pongal. Although it is primarily a Hindu festivity, Muslims and Christians also celebrate, for it is as much to do with the state's self-image as religion. It takes place, over ten days, at the end of August and the beginning of September, in the Hindu month of Bhadra, when the monsoon has finished and the granaries are full and there are flowers everywhere. During Onam Kerala looks back to its golden age. There is a folk song that goes:

> When Mahabali ruled the land
> Everyone was equal.
> Happily they lived.
> Danger befell none.
> There was no falsehood, fraud
> Nor untruth.

Mahabali (as he's known in Kerala, though he's plain Bali in the Puranas) was the ruler of the Malabar Coast in ancient times. So long ago, in fact, that his reign took place in the second *yuga*, the Treta age[6]. Mahabali, the son of Virocana and grandson of Prahlada, was an *asura*, which is often translated, misleadingly, as a demon. An *asura* was basically a rival of the gods and not necessarily evil. Mahabali, in fact, was far from evil; he was a wise and good ruler and was greatly loved by the Malayalis. The *asura* king was considerably more popular than the lesser gods and, besides the Malabar Coast, his kingdom grew to include all of the heavens, all of the earth and all of the sky which, understandably, outraged the lesser gods who appealed to Indra, the Lord of the Firmament. Indra, in turn, asked Vishnu to deal with Mahabali. Vishnu disguised himself as a Brahmin dwarf called Vamana and set off to visit Mahabali in Kerala. When he got there, he asked Mahabali to grant him all the land that he could cover in three strides. Mahabali, amused at such a request from the stunted figure, agreed. Vamana started to grow and grow until he was as big as the universe. With just two giant strides he covered the entire earth, the heavens and the sky. Mahabali, realizing that Vamana was none other than Vishnu and that he had been beaten fairly, offered his head for the third stride. Vishnu stood on Mahabali's head and pushed the *asura* down like a tent peg, right down through the ground to the nether world where he was condemned to stay for ever. But the Malayalis begged Vishnu to let their beloved king return to them once a year. Vishnu granted their wish. So, at Onam, Mahabali returns, shooting back up through the soil and bringing with him the luscious spring as a reminder of his plentiful reign. The Malayalis build little pyramidical mounds of flowers, called *kolams*, in their courtyards. These represent the old king bursting up through the ground, as if in an eruption of petals. Several of these *kolams* were to be seen from the train as it moved down the coast. The salesman told me that, in the evenings, young girls perform a hand-clapping folk dance called *kaikottikali* around the *kolams*. Describing the dance he mimed a few steps, causing his aunt to giggle and cover her face. In *On a Shoestring to Coorg*, Dervla Murphy sees the Mahabali legend as nostalgia for the old pre-Aryan days, before caste reached the South. I was struck by the legend's *Golden Bough* quality.

The hotel that the salesman had recommended was a brand-new one. In fact, the builders were still working on it. But it was perfectly adequate and reasonably priced. I had a quick shower, then changed into clean clothes and went for a walk. I bought a banana with a brick-red skin. I had to peel it with a knife and the flesh tasted like soft wood, not sweet at all; I wondered if it was a cooking banana but I had seen other people eating them raw.

Trivandrum seemed a pleasant city, southern in the way that Madras is but Bangalore isn't – lots of very dark people. The Padmanabhaswamy temple was closed to non-Hindus. Even Hindu visitors had to wear special lungis to go in which they could rent at the entrance. There weren't any other Europeans to be seen. There was a *khaddi* fair to celebrate Onam, rows of tents selling handloom cottons, like trade stands at Badminton. I thought I'd look for some checked lungis and, if I found any that I liked, have Mr Prakash the *darzi* turn them into shirts for me. As the average lungi was two square metres there was plenty of material. Or if I saw any cotton on a roll that I liked I'd buy that. There were so many tents with such similar fabrics that, after a while, it got boring. I was rummaging through a box of lungis, folded into little square packets, when a tiny brown hand rested on mine.

A young girl with a solemn expression wanted to show me some batik. I wasn't interested but found it odd that she held on to my hand for quite a long time. Leaving that tent for yet another with more or less the same selection all over again, I felt a tiny brown arm link around mine. It was the girl from the last tent. She still had a solemn expression, but looking at her properly, I could see that she wasn't a young girl at all but a midget aged about forty. She was unusually dressed. She had on a white nylon overall like a lab coat and orange plaid slacks and white socks and sandals, not chappals but the sandals that English children wear to school, and her hair, which was the rusty colour that beggar children's hair goes from malnutrition, was tied in a long plait. She didn't smile or speak at all. Without having anything specific to go on, I could sense that there was something wrong with her. She just attached herself to me and, whenever I managed to free my arm, within seconds, she was back on it. It was embarrassing and creepy. I couldn't exactly say, 'Unhand me, miss,' but I wasn't at all comfortable about the situation. I left the tent and decided to leave the *khaddi* fair altogether, making my way back to the hotel through the bazaar. The midget clung to me. She certainly wasn't a beggar and if she was a hooker, she didn't make any of the provocative gestures that one would have expected. Her silence and trance-like movements suggested clinical depression. We came to a busy road by the Connemara Market and I shot across it. I shot back again and it seemed to have worked – I'd shaken her off. However, when I reached my hotel I found the midget waiting by the entrance. She must have taken a short cut. I started to think of the film *Don't Look Now* and hoped that I wasn't dealing with a psychopath. I felt a *frisson* of anxiety. I walked past her but as I did so I noticed that her eyes were welling with tears. I didn't really know what to do. If she'd wanted someone to talk to, she would surely have spoken. If she'd wanted money, she'd have asked. One of the bearers shooed her away. I asked him if she was all right and he gave a loud snort that could have meant a number of things.

In the lobby of the hotel there was a bookshop. I glanced at its window and saw that it was selling second-hand 'airport' books; Jackie Collins novels, Jeffrey Archers that people must have left in their rooms. There were also a few trays of luridly coloured sweets: *burfi*, champagne toast, night queen, Mysore Pak; all of which taste pretty much alike and delicious if you just eat one – more than one and you feel sick; in that respect they're like Cadbury's Creme Eggs. What surprised me about the shop was that it accepted credit cards and was full of customers. So I went in. There were piles of 'girlie' calendars from Australia, the kind that hang in garages. There were posters of topless girls on bicycles, strapping Australian girls, more sporty than sexy, as if they just found it more comfortable to ride their bikes without T-shirts on. Coffee-table books on glamour photography, the history of lingerie. Pseudo-medical books on marital intimacy. Misty David Hamilton postcards. The sort of thing that is hardly considered pornographic at all in the West; more what you'd find in a remainder bookshop. But, in a country where *Playboy* magazines are seized by customs officers, these were hot items and affluent-looking businessmen were snapping them up. It was clear that this was a recent consignment. Some of the men were buying several copies of the same calendar, perhaps to sell on or, more likely, as presents for friends.

I had hoped to see a Kathakali performance in Trivandrum but there wasn't one that night. I'd noticed that a band was going to play in the hotel restaurant that evening so I asked the receptionist what sort of music it would be. 'George Michael style, OK? You better believe it!' was his answer. I decided to eat early and avoid the cabaret. The restaurant was very dark and I was the first customer of the evening. The menu was North Indian and Chinese. I ordered tandoori prawns with *roti naan* and a lime soda to drink.

I was waiting for my food to arrive when a tall and very old man entered the restaurant. He looked like a Eurasian or a pale North Indian but he could equally have been Greek or Italian, it was hard to tell. He was something of a VIP because two waiters and the restaurant manager bustled around him, pulling out his chair and straightening the cutlery on his table. He was wearing shorts and a polo shirt and Pathan chappals like Major Trivedi's. His bare arms and legs were spindly but his body was a wide flat carapace. He was in his late seventies or early eighties and his hair, brushed forward like a Caesar's, had been dyed with blue-black ink. 'I expect you'll be going to Kovalam. That's where the young people are.' It was a lower-middle-class cockney accent. Or could it have been Australian? Ah, I thought, the pornographer.

I replied that I was heading for Kovalam in the morning.

'I lived there last summer. It's a bloody dirty place.' I told him that it's supposed to be one of the finest beaches in India. He laughed. 'No, mate. It's the dirtiest bloody beach in India.'

I asked if he lived locally. 'No. Thought about it but it's too dirty for me down here. I gave it a go but I've had enough. I'm going up to Mercara, that's in Coorg. Cleaner up there. Not so many people, not so many Indians.' I said that I liked Indians. I didn't find them at all dirty in their own houses. In fact, most of the Indian houses that I'd stayed in were considerably cleaner than Western houses.

'Don't you believe it, mate. They don't use toilets, you know. Don't ever touch an Indian.' Having exhausted this topic, I asked him if he was Australian. 'Well, I've lived there, yeah. But I was born here, would you believe? Never lived here much though, not until recently.' What I could make out of his life sounded extraordinary. He'd lived in Acapulco, in Venice Beach, California, in Bangkok, in Sydney. In the fifties, he'd lived in London. Somewhat improbably, he enquired, 'You've heard, I suppose, of the Chelsea Set?'

It was in London that he'd picked up a strange illness that no doctor could treat. A Harley Street specialist had advised him that cold weather would kill him so, ever since, he'd lived in hot places. I asked what he'd done for a living. He grinned. 'This and that, mate.' A waiter brought my prawns. The old man looked concerned. 'Jesus, you're not going to eat that!' I said that I was and he shook his head gravely. I noticed how wrinkled his neck was and the vulturish angle of it.

His food arrived. 'Mexican chicken. I give 'em the bloody recipe so they can't bugger about. Chicken's clean meat. That is, the meat can be cleaned, red meat can't. Stale blood, mate, that's why it's red. And chillies'll wipe out bacteria. I'll tell you, Indian food will kill you.' I repeated my assertion about Indian cleanliness.

'The young girls,' he said with a faraway expression, 'they're all right. I mean, very young. They're naturally clean. But once they get older, start bleeding, they're ruined. They don't stay clean, don't wash properly. They're as bad as the men. It's blood that carries germs. Where are you going to stay at Kovalam?' I said that the Rockholm had been recommended to me.

'Well, it's clean. But you'll never sleep.' I asked why not. 'The waves on the bloody rocks, mate. Crashing all night.' He recommended a restaurant on the beach, called 'My Dream'. 'You can tell 'em you know me. Mr Aubrey, tell 'em. They'll treat you right.'

I travelled the eight or nine miles from Trivandrum to Kovalam by auto-rickshaw. It was a delightful journey through the coconut groves. There seemed to be a local craze for tie-dyed lungis, worn down to the ankles, not doubled. Lungis in general were worn by both sexes though the women's lungis (*mundus*) were tied slightly differently so that they skirted out. As we got nearer to Kovalam, families of stone-breakers sat by the side of the road, bashing lumps of granite with hammers, sometimes sitting under umbrellas or movable sun-screens made of sacking. It looked a ghastly job. Then there were hoardings everywhere advertising hotels. We climbed a steep hill and, below us, through the coconut palms, there was the sea. It looked very rough. The rickshaw-wallah agreed. 'Plenty are dying.'

The Rockholm was a sand-coloured modern building down a narrow lane. From the road it didn't look
very promising but my room was simple and comfortable (and half-price in this close season) and the view,
across the rocks in a secluded bay (a lighthouse on one
headland and, down the coast, a fine white mosque),
was splendid. Kovalam Beach itself, on the other side
of the lighthouse, was smaller than I'd expected and
crowded. Most of the crowd were English students,
who would have spent the last six weeks or so in the
damp North and had come to Kovalam to get some
sunshine before returning to Blighty and college at the
end of the month. My heart sank at the rows of cafés
selling Western food and blaring out Dire Straits and
Bruce Springsteen. There were organized games of
frisbee and volleyball but most people were splashing
in the surf or sunbathing. A number of pi-dogs lolled
beneath thatched beach umbrellas. At the café called
'My Dream' I ordered my lunch, mentioning that Mr
Aubrey had recommended the place to me. The
waiter's hand trembled. I wondered if I'd said the
wrong thing. The kitchen staff kept peering at me with
inquisitive, worried expressions. When I asked for the
bill, they told me that the meal was on the house. But I
insisted on paying and decided, to save us all from
embarrassment, not to eat there again.

I swam for a while, then sprawled on the beach. As
many of the students seemed to know each other I felt
rather lonely and, listening to their conversations, I
felt old; at least too old to consider Tanita Tikaram a
genius. I noticed Guddu, the Madrassi protest singer,
talking to two topless girls. I decided not to reintro-
duce myself unless it was unavoidable but Guddu
failed to notice me anyway. The girls seemed more
interested in his tightly held dreams than I had been.
Perhaps he'd found his audience. Little boys tried to
sell me coconut oil. Women came along selling fruit. A
dead-ringer for Chuck Berry was selling sunglasses.
Another man sold lungis and I bought one with a

hammer-and-sickle motif. Migrant Rajasthanis sold embroidered hats, skirts and bags. The local people were Moplahs[7], descended from the ninth-century Arabs, who settled on the Malabar Coast and the Dravidian women they married.

I sat on the terrace of the Rockholm and ate a good but fiery dish of curried mackerel (*meen charu*) with mashed tapioca that was like mashed potato but starchier, like the aroids that are eaten in the Caribbean. I'd told the waiter that I wanted to taste local cooking and he'd suggested that I eat what the chef had prepared for the staff's evening meal. There was a good deal of interest in me as I ate the fish. I think that they were surprised I could cope with the chillies. After that, whenever I ate at the Rockholm, the waiter would recommend some dish that wasn't on the menu. I felt quite privileged. The other guests were more my age. The students stayed down at the beach. It must have been noisy down there. There were two French sisters, very alike, who resembled the Duke of Wellington on the five-pound note. They ate their breakfast on the terrace, sitting with straight backs, both wearing fine brocade dressing-gowns and smoking heavily. There was a homosexual couple from Italy. One was bald and like Elton John to look at. I felt sorry for him because he was horribly sunburnt. His friend was good-looking with long black hair. He was effeminate, in a graceful way; not camp because there was a seriousness about him. My guess was that he was a dancer; he had very elegant deportment. The only absurdity was that he had taken to wearing local costume and the tie-dyed lungi that he swished lightly about in looked like drag.

Just after dawn, the small fishing boats left the village in a flotilla, carrying their nets out to various points in the bay. The boats were made of five poles tied together, more like surfboards than canoes and, coming back in, they seemed to balance on top of the waves. There were also individual fishermen who stood on the rocks. They used very little equipment, just hook, line and a stone as sinker. Nor did they catch much. Perhaps that wasn't the point.

I walked down to the main stretch of beach. At the far end there was a man dancing, dressed in colourful rags and flowers, like a mummer. But he'd gone by the time I got there. I sat at a café and drank a lime soda. At the next table were two English women. One was middle-aged, grey-haired and gap-toothed. The other was in her early twenties, plump and pink with the palest fair hair. I asked them if they'd seen the dancer. 'What, Worzel Gummidge?' asked the older one and I nodded. 'Oh, yes. He's often here. It's Harvest Festival.' They were mother and daughter. The daughter's name was Tilly and the mother's name was Enid – though all the waiters and fruit-sellers called her Mummy. Enid's husband was an army officer in Germany and Tilly had been at the Royal School in Bath. We talked about Bath for a while. Tilly defined herself as a 'Sloane Ranger', which I thought odd, like saying 'Hallo, I'm a Champagne Socialist' or 'My name's Terry and I'm a Lager Lout'. Tilly had been working in London and had supposedly saved up enough money to buy a round-the-world air ticket. It turned out that she'd left behind an enormous overdraft and an angry bank manager. Somehow the bank manager had been given Tilly's poste restante addresses and a series of nasty letters had awaited her all across Australia and Asia. Legal procedures were threatened and, panic-stricken, Tilly had contacted her mother. Enid had spoken to the bank and found out that the situation was indeed grave, then decided that the best thing she could do was to bring Tilly home personally. They'd met up in Thailand. Enid found Tilly well and staying, for next to nothing, in a hut on a beach. Within a week Enid had decided to join her daughter travelling and to ignore the urgency of the bank's demands. She had enough money for both of them. It would mean staying in very cheap places but that was all right if they avoided big cities. It seemed to me that Enid was the one who didn't want to go home. She seemed to be having a real adventure. Perhaps years of army life and conventional behaviour had made her restless. Tilly was quite sweet, still completely irresponsible and not a bit repentant. She'd bought lots of jewellery, semi-precious stones, silver bracelets. She'd also had five silk ballgowns made and sent home. Enid thought it rather funny, she wasn't cross. 'Oh, Mummy's completely cool about it.'

Enid had the booming voice of an old-fashioned memsahib, which is probably normal among officers' wives, and, though she got on extremely well with the locals, making them roar with laughter, many of the English students were wary of her. I overheard two Northern girls muttering about Enid being 'a Tory racist'. She may well have voted Conservative (though she never discussed politics with me) but there was nothing racist about her. In fact, she was a favourite with the fruit-sellers. 'Oh, Mummy!' they'd cackle in response to her stories and some of them, having sold their wares, would while away the rest of the day in her company. Tilly sunbathed beside her and read *Riders* by Jilly Cooper. Their next stop was Goa. Then, away from the beaches, to Nepal. 'Mummy's turned into a hippy, I think. She wants to go to all the freak centres.'

Kathakali is the famous dance-drama of Kerala. Stories from the *Ramayana* and the *Mahabharat* are acted out by extraordinary dancers in the most spectacular costumes. The whole effect is, superficially, more Chinese than Indian. The texts, comprising songs and narrative passages, were sometimes written by the local royalty. Balarama Varma, the Maharajah of Travancore for most of the eighteenth century, wrote six of them. Other kings were known to have acted and danced in performances that they'd written. I suppose it was all a bit like the spectacles at Versailles and the courtly masques of the sixteenth and seventeenth centuries. A proper Kathakali performance lasts all night. If there'd been one to go to, I'd have gone. But there wasn't so I went to a demonstration of Kathakali instead. It took place on the roof of the Neptune Hotel. I arrived early to watch the dancers getting ready. In the past, they told me, masks were worn but these have been replaced by elaborate make-up, created from natural substances; leaves, sap, crushed flowers and powdered minerals, all with their religious and medical significance. Great head-dresses go on top. The movements of the face have become central to the drama. The nine *rasas*, dramatic emotions (tranquillity, fear, loathing, desire, wonder, courage, pathos, anger and ridicule), are expressed with the weirdest distortions of the facial muscles and, if the lecturer hadn't announced each one, I'd never have guessed them. They all seemed to express the same thing to me – that the dancer was about to sneeze. There are ninety or so hand movements, *mudras*, but their combinations are infinite. One pretty *mudra* shows a bee buzzing around a lotus flower. How on earth would one have deciphered that? The whole thing is so stylized that Kathakali dancers start learning their craft, at special institutes, from the age of ten. It's as long as seven years before they can perform. Only men take part though they may play female characters.

The demonstration consisted of a lecture and a short excerpt from a much longer drama. The lecturer explained that a full-blown Kathakali consisted of three elements: the sung narrative, the drum accompaniment and the danced mime. The narrative is sung by a man called a *Ponnani* who strikes a gong. He is assisted by a cymbalist called a *Sankiti*. The two drummers are the *Chendakkaran*, who beats a cylindrical drum, and the *Maddalam*, whose drum is barrel-shaped. The dancers don't speak or sing (though, sometimes, if portraying a demon, one may hoot like an owl) but emphasize their movements by stamping their feet and sounding the bells that are attached to their ankles. What was going on on the hotel roof was a much reduced version of all that but the dancers' costumes and strange descriptive movements and the single pounding drum did convey something mysterious and hypnotic. I couldn't make the story out at all and could only suppose that, attending a Kathakali performance in its entirety, one would get more out of it, losing, I would imagine, one's sense of normal time. It might be possible to enter the drama's own universe. Either that or fall asleep, worn out and frustrated by incomprehension.

I walked along the coast to the Moplah village. The mosque wasn't an old building; it was like an art deco cinema. I was surrounded by children who wanted to try on my hat and have their photographs taken. Grown men were solemnly playing marbles. There were fishermen, sitting on dunes, mending their nets and small fish were spread out on the ground, in large neat squares, to dry.

I thought I'd have a shave and haircut at the village barber's. The shop was a thatched hut but inside it was all pastel colours – light-blue walls, green furniture, pink around the mirror; similar to the pastel decoration that one finds when old pubs have been converted into cocktail bars. The village hipsters congregated there to talk about movies. Although they tried to include me in the conversation, it was very faltering. They asked me if I'd seen *Die Hard 2*. Then it was decided that I resembled its star; one of the hipsters pointed at my head and, as if he'd made a great discovery, announced, 'Bruce Willis.' This caused some debate with my lathered face receiving a lot of attention. A senior hipster had the final word. 'Gene Wilder.'

Outside the barber's shop was an 'old timer' with two remaining teeth and round pebble glasses. He made a strange signal to me, a mime of smoking a cigarette noisily. I presumed that he was asking for a cigarette and tried to explain that I didn't have any. He pretended to drink from a bottle. I hadn't brought my water bottle with me. Then he started sticking his thumb right down his throat (as if trying to make himself sick) and making a horrid retching sound. I walked on hastily.

I needed an auto-rickshaw to take me back to Trivandrum. It meant walking along the beach to the grandest hotel at Kovalam, outside of which there were always plenty. On the way I passed countless handicraft shops. Most of the stuff they were selling came from Northern India. As we were almost as far south as it was possible to be in India, it struck me that the merchandise wouldn't have much souvenir value. Like bringing Dutch clogs back from Sicily.

The rickshaw-wallah brought a friend of his along for the ride. The rickshaw-wallah's name was Guppy and his friend was called Harish. They were both in their thirties. Guppy wore a khaki shirt, the standard rickshaw-wallah's garb. Harish wore a bright Hawaiian shirt with white roses against a pink background. They were unusually happy, I thought, smiling and giggling. I soon found out why. Harish explained that they had been smoking dope; they were, he told me, completely stoned, out of their heads, in fact. I decided that it was safe to travel with them. Guppy couldn't be any more dangerous stoned that the average rickshaw-wallah at the best of times. If anything he was likely to drive slower.

The slightest incident caused torrents of laughter from them. We passed a buffalo with such an amusing expression that Guppy had to stop the engine. 'Did you see its face?' I said that it was just a buffalo. 'No, no, no. It was exactly like my wife's brother. You will please make photograph, then send me a copy. I believe it is a miracle.' Harish said that, actually, the buffalo did resemble Guppy's brother-in-law but in its movements and its slow lugubrious attitude. He didn't think a photograph would capture the likeness.

Harish spoke very good English. I commented on it. 'Well, I should do.' Guppy rocked with mirth and echoed him. 'Well, he should do!' I asked why. 'Because I lived in England for three years!' Again there was uncontrollable laughter from both of them.

'Where did you live?'

'North Yorkshire!'

I asked whether there were any other Malayalis up there. He spluttered. 'None, my friend. None at all!' Guppy found this about as funny as the buffalo's resemblance to his brother-in-law had been. We had to pull up to the side of the road so that he wouldn't miss any of the story. What had he been doing there?

'I was a bloody farmhand!'

'A bloody farmhand!' Guppy slapped his leg with amusement.

It sounded so improbable that I thought he was joking. 'No, my friend. It's the truth.'

Harish told me that he had met an English girl at Kovalam and had married her. They had lived fairly contentedly with his parents who ran a small textiles shop just outside Trivandrum. Then the English girl grew homesick and they decided to move over to live with her family in rural North Yorkshire.

The girl's parents had not welcomed Harish ('I think they were racialists') and made it clear to him that they didn't consider the marriage to be a legal one. Furthermore, they set about convincing their daughter that she was still single, even though the authorities, in both countries, recognized the union.

After three years of cold winters and even colder shoulders, Harish had decided to return home. He'd made very few friends of his own. The other Asians that he'd met were as unfamiliar with Keralan life and culture as the English themselves.

His father-in-law had given him work on the farm but paid him as little as he could, deducting more than half of that for board and lodging. His fondest memory was of harvesting potatoes. The smell had made him high. Guppy was amused but incredulous. 'English potatoes are making you stoned? This I cannot believe.'

'It is true! All the time I was so high.'

Guppy asked me if this was so. I said it was new to me. 'That is because you are used to it already.' They laughed all the way to the station.

At Quilon[8] I stayed overnight at the Tourist Bungalow, away from the town centre. It had been the British Residency (Lord Curzon had stayed there) and it seemed to me that nothing had been changed, except that the grounds had been turned into a pleasure garden and that meant loud film music. It was on the shore of a lake and one could hire a rowing boat. Normally it was possible to eat at the Tourist Bungalow, but the staff were off for the Onam holiday, so I went back into town to look for food.

Quilon is a little market town today though it was once a thriving port[9]. There must be a printing works there making the posters that you see in Indian offices – a sunset over the sea and some platitude like 'Today is The First Day In The Rest Of Your Life' – I had never seen so many of the things. I found a *dhaba* and the waiter recommended fried chicken and *appams*. All chicken in India is stringy but the meat was breaded with a peppery garlicy mixture and served with slivers of raw onion and chillies and lime. The *appams* were like very thin crumpets or French crêpes – also similar to Ethiopian *injera*. Two men at the next table were having brains in a very red gravy.

There was a man in the bazaar selling one-string fiddles. He played the crowd a few tunes. Rhythmic hillbillyish melodies that hardly sounded Indian at all but sometimes Irish and sometimes like raw country blues. It was a stirring sound. I was tempted to buy one.

I was going to travel by boat through the backwaters to Alleppey and I'd read that it was advisable to take plenty of food. It wasn't, apparently, possible to buy food on the journey. So I bought some oranges and bananas and biscuits, my usual travelling picnic. The boy who sold me the biscuits attempted to overcharge me by five times the price that was printed on the packet. When I pointed this out he tried to explain. 'Old price, old price.' Then they must have been old biscuits and I didn't want them. 'No, no, sir. Fresh.' He pointed to a date printed next to the price. I pointed to the price again and paid him accordingly.

I went back to the Tourist Bungalow and got in to bed.

The film music played until two in the morning. I couldn't sleep. I sat up grumpily, reading *The Vampyre* by Polidori and ate all the food that I'd bought for the journey.

On my way to the jetty, I passed a Syrian Christian funeral procession[10]. The coffin was carried in a sort of glass palanquin. I wanted to stop the rickshaw and watch but there wasn't time. I bought some more food at vastly inflated prices and waited with a crowd of young Europeans, most of whom had come from Kovalam. It isn't necessary to stay overnight at Quilon, an early bus leaves from Kovalam every morning and arrives in Quilon in good time for the backwater ferry. My midnight feast had given me a stomach-ache and I'd had to use a particularly gruesome public lavatory. The stench had made me feel sick and I had to sit down when I got to the jetty, to regain my strength. As soon as the ferry arrived, most people crowded on to its metal roof. I found a seat below. I was worried that I was going to be sick. I started considering the possibility of food poisoning, the lavatory smell wouldn't have caused such a lasting reaction. I felt queasy and miserable and dreaded a recurrence of the grim gastric flu that I'd had in Tamil Nadu. We pushed out into Ashtamudi Lake, a shining glass disc. A pair of fish eagles swooped about. Two men in a canoe rowed past, reminding me of George Caleb Bingham's painting, *Fur Traders Descending the Missouri*. Gradually the serenity and quiet beauty of the backwaters worked like medicine. From the expanse of the lake we moved into narrower stretches, no wider than roads. There were houses built on strips of land. Children waved to the boat. People stood washing in the blue water. More canoes and ragged boats with big brown sails passed the ferry. It was an extraordinary place, a cross between the bayous of Louisiana and the landscape on Willow Pattern china. There were water lilies and lotus flowers in the water. Some of the stretches were nearly clogged with a weed called African Payal. Chinese fishing-nets, spidery Heath Robinson contraptions, stood among the palm trees. Black pigs rooted along the grassy strips. An elaborate portrait of Lenin (with the kohl-rimmed eyes of a Bombay film star) decorated the side of a house. Whenever the engine stopped the only noise was the cawing of crows. I went up on to the roof. The only Indian passenger was Guddu and this time he recognized me. He was taking the ferry to Alleppey, then taking it straight back to Quilon again. 'It is just a diversion.' He wanted to spend more time at Kovalam. A lank-haired girl, wearing a mirrored Rajasthani skirt, was playing a guitar. It must have been a cumbersome piece of luggage. She sang Suzanne Vega's 'Marlene on the Wall' very badly; it was an idiotic song at the best of times and the girl had a silly mannerism of switching octaves at the end of a line (resulting in over-emphasis) that made it even worse. Guddu enjoyed it. 'This girl I know,' he informed me proudly, 'her future as a recording star is assured.' I suggested that he borrow the guitar and play us one of his songs. He went all bashful. 'I'm not a guitarist.'

'I'm sure you could tell that girl the chords.'

'No, no. You see, I write the words only. I leave it to the film studios to set them to music. That is the standard practice for song-writers in this country.' The lank-haired girl played a series of ghastly songs; some that weren't that bad to begin with ('Wild Horses' by the Stones) she nevertheless managed to wreck with the octave switching. The prow of the ferry was the quietest place to be. So I sat there, on my own, enjoying the tranquillity, for most of the nine-hour journey.

At sunset I was joined by a girl from Wolverhampton. Her name was Rachel and she was a stout dark girl in her late teens. She had a vaguely ursine manner (perhaps more badger than bear) that was accentuated by her muscular hairy limbs and quick black eyes. She was going to study fashion design at Brighton. That surprised me because her whole appearance suggested a more down-to-earth career; I'd have guessed that she was a chemistry student. She had been travelling around India with her boyfriend Matthew and another traveller that they'd teamed up with in Rajasthan. When she told me that I realized how much of a loner I'd become. I'd never have considered 'teaming up' with anyone. It wasn't unfriendliness, it just hadn't occurred to me. Rachel, in turn, was amazed to hear that I'd been staying with Indian families. Matthew had decided that India was fine, the problem was the people. She tended to agree. They were so dishonest. Eric, their friend, got on better with them than they did. He was older than Matthew and Rachel and had been to India before.

We arrived at Alleppey in the dark. Saint George's Lodging was supposed to be good value. A single room with an attached bathroom was only twenty-five rupees a night. The three of them decided to stay there as well. Matthew was tall with a chubby smiley face. He was dressed in surfer fashion (at least an English fashion chain's notion of surfer fashion): a T-shirt with the logo 'Fat Willy' on it, gaudy baggy shorts and checked 'vans'. Eric was my age, a sunburnt Scot. He had red hair tied in a neat pony tail and carried his luggage about on a foldable trolley. He was an actor and drama therapist. We set off towards the lodge, using the map in the *Lonely Planet*. As we approached the town centre, we discovered that a parade to celebrate Onam was about to take place. Saint George's Lodging was the top three floors of a large city block. There was a sign at the top of the stairs: *Your Home Away From Sweet Home.* We signed in and were told that dinner was unavailable so we decided to find somewhere to eat in town after we'd dumped our bags. I was just being shown to my room when there was a powercut. The bearer went back to reception to get a candle. What I saw of the room appealed to me, a monk's cell.

Outside the whole city had blacked out. People had gathered along the pavements to watch the parade. The only available lighting came from torches and candles but it went ahead anyway, a ghostly procession that ought to have been merry, with bright yellow flags waving. The marchers, most of whom seemed to be from trade unions, trooped cautiously along, like a jungle platoon behind enemy lines. Very few of the banners that one could read were in English but the whole thing appeared to typify the Keralan *mélange* of left-wing politics and religion. Eric thought that there might be power nearer the jetty so we went back the way that we came. The streets got more and more crowded.

There were several drunks. By and large, a drunken Indian is nothing to worry about; alcohol brings out a floppy silliness, that's all[11] – one rarely comes across the confused and pent-up fury that can make a Northern-European drunk so threatening. But, as we pushed our way through, one young man lurched forward to put his hand on Rachel's breast. It looked to me as if he was trying to steady himself more than molest her but it was hard to tell. Rachel's immediate reaction was to strike him across the face; the man was so plastered that her slap knocked him over.

As he lay on the ground, Matthew kicked him in the mouth, repeatedly, until blood spouted from his lip and ran down his neck and soaked into the collar of his white shirt. I was shocked. It seemed excessively violent and sickening, out of all proportion to the man's offence. His companions pulled back, as horrified as I was. I muttered to Matthew that he could have just told him off. 'Bollocks I could have,' he snapped back. Rachel, trembling, said that it was always happening. They had both reached boiling point. 'They don't treat their own women that way. They're such fucking lechers with white women.'

It surprised me that she persisted in wearing a thin cotton singlet without a bra. Rachel could have worked out what was acceptable, or unlikely to draw attention, by observing the way Indian women dress. One wouldn't expect her to wear a sari but she should have realized that what might be all right to wear on a beach was unwise to wear on a busy city street at night. That isn't to excuse the behaviour of the men who'd grabbed her – but if such confrontations had become a problem for Rachel, it seemed to me that the situation was avoidable. We walked on without talking, numbed by Matthew's outburst. It was all the more disturbing to me because, to be honest, there'd been times when I'd wanted to hit people myself. Rickshaw-wallahs who'd drive me miles out of my way (in Bangalore where I knew the routes well) to bump up their meters; the persistent money-changers, hustlers, all the hopelessly transparent con men who plagued one at every corner. So often I'd felt that the last recourse, the only way to say 'stop bothering me' would be violence (even threatened violence) but I'd always managed to keep my cool. Now I felt guilt by association, as if I myself had broken a self-imposed rule. I wanted to get away from Matthew, not to be seen with him. Rachel's and Matthew's circumstances were such that all the Indians they had met were people who looked at them as Europeans instead of as individuals. Insulated by one another's company, their only encounters had been small business transactions; there were no Trivedi families in their experience of India; they must have felt as if they were running a gauntlet of petty entrepreneurs and low-lifers. Something, that had been about to snap, had snapped.

We eventually found a café with its own generator. All the proprietor could offer were *dosas* or *idlis*. Most of the staff, he explained, had left to watch the parade; if we hadn't just walked in, he would have closed for the night. Matthew didn't know what *dosas* or *idlis* were and didn't like the sound of them when Eric told him. He was in the middle of protesting when the lights of Alleppey came back. So we moved on to another restaurant where he could get egg and chips; he needed comfort food.

My room was hardly furnished. The bed was a mattress on a concrete platform. There was a smell of disinfectant. I spread my mosquito net and went to sleep. At two I was woken by a sound like lino being torn off a floor; it took me a while to work out what it was. Somebody, right outside my door, was clearing his throat in the loudest possible manner. It took him a good five minutes to do. It's more like clearing the lungs than just the throat. I'd watched men performing this elimination, the whole neck and chest racked with convulsive spasms. No sooner had the man finished than somebody else started. Not quite as loudly but loud enough to stop me from going back to sleep. Ten minutes after that a third man starting 'hawking', the loudest of all, a noise that was similar to a leopard's snarl. I couldn't understand why it had to go on outside my door and went out, determined to move

'Johnny Weissmuller' along. I found out that the wash basin for the corridor was on the wall next to my door. Men who'd taken part in the Onam parade were returning to the cheaper rooms, without attached bathrooms. They were whispering and tiptoeing about, behaving considerately towards the other guests – until it came to throat-clearing which just can't be done quietly. This obsession with mucus is hard to understand. In certain areas the dust might have something to do with it. There are also breathing exercises that figure in yoga and breathing itself has religious significance (*Prana*). Perhaps the elimination of mucus is to ease breathing. But women have to breathe as well as men and I'd never encountered a female 'hawker'. I'd read that many Hindus believe sperm is produced in the head; any mucus is looked upon as 'spoiled sperm' to be got rid of as quickly as possible. I had asked Major Trivedi if that was, in fact, the case and he got rather cross. 'Who writes such nonsense?' I read him a passage from *On A Shoestring To Coorg*. 'You see, the world regards the Indian people as unhygienic and backward. Western writers are broadcasting such falsehoods.' However, mucus does hold a real horror for most Indians. To carry a used handkerchief in one's pocket is about as unthinkable as carrying used lavatory paper about. I realized I'd just have to put up with the disturbance and eventually went back to sleep around three. The early risers woke me again at five, the first mucus elimination of the day being just as rigorous as the last one at night. There didn't seem any point in trying to sleep on.

I walked to the jetty to catch another ferry up to Kottayam, a shorter trip than Quilon to Alleppey. This time I was the only European on the boat. It was much less crowded and I managed to get a seat to myself. Using my bag as a pillow, I stretched out and dozed all the way there. Waiting for me at the Kottayam jetty was Suraj Bhavasarman, a teaching associate of the Trivedis.

He'd come home for Onam. Unfortunately the flu that had struck the Trivedi household had caught up with him. He looked much too ill to be walking about. His older brother Kumar was with him and an auto-rickshaw-wallah from their village. Suraj explained that his brother would accompany me to the Arunmula boat races and left us, to get back to his sick bed as quickly as possible. Kumar – who had a boxer's face, a broken nose and puffy eyes – was a reporter for a local paper. He decided that the best thing would be for me to leave my bag at his office.

We had to hurry as the races started within an hour and it was a long way to Arunmula. Downtown Kottayam seemed to be mainly jewellery shops. I bought some film while Kumar deposited my bag. Off we set. The rickshaw-wallah, whose name was Ramu, was a cross-eyed smirking man. He drove with the customary recklessness and soon we were leaving Kottayam and hurtling along ragged country roads and wooded lanes. Kumar chatted a lot, he was more talkative than Suraj. He liked poetry. 'How is Ted Hughes?' he asked me, enquiring after my opinion rather than the poet's health. Hughes was a great influence on many Malayali poets. Was I familiar with R.K. Uma? I replied that the only Indian poet I'd read was Dom Moraes. 'R.K. Uma writes in Malayalam only.' I explained that I didn't know the language. 'But her poetry has been translated into English. An Australian professor has translated some poems. Even in Britain, I am sure, they are published.' I told him that I hadn't come across these translations. He shook his head and said that it didn't matter. 'You will read the poems tonight and you will have the pleasure of meeting Srimati Uma herself.'

'Very famous woman,' Ramu assured me.

'In our house she stays.' Kumar was proud of this literary lodger. 'Always in Malayali papers you see her poems. All over Kerala she is known.' I asked Kumar if he wrote poetry himself. 'No, no. Novels, plays, film scripts. Poetry, no.' It turned out that he'd written eight novels. As he was in his early twenties, this surprised me. Were they all in print? He waved his hand as if to dismiss such trivialities. 'None are yet published.'

'He has written them,' Ramu told me, miming with his free hand to imply that Kumar's manuscripts weren't typed out.

'Film is where I am heading,' said Kumar. 'I am developing a series for television. The avatars[12], manifestations of Vishnu. It will be similar to the *Mahabharat* you have been watching. I myself am to play Krishna.'

'Money, my god!' chuckled Ramu. 'All will be rich then!'

'Yes. It will be shown on BBC and you can say that in Kerala you have met Kumar himself.' When would the scripts be ready? 'I said that it is where I am heading. I am still developing the idea.' We came to a bridge across the river Pamba. 'Down that river are the races,' announced Kumar and we turned in the direction that he indicated.

A few miles further and the roads were clogged with traffic. Buses, cars, bicycles, pedestrians. We decided to park the auto and walk the rest of the way. We were behind a high-school marching band, in shiny red-and-white uniforms, who had already finished performing and were now rushing to watch the races. Ramu smirked at them and, turning to me, said, 'English style.' The races took place beside the Parthasarathy temple; they were to commemorate the installation of the deity who is an aspect of Krishna as a charioteer. The atmosphere was similar to that of any well-attended regatta but, as the temple is a pilgrim centre, there was also a religious dimension. Numerous sadhus hovered about. One old sadhu had woven his matted hair into the shape of a boat, an idea that could catch on with members of the Leander Club. Kumar, waving his press-card, led us into the largest enclosure. On both banks, between the tall trees and the water, swarms of spectators had gathered. Many were actually standing in the river. We positioned ourselves in the press gallery – our view was the best possible. Directly above us sat the Governor of Kerala and his guests. A selection of silver trophies stood on a trestle. Television cameras pointed down at the river. Small boats of all kinds moved between the spectators, selling fruit and soft drinks. A police launch chugged about, the policemen pushing the crowd back towards the shore. Bands played lovely music, half-Dixieland, half-Indian folk music. Two clowns with made-up faces and funny hats splashed in the water, performing routines and singing. The crowd shouted the refrain. The policemen prodded the clowns with their lathis, as if they were part of the comic routine. Which they might have been because the audience laughed and clapped.

There was a long boat with an eagle's head carved on its prow and about fifty oarsmen. I presumed it was one of the racing snakeboats but was told that it was a purely ceremonial craft. Soon the real snakeboats would arrive. Every village in the area owns a snake-boat (*chundanvallam*), so called because it resembles a water snake darting across the water. A snakeboat varies in length between a hundred and a hundred and fifty feet. The prow is raised several feet above the water and the snakeboat is decorated with bright pennants. Crews of a hundred or more men, dressed in white lungis and headbands, row; each boat coxed by the village headman who sits under a red umbrella. The snakeboats glide to the starting point, everybody cheering as they pass. They race in heats, with the headmen chanting songs about Lord Krishna and the oarsmen joining in the chorus. Some of the bigger boats have drummers aboard.

It was a stunning afternoon with the blue of the sky reflected in the river, the dazzling green of the trees and all the colours along the banks. The boats moved incredibly quickly when it came to the racing. They really did look like huge serpents skating along.

The qualifying heats were dealt with fairly promptly. Close to where we were standing, a sports commentator from All India Radio held everyone's attention; a middle-aged man with a pencil moustache and the sort of grin that really does stretch from ear to ear; he reminded me of an H.M. Bateman cartoon. 'Very famous,' Ramu said and he certainly seemed to be. People reached forward to touch him and were pushed back by a bodyguard.

There was a longish wait for the final. A naval helicopter demonstrated air-sea rescue methods. Kumar fetched three coconuts with orange shells, the liquid inside tasting almost fermented. On the opposite bank six brightly caparisoned elephants, great tuskers, came through the trees, then stood in line at the water's edge. The All India Radio personality burst into song. He had a trained baritone voice. The crowd was enraptured. I asked Kumar what the man was singing but he hushed me, too enchanted to answer. Ramu said that they were 'well-known songs, very old, very sad'. One must have been the equivalent of 'Old Shep' because quite a few people were dabbing their eyes. Eventually the final took place. The governor made a long speech before presenting the prizes. Spoken Malayalam, which is sometimes compared to the noise of peas rattling in a tin cup, does sound extraordinary, unlike any other Indian language. It has a lot of 'clanging' sounds ... 'clangclangalang langaclangclang'. The six elephants waded across the river, the water reaching their gigantic shoulders, the All India Radio personality bade his listeners farewell and the crowd started to disperse.

When we got back to Kottayam, Kumar insisted that I meet his editor, a Syrian Christian called Mr Ouseph. Mr Ouseph had visited London earlier in the year. He was a good-natured blunt man who was ready to admit that he'd hated Britain and couldn't see why anyone would leave Kerala for such a place.

I asked him if there were many Malayalis in London. 'Yes, yes. I would say there are thousands.' Kumar said that few of his relatives had ever left Kerala, let alone India. 'Of course they have not,' said Mr Ouseph, 'but that is because your family are Nambudiris. Why would a Nambudiri leave? What sense would the rest of the world make?'

Mr Ouseph told me of a church in the East End that is Greek Orthodox during the week and, on Sunday evenings, Syrian Christian. Walking to the church on a raw February evening, swathed in an anorak ('only my nose sticks out'), Mr Ouseph had been recognized by an old school-friend. It had been twenty-five years since they'd last seen each other. 'It must have been my nose this fellow remembered!'

The Bhavasarmans lived about twenty miles the other side of Kottayam. As Mr Ouseph had said, they were a Nambudiri Brahmin family[13]. Kumar asked me if I knew Brahmins and I said that I'd met plenty, the Trivedis were Brahmins. 'Nambudiris are the most old-fashioned.' I couldn't decide whether he was anxious in case I'd behave in some way that would offend them or that I'd consider his family provincial. He seemed uncomfortable so, to put him at ease, I asked him what novelists he liked. 'D.H. Lawrence I admire. How is he to you?' I replied that I used to like Lawrence's novels but now I preferred his poetry. 'Is that because he is perverted in his novels?'

The Bhavasarmans' house was in a rubber forest. We arrived after dark. There seemed to be more than the usual number of stars in the sky, the woods could have been floodlit. Mr Bhavasarman stood in the courtyard with Suraj, who still looked ill but said he felt better. Mr Bhavasarman was a small powerful man, rather like Picasso, with a remarkably round head; he wore an orange lungi and a sacred thread over his left shoulder. On his forehead he had smeared a red dot and a grey stripe, a red patch high on his chest and one on each arm just below the shoulder. 'Our parents do not know English.'

The house was like a tiny motel in that each room had a door that opened into the yard. A fat yellow dog came out of one door and barked at me. 'This is Bruno,' said Kumar. 'English dog,' said Ramu, I couldn't think why. I asked Suraj what sort of dog Bruno was. 'Our village sort.'

Mrs Bhavasarman, a pretty, shy woman came through another door, pressing her palms together and tilting her head forward. She wore a purple choli under a white sari. Behind her stood R.K. Uma the poetess, in her mid-thirties, very tall and wearing an ankle-length blue smock. She had large round glasses with thick frames and a pleasant toothy smile. Her hair was loose and hung in thick Botticelli waves, strands of grey among the black. 'Welcome, welcome. Are you very tired? Will you eat? Come.'

Several young children appeared at another door. Were they Suraj's and Kumar's younger siblings? 'No, village children. We have television, you see. All come to watch.'

'This one is my boy,' Ramu told me, grabbing a small child who hid his face with his hands.

We ate at a low table in the kitchen, sitting on rustic benches that were carved to resemble flattened animals. Suraj, Kumar, Mr Bhavasarman and I had dinner together. R.K. Uma and Mrs Bhavasarman served us but would eat later on, the women ate separately. Just before we started eating Mr Bhavasarman threw a handful of rice out of the kitchen door. 'For the crows[14],' explained Kumar. We ate off banana leaves. Nambudiris, and other Malayalis, eat in a strange way, using the palm instead of the fingers and rolling the food into round pellets like snowballs, tossing them into their mouths. Liquid from the food tends to run down the wrist. This is licked off without embarrassment. It's not very elegant but, performed with dexterity, is a practical way to cope with the mushy vegetarian food. There were pieces of plain banana and fried banana crisps. There was a peppery *sambar, aviyal* (a jackfruit curry) and another very hot curry of ginger and coconut, rice and popadams. To drink there was water or a hot infusion of cumin and coriander seeds.

There wasn't much furniture in the house but each room was painted a different colour and the stone floors shone like pewter. A swing seat, the sort you might find on an American porch, hung in the television room. Nine village children lay on the floor glued to a news programme.

R.K. Uma talked to me. She explained that she was raised a Nambudiri but was now a follower of a guru near Kanniyakumari. She made a living teaching literature at a college near Kottayam. She was passionate about American poetry. The names she reeled off were only vaguely familiar. Ferlinghetti, Corso, Snyder I just about knew. And Sylvia Plath, of course. Anne Sexton. But most of the names meant nothing at all to me. I explained that I didn't really keep up with poetry. 'Malayalam is an expressive language, full of music. Verse takes on an urgency. It is suited to extremes of feeling, raw expression.' I'm not very keen on raw expression myself but of course I didn't say so. I said that observation interested me. R.K. Uma dismissed this interest with a toss of her head. 'Observation, observation. Now it is our duty to challenge!' What a pity, I said, that I didn't understand Malayalam. 'The translations you can read! By an Australian, himself a poet. Sometimes the meaning has been changed. Only slightly, where the concept behind the original word cannot be translated. Actually, I would like your opinion of these translations.' She produced some typed sheets. She had several copies of one of the translations and told me that I could keep it. She wanted me to read it there and then. I have always found it difficult to read people's poems. Particularly when they're waiting for one's reaction.

> How can we live like this,
> stripped of our innocence?
> Without innocence,
> we can feel almost nothing.
> Fear dries the mouth,
> anger hurts the head,
> we swallow disgust,
> complain of nausea.
> We know we are grieving
> because we want to sleep.

She gave me time to read it, then tilted her head, waiting for my opinion. I replied, truthfully, that I found it direct, the language straightforward. Was it written in response to a situation? It struck me as political. She threw her head back. 'Political in the strictest sense, no! But if you mean the outcry of human feeling, then it is a protest.' Against what? R.K. Uma looked at me witheringly and echoed my question incredulously. 'Against what?' I back-pedalled, trying to provide my own answers, hazarding poverty, political corruption, the decline of spirituality – all to no avail. 'Those are immutables. Why would one protest against immutables? It would be like charging a stone wall. No, no. The poem already says what it is about. It is protesting the loss of innocence, purely the loss of innocence.' Individual innocence, cultural innocence? 'Both of those. And more. For as we move forward we lose so much. That you must be aware of, it is just the same everywhere.'

Mr Bhavasarman, who was standing by, picked up my Walkman. I'd been listening to Maria Callas, a compilation of arias. He chewed betel and walked around, sometimes waving his arms and fluttering his fingertips as if pretending to fly. He spoke to R.K. Uma who translated his question. 'He wants to know if this is cathedral music. He has heard on television similar music that was from a great cathedral.' He liked the tape so much that I gave it to him.

In the morning, first thing, I went for a stroll with Suraj, who said he was completely better, and R.K. Uma, who seemed to be in a less declamatory mood. It was an idyllic place. The house was surrounded by fruit trees. Suraj showed me a pepper tree. There was a kitchen garden and a snake shrine, not very big, like the untended garden of a small town house in England. In the middle stood a statue of a three-headed cobra. Were there real ones? 'Sometimes there are. We give them milk when they come.' The rubber trees had been slashed and white plastic cups were taped beneath the slashes. R.K. Uma picked wild flowers as we walked along and told me the Malayalam names of each one. She knew them all, their medicinal properties and any folklore that was associated with them. Did flowers crop up in her poetry? 'All the time,' she smiled. I wished I'd seen translations of those poems. 'They are not translated.'

'Very beautiful,' said Suraj; then, turning to R.K. Uma, asked, 'Isn't it Wordsworth that they are compared to?'

'Shoot, shoot,' she replied, embarrassed by such flattery.

'You should have asked the Australian to translate them.'

'You see,' she explained, 'the names of so many plants we didn't know in English. Or we could find only botanical names. Therefore they remain untranslatable.'

'Those are the poems that appear in newspapers.' Suraj told me. Evidently R.K. Uma wasn't the uncompromising radical that I'd taken her for. Also I suspected she was more talented than the translations would lead one to think.

I asked Suraj if his father owned the land. 'Most of this land, yes.' And did he employ the villagers? 'Well, when the work is to be done. Otherwise they all have jobs, different kinds.' So what caste were the villagers?

'Low caste,' answered Suraj evasively.

Are Pulayans the same as Sudras?

'Similar,' said R.K. Uma. I got the impression that caste was a sensitive area.

'You cannot understand the caste system, a non-Hindu,' stated R.K. Uma to confirm my impression.

I asked about 'Unseeables', were there really such people in Kerala? Suraj was dismissive. 'Nowadays, I don't think so.'

But R.K. Uma said, 'You mean the Nayadis[15]. I think they still exist. Where I lived as a girl there were Nayadis. Of course I hardly saw them. Certainly they are dying out. But I would think there are some in the state.'

'The people who've become Christians, they could have been Nayadis,' Suraj thought. We came to a tank, a stone-lined square pond. It was about half full. 'Summer evenings we spend here.' It was quite a long way from the house. Suraj explained that there were three tanks but this was the largest and the favourite. We passed a lake that was covered in lotus flowers, so precisely formed that they looked sculptural, almost artificial. The water on their round green pads formed tiny droplets like glass beads. 'That is because there is fur all over the leaves.'

When we got back to the house there was a little wizened man in the yard; he looked just like a monkey and turned out to be a coconut-picker. Bruno was chained to a wall, Suraj told me that he would bite the man if he was loose. 'Would you like a coconut?' asked Kumar. I nodded and the man removed his head cloth which he used to tie his ankles together; then he shot up the trunk of a palm tree as one might climb a rope. He came down again with a sizeable nut and told Kamur that it contained plenty of water but no flesh.

Kumar handed it to his mother who went into the kitchen, then came out with the coconut-water, and some crushed mint leaves, in a stainless-steel beaker. 'He is a singer,' said R.K. Uma. 'You must hear him.' She asked the coconut-picker if he'd sing for us and he laughed. Suraj went into the kitchen and came out with a metal water pot. 'That is his drum, you see.' The coconut-picker squatted on the gravel with the pot, upside-down, between his knees. He strummed it with his finger-tips, producing an unexpected zithery sound. When he'd established a rhythm he started to sing, a jaunty folk song that came back over and over to the same refrain. It must have been the equivalent of a calypso. His voice was high and full of wit. He sang on the verge of laughter all the time and sometimes he actually did laugh, incorporating it into the melody. The Bhavasarmans laughed as well. I asked what he was singing. R.K. Uma told me that it was an old song to which he'd added new lyrics. 'It is satirical, about a local wedding. The humour of it I can't translate. You would have to know the families.'

Mr Bhavasarman played the Callas cassette at full volume on Kumar's tape deck. As soon as one side finished he'd turn it over again. Visitors kept dropping in. Mrs Bhavasarman's sister who looked very like her and was dressed almost identically, the only difference being a green border on her white sari. Various pedlars, including an ayurvedic medicine salesman, an itinerant homoeopath (a *mandula*) who was also highly regarded as a fortune-teller. He held my hand and muttered something about Patna. 'He is saying that you will return to India in a few years time and visit Patna,' Kumar told me. Ramu came to drive me back to Kottayam. As we rattled away, I could still hear 'Un Bel Di Vedremo' wafting through the rubber trees.

From Kottayam to Cochin I travelled by bus, north along the Vaikam Road. The bus stopped at Mundukayyam on a slope below the Embbassi Hotel. A torrent of sewage rushed down a trench behind the Nandini Milk Bar and the trees were seething with fruit bats, creatures from the realm of insanity, whistling and chattering like demons.

At the Ernakulam bus stand I was met by Major Trivedi's old friend, Professor Koshi Jacob, a Syrian Christian, who shook my hand and asked me to call him by his nickname, Jakey. He was a fat man in his forties, wearing a chocolate-brown safari suit. He had a toothbrush moustache and perfectly round eyes, like buttons on a teddy bear's face. A fixed expression; kind but humourless, trustworthy, cautious; the reassuring look of a beloved toy. Jakey looked at my bag and said, 'Oh dear, oh dear, oh dear.' Was there enough room in the car? 'That is not a problem, the back seat is empty. The problem, you see . . .' he paused and took a deep breath, 'is that I have a heart condition. I cannot carry your bag to the car. Please don't think me impolite . . .' I said that I wouldn't think anything of the kind and we walked to his car. He swung his arms as he walked, little toddling steps. The door on my side wouldn't open. Jakey tried unsuccessfully to open it from the inside. He got out again. 'Oh dear, oh dear, let me see.' He pulled at the handle with such force that it broke away. This left him breathless and flustered. I got in on his side.

We drove along Marine Drive. It was a lovely day. Ernakulam is the city on the mainland which, along with the islands of Willingdon, Bolgatty and Gundu in the harbour and Fort Cochin and Mattancheri on the southern peninsula, makes up the metropolitan area of Cochin – rather like San Francisco and the Bay Area. Jakey drove at fifteen miles an hour. 'First we must go to the police.' I wondered if he was going to report his broken car door. 'You see, you are not staying in a hotel. When you stay in a hotel, they take your passport details . . . that is, you see, the law . . . I must tell the police where you are. As it happens, the police station is right here. The commissioner is a friend of mine, there will be no problem.' We turned right into a barracks. Various policemen stood around with rifles. Policewomen, wearing khaki saris, moved from building to building with clipboards and papers. Professor Koshi Jacob was well known, his car was saluted as it entered the compound. A policeman stepped forward to open the car door for the professor, came to my side and, finding no handle, looked bewildered.

I got out on the driver's side and followed Jakey to the commissioner's office. The commissioner was another Syrian Christian, a blue-jawed curly-haired giant surrounded by small thin *chaprassis* (messengers). It was an impressive office; a vast desk covered with papers and glass paperweights; wall charts, blown-up street maps of Ernakulam; shields and silver cups; a display case full of swords. Jakey and the commissioner greeted one another with formal courtesy; mutual respect, I sensed, more than friendliness. The commissioner glanced at my passport, then closed it again instantly. 'There is no need for paperwork. Now, will you have coffee?' He clicked his fingers and an underling sped from the room. 'Your dear parents, how are they?' Jakey replied that his parents were well, then told me that the commissioner's father and his father had been school-friends. There was a minute or two of silence and I could hear Jakey breathing. 'Yes, it is true. The very best of chums,' the commissioner announced eventually, when the peon returned with three cups of sweet milky coffee that must have come from an urn. 'We are almost a family.'

As we drove inland, through the main streets of Ernakulam, towards the suburb where Jakey lived with his elderly parents, I was impressed by the wealth of the city. It wasn't a city of palaces like Mysore but it was full of emporia displaying luxury goods, Western-style fashions, electronic appliances. Jakey told me about his time in Bradford, where he studied business administration for a year in the 1970s. 'As you know, Bradford is not a beautiful city. But . . .' We stopped at a traffic light. 'I found it pleasant enough. If I became homesick for Indian food, all the ingredients were available.' There were lots of Pakistanis and Northern Indians, no Malayalis at all. London was the city for Malayalis. 'You see, in that way it was good for me . . . I branched out. Of course I went to London often.' I asked if he'd visited the church in the East End that Mr Ouseph in Kottayam had mentioned. Jakey said he'd preferred to attend Anglican churches. 'I made many English friends. You will see my photos.'

Jakey's father was also a professor, a retired biologist. He was well into his seventies, a short nimble man in a bush shirt and white lungi; he had an incredibly firm handshake. Jakey's mother, much the same age, was even smaller, around five foot. She wore a checked *mundu*, like a sarong. Jakey had told me that her English was rusty. It surprised me that two small people had produced such a hefty son; Jakey didn't look very much like either parent. Their house was new, a little marble villa. It wouldn't have looked out of place in America. Not much furniture but what there was looked very old and of good quality and its sparsity showed off the elegant proportions of the rooms. Jakey explained that, for a long time, they had lived in the country[16], with his father's older brother, but it had become too crowded. 'Old people need peace and quiet. We moved here three or four years ago. Now this is the up-and-coming area of Ernakulam.'

Down the stairs came two young children. 'My niece and nephew. They are staying this week. Saira, Chandi, come and say hallo to Uncle Joe from England.' The children had been asleep and were rather bashful. Saira was seven, with her two front teeth missing, a pretty little girl. Chandi was about three, he ran to hide behind his grandmother. Both wore Western clothes. Saira spoke perfect English. Within minutes she was singing:

Here we go looby loo,
Here we go looby lye,
Here we go looby loo,
All on a Saturday night.

Jakey slept upstairs but had what could only be called a den downstairs. It was to this den that I was beckoned to look at his photographs and souvenirs from England. It was the most unlikely room for a middle-aged professor: a Margaret Tarrant print hung, in a large Oxford frame, on one wall; a fair-haired Jesus surrounded by little middle-class English children and farm animals. Had he brought that back with him? 'Oh, no, no. All my life I have had that picture . . . but you are right, it is originally English.' A bookshelf full of thrillers. Hammond Innes, Alastair Maclean, James Hadley Chase. A Norton Anthology of English Literature. An A–Z of London. A frieze of beer mats and a Heineken towel. Postcards of London, comic postcards (not the bawdy kind), a poster of the Prince and Princess of Wales on their wedding day ('After my time, of course. Kind friends have sent it. One day it might be valuable, don't you think?') and various framed diplomas and certificates.

'I expect you are reminded of home. Let me put on some music so that we can relax.'

Beside the window was a tape player. He slipped a cassette in, declaring, 'This I know you will like.' Mary Ford's and Les Paul's 'Mockingbird Hill' chirruped merrily, followed by the New Seekers version of 'Put Another Nickel In The Nickelodeon'. 'You see, the first time I was ill was in Bradford . . . two months I was in hospital. This is a tape from hospital radio. I was given it when I left . . . they knew all my favourites.' He nodded his head to the tunes. After the New Seekers came Clive Dunn's 'Grandad' ('this one Saira likes so much'). Most of Jakey's photographs were of English friends and most of them old women, Thora Hird types. Occasionally a slimmer Jakey stood with his arm around one of them. There were several photographs of London. Tower Bridge, a guardsman in a busby. One picture was of Jakey smiling, somewhat nervously, surrounded by crop-headed young men waving red and white scarves – not quite skinheads, more what used to be called 'Crombies'. Jakey said that that one was taken in Trafalgar Square. 'A fellow Keralan was taking my photograph. These fellows rushed over to be in it as well. They were from Manchester . . . I think they had been drinking.'

After putting her grandchildren to bed, Mrs Koshi Jacob produced a magnificent dinner. There were cold fillets of pomfret in a spicy batter and *meen vevichathu*, pomfret again, but served warm in a chilli sauce. Hot chapattis, a great steel bowl of fluffy par-boiled rice. After the fish, came 'shtew', a light chicken and coconut casserole flavoured with cloves. With this 'shtew', there was *thoran*, a curry made from what I presumed was jackfruit but was, it turned out, shredded papaya. Creamy curds. And, to finish, bananas – foot-long bananas with black seeds running through them. Both Jakey and his father sat bare-chested at the dinner table. The old man had a well-preserved muscular torso. Jakey, in comparison, was terribly fat, great breasts and rolls of flab.

After dinner we watched television. There was the usual compilation of film clips. I saw, in grainy black and white, a familiar face. 'Is that Tiptoe?' I asked Jakey. 'Yes, that's her. When she first started.' She was outstandingly beautiful. The film bore some resemblance to *My Fair Lady*; it was a costume drama and Tiptoe and an older man were dressed in European Edwardian clothes – Tiptoe in a white muslin dress and the man in a tweed suit. They were dancing about in what looked like a library. The man, a professorial type, would roll down charts covered in Devanagari script and point to individual words. The song was in Hindi but it had an English refrain: 'Thank you, thank you, sir!' shrilled Tiptoe at the end of each verse and the Higgins character replied, 'Don't mention it, my dear.'

Jakey's father asked if I would join them in prayer before going to bed. 'We pray in Syrian, of course, but you will be with us in spirit.' When the time came, we gathered on the upstairs landing. Jakey told me what was going on, when the Lord's Prayer was being said. Mrs Koshi Jacob read from the Bible. Syrian sounded vaguely like Greek, nothing at all like Malayalam. Then, in sonorous English, Jakey's father proclaimed: 'The grace of our Lord Jesus Christ, and the love of God, and the fellowship of the Holy Ghost, be with us all evermore. Amen.'

I caught a bus to Marine Drive. The bus was quite full when I got on, I had to stand. More and more people got on until it was so crowded that I grew alarmed. The smell of coconut oil in people's hair made my head swim. I could hardly breathe. I managed to squeeze my way off the bus and went the rest of the way by auto-rickshaw. From the jetty opposite the Sealord Hotel, I took the motor-launch to Fort Cochin. It was a hot bright morning and the light on the water bounced about playfully. The ferry moved among great big ships, scruffy little tramp-steamers, dhows, sailing clippers and, darting about like water beetles, the little narrow boats that I'd seen on the backwaters. It was as if maritime history had been confused by too much sunshine and all the business of the harbour looked as easy-going as model boats on a pond in a park. We pulled up in front of some Chinese fishing-nets. These ones were in use, great spindly versions of medieval siege catapults. A team of men hauling and a great deal of shouting, all for a paltry catch. Perhaps the tides were wrong, perhaps they were only demonstrating how the nets worked. I bought a coconut. Next to the coconut stall was a man who fried fish. You bought the fish from the men who worked the nets and took it to this fellow. When it was cooked he served it to you with slices of double-roti, chopped onion and chillies, a squeeze of lime.

It was a pretty, shady area and the buildings looked quite Dutch with their scooped tiled roofs. Nearby was Saint Francis's Church, the oldest European church in India. It had been built, out of wood, in 1503, by Portuguese Franciscan friars who had accompanied the explorer Pedro Alvares Cabral. In the middle of the sixteenth century, when the Portuguese were firmly established on the Malabar Coast, it was rebuilt in stone. Vasco da Gama had been buried there. Later his remains were taken back to Portugal but his tomb remains as a memorial. Then the Dutch took over and, in 1779, largely rebuilt the church. Finally, in 1795, the British turned it into an Anglican church and now it is Church of India, the direct offspring of the Church of England. There were old-fashioned punkahs instead of ceiling fans, a punkah-wallah must sit outside pulling the ropes. They weren't in use otherwise I'd have gone to look for him. I never did see a punkah-wallah. Near the church were some large bungalows with chocolate-box gardens. On one verandah dozed a pair of beagles.

A middle-aged Englishman with a rucksack staggered up to me, sweating profusely. 'Is this the synagogue, then?' I said that it was in Mattancheri, this was Saint Francis's Church. The Englishman said that he'd been told it was a synagogue. He was obviously in a bit of a muddle. 'You bloomin' sure, then?'

'Yes, I've just been inside.'

'And you didn't see any Jews? You sure?' He was an unlikely backpacker, I thought, looking at him: a red face mapped with broken blood vessels, a great bulbous nose, tired red-rimmed bloodshot eyes. A bald head and Coco the Clown's orange hair. He wore a black T-shirt with a picture of Bob Marley on it, very tight across the stomach, a money-pouch, uncomfortably tight checked polyester slacks (with the flies undone) and he was carrying a white sun hat like a cricketer's.

'The synagogue's not that far away.'

'Nah, I'll go into this church then instead. Sit in the shade, like. I've seen Jews before, haven't I? Didn't come to India to look at Jews.' Then he asked me the time and if I knew anywhere he could get a beer. 'Bloomin' parched, I am.'

The Rajah's Palace, in Mattancheri, wasn't at all palatial, a two-storey quadrangle in a seventeenth-century Dutch style. Like the church, it had been rebuilt by successive waves of European traders. The Portuguese built it in 1557 as a present to the Rajah, Veera Kerala Varma (1537–61). It was important to be on good terms with the Rajah. A century or so later the palace was renovated by the Dutch. It is often referred to as the Dutch Palace. The palace has a sensible bourgeois appearance – maybe the Dutch wanted the Rajah to conform to their own notions of respectability and civic duty. Inside, however, all sorts of splendours were on display. In what was the Coronation Hall, a long low room on the first floor, were the royal palanquins, ornate costumes and turbans, lances and swords. The walls of the bedchambers were covered with exceptionally fine murals, badly in need of restoration but still remarkable. There were scenes from the *Ramayana* and other legends. Lord Krishna, with octopus arms and a satisfied grin, basking with the cowgirls in the Brindavan forest. That must have set the stolid Dutch burghers tutting. It always amused me to think of the cowgirls; in my mind's eye I saw the blue-faced god frolicking with a bevy of honky-tonk angels, all looking like Jane Russell in *Son of Paleface*. In the middle of the quadrangle there was a temple but I didn't go inside.

I walked from the Rajah's Palace, through streets away from the seafront, past interesting antique shops – I noticed painted bamboo screens, biblical scenes done in a naïve approximation of a High Renaissance style, I couldn't tell if they were old or not – insurance offices, *dhabas*, spice warehouses, until I came to the area called Jew Town. The streets were narrow and European-looking although the colonial atmosphere wasn't as strong as it had been in the area around the church. It reminded me somehow of New Orleans or Marseilles, the slightly seedy waterfronts away from the big docks, where there might be brothels and dingy bars. But all that I saw were 'pure vegetarian' cafés and white-clad figures moving drowsily about. The air was full of pungent dust, I felt as if I was breathing powdered ginger or cinnamon. I soon realized that spices weren't the only commodity for sale. As I passed through the slow-moving crowds there were muttered offers, 'hashish, hashish' and 'Kerala grass, Idukki grass'.

I had to ask for directions to the synagogue. It was up a narrow dead-end street. The synagogue dates from 1568[17] but was destroyed during a Portuguese raid (against the Dutch who were gathering force as rival traders by this time) in 1662. Two years later, under Dutch rule, it was rebuilt. The synagogue belongs to the White Jews, now a tiny community with most of its members having moved to Israel. There are less than thirty White Jews left. The Black Jews, including the Ben-E-Israel community up the coast in Bombay, probably number a couple of thousand still. I was told that quite a few had gone to Israel but had been treated badly and had since returned. The synagogue was a charming building. Like the Rajah's Palace, it had a plain exterior; inside it was pleasantly ornate. There were a few Indian tourists looking around. The floor of the synagogue was covered in blue-and-white Cantonese tiles, like endless variations on the willow pattern, no two tiles are alike. There is an amusing story about the tiles and their provenance. Apparently, the Rajah whose palace was near by, through his allies the Dutch, had imported a large quantity of fine Cantonese tiles to pave his Durbar hall. The White Jews thought that they'd do nicely for their synagogue floor. So word got to the Rajah that bull's blood had been used in their manufacture and he was so disgusted that he refused to have them in his palace – hence their presence in the synagogue. Belgian glass lamps, a nineteenth-century addition, hung from the ceiling.

Showing visitors around the synagogue was Mr Cohen, an elder. There is no longer a rabbi but Mr Cohen is allowed to conduct marriages. As most of the White Jews are very old now, this doesn't really come up much, though I suppose that visiting Jews might choose to marry there, legalities permitting. When the last Jews die (or leave to join their relatives in Israel) the building will be preserved by the Indian government. I felt lucky to have just witnessed the last days of this unexpected and fantastic community. Mr Cohen asked me if I was Jewish and I told him that I had a drop of Jewish blood on my mother's side, Sephardic, from Holland. 'We are Sephardim,' he said welcomingly. There were two teenaged boys photographing the synagogue, rich Americanized Indians with sophisticated equipment. Overhearing this exchange, they approached me and asked me if I was from Amsterdam. When I told them that I wasn't, one of them grew quite indignant. 'You told that man you were from Holland, I heard you.'

'I told him that I had an ancestor from Holland.' He was still indignant. He looked at me coldly. 'You are Dutch.'

Near the synagogue were a few White Jewish residences and, snooping through the window-grills surreptitiously, I saw several geriatric Jews, the old men wearing white lawn kurtas and the women madras-check saris. They were very fair-skinned but otherwise much like any other aged Indians. I was slightly disappointed by their clothes, having read of bright tunics and waistcoats and turbans (worn, as

259

Western Jews wear skull-caps, in the synagogue) and I think I'd been expecting something more exotic. It brought home to me how much more colourful Thurston's Edwardian India must have been. As I walked on, a White Jewish girl, about twenty years old, passed me. I could tell from her clothes, unmistakably mass-produced Indian 'Western' garments, that she wasn't a tourist. Her hair was in two plaits and she carried a pile of books. I wondered what it must be like to live in such a fading world and then felt depressed by all this finality.

I walked to the Jewish cemetery. It wasn't mentioned in any of the tourist guides but Mr Cohen had told me the way. I had to go through the main streets of the local spice trade. Many of the businesses had names above their doors that, at first glance, looked Jewish but could equally have been Syrian Christian. I found the cemetery. Just outside it was a *chai* stall with two men crouching in its shadow. One of them made the strange all-purpose kissing noise that railway coolies make, that can mean 'mind out' or 'come here', as a whistle can. I ignored him, guessing that he wanted to change money or sell me hashish, and walked on. The graves were hangar-shaped, half-cylinders. There were lots of them and, reading the inscriptions, it seemed to me that the White Jewish community must have been continually infused with new blood from Europe. There were lots of Portuguese sounding, typically Sephardic surnames. The most recent graves were inscribed with first names like Lily and Nellie, nineteenth-century English names. I found it hard to believe that the first language of these people would have been Malayalam. As I wandered along the rows of graves, a man came running towards me. I guessed that he was the guardian of the cemetery about to ask for a small admission fee. He was breathless when he reached me and kept gasping. He looked very nervous and was sweating. His English wasn't very good. 'You, Whittington?'

'I'm sorry, I don't understand.'

'Whittington?'

'No.'

'Brown, huh?' I explained that I was just looking at the cemetery. No-one was expecting me. I could only suppose that some white men called Whittington and Brown were due to be shown around by this man. 'Brown?' He hadn't understood me. I was wondering how best to explain myself when he grabbed my arm. Now there was a note of urgency in his question, he was pleading. 'Whittington? Brown? Brown?' I shook him off, wondering if he was mad. He pulled a brick-shaped parcel out of his lungi. He opened the top of it, as one would open a packet of sugar. It was heroin: there must have been a pound of the stuff. That was what he'd meant by 'Brown' (though 'Whittington' still eludes me. Had he been saying 'Willingdon', the name of one of the smaller islands in the bay?). I managed to convey that I wasn't interested and he turned and ran. As I approached the *chai* stall on my way out I could hear a blazing row. There were more people around it than before and I saw the man who'd beckoned me was about to come to blows with the man who'd approached me in the graveyard. As soon as they saw me they all fell silent and watched me intently as I went by.

When I returned to the marble villa, Saira's and Chandi's mother, Jakey's sister Rabka, had arrived. Rabka was younger than Jakey and looked like her father. She worked, at executive level, in a Trivandrum bank and had a doctorate in economics. For dinner we had *erachi olarthiathu*, a beef dish similar to *rendang*, the dry curry of Thailand. Lumps of meat had been cooked in a sauce that was reduced and reduced until it formed a hard candy-like coating. The flavour of coconut was very noticeable and it was garnished with roasted coriander seeds, a typically Keralan touch, I was told. At prayer-time, Rabka sang a hymn. Jakey told me that I'd recognize the tune. It was the evangelical American hymn 'Shall We Gather At The River'.

Before I left the Koshi Jacobs' household Jakey's father asked me to plant a coconut palm in their garden. 'This tree we shall call henceforth Joseph.' The train was due to leave Ernakulam at three o'clock. Jakey and his parents came to the platform to wave me off. We bought some Himachal Pradesh apple juice, very cold but so tasteless that it might have been watered down. The train came. I thanked the Koshi Jacobs for having me and said goodbye. To my surprise, Jakey's father burst into tears.

I sat down beside a family group, presided over by a flat-nosed man with extraordinarily muscular arms – even his wrists rippled – holding a small replica of himself, his infant son. Two pretty, frail sisters, one of whom I assumed to be the man's wife, and two neat little girls, his daughters or possibly (because they didn't look at all like him whereas the baby boy was identical) nieces. The family were rather fascinating in a compositional way. They made me think of Picasso's pink period ('Les Saltimbanques'). It was the way they balanced and seemed self-contained. I longed to photograph them but there wouldn't be an opportunity and, besides, the quality I wanted to capture would have disappeared if they'd posed for the camera. A frail old man wearing a white dhoti came on and sat next to the window. His only visible luggage was a gigantic book, like a volume of an encyclopedia, very old and dusty and filled with minuscule script that I guessed to be Malayalam.

Shortly after the train had started moving, the middle-aged Englishman whom I'd met in Fort Cochin stumbled into the carriage. He'd had difficulty finding his berth which, it turned out, was below mine. He took off his rucksack sighing, 'Jesus, that's better,' and sat down, his flies gaping open to reveal some very insanitary Y-fronts. This display caused a stir among the other passengers. I leant over and told him. 'There's nothing I can do, they're broken. Weren't much cop to begin with, really.' It was, unmistakably, a Bristol accent ('really' pronounced 'ree lee' and used more as punctuation than a modifier). He put his hat over the opening and said that he'd get some new trousers in Bangalore. I suggested he go to a *darzi* and have some made, that way he could be sure of the fit. I wondered if I sounded pompous, a self-styled India hand? The Bristolian smiled goofily. 'What, tailor-made, like?'

'Yes, but it's not necessarily as grand as it sounds. Most Indians get their clothes made by *darzis*. Ready-made clothes are usually more expensive.'

'What, those chaps with sewing-machines?'

'Those are *darzis*.'

'I thought they were just mending. You know, sewing patches and that. Didn't think they were making clothes. Stands to reason, when you come to think of it, really, do'n'it?' His name was Donald and he'd been in India two months. He came, in fact, from Yatton so I wasn't far out. He'd been unemployed for over a decade. His mother, with whom he'd lived, had recently died and had left him six thousand pounds.

'I don't know where she'd been hiding it, to tell the truth. Far as I knew, neither of us had any dosh, like. Most bloody money I've ever had in me hand and that's the truth. I thought to meself, really, six thousand, when it comes down to it, like, that's not a lot, in actual fact. I thought: Not a lot in England, no, but – this was me train of thought, see? – you take that abroad and you can live like one of the bloomin' Train Robbers. What've I got to lose, really? So I thought, Not Africa. Bloody AIDS and all that, don't have to be a poof or nothing out there, still get it, mind? Lions! And what'd you bloomin' eat? India, I thought. Well, I know the food's all right, i'n'it? And, really, it was part of Britain, like? Can't go too wrong, I said to myself. I've always got on with 'em. Funny thing is, down from me mum's – well, where we used to live – there's a newsagent, see? Run by an Indian. So, just before I come out here, like, I go in and ask him what part of India he comes from? Just as you would, like. You know what he says? Bloomin' Kampala! I says to him: you takin' the piss? Friendly like.

'It's all right here, mind, i'n'it? If you're English and that. Treat you like a bloomin' lord. I've got to laugh, really. If they knew, right? If they knew what a bloomin' dosser I was at home, like! No, it's the bloomin' Raj, see? All white men are superior, really, in their eyes. Rich countries and that. Don't matter about you individually, see?' I felt that Donald was over-estimating the Indian acceptance of Westerners. I asked where he'd been so far. 'Well, I was in Goa. Lovely. Rainier than they say, mind. Di'n't matter though, kept it cool. Got this stuff called fenny. It's moonshine, really. Bloomin' lovely. Tastes of nuts. Out of your brain, like, for a lot less than a quid. I says to myself: this beats your bloomin' snakebite! I'd have stayed, mind, but things got a bit out of hand, really. I've got to laugh, same wherever I go.' I asked Donald what had happened but he grinned and said, 'You don't want to know.' After Goa he'd gone to Kovalam. There things had got out of hand considerably quicker. How? Drunk and disorderly, I guessed but didn't say so. Donald tapped the side of his nose. 'Ask me no questions and I'll tell 'ee no lies. You want to be careful, mind. Best to keep moving.' We both read for a while. I noticed Donald's lips moving as he read.

Though he was, I'd imagine, in his fifties, there was something adolescent about him, even childish. His behaviour was that of a scamp. If he was an alcoholic (and there was every indication) he was a particular and quite rare type: the man who drinks to postpone growing-up. He wouldn't have been a brooding or gloomy drinker nor would he be prone to outbursts of violence or misjudged passion; he'd have been the pub comedian, the clown beside the beer crate at the back of the coach, happy with his role. Until the others had settled down and he found himself older than his drinking companions; then older still and something of a bore. I've known a few of his kind. I've seen one give up drink through Alcoholics Anonymous and turn instead to charity fund-raising – he could give up the booze but the urge to make a fool of himself was stronger. He showed up at marathons dressed as a duck, got his picture in the local paper. Still he never grew up – because he couldn't and that was his real maladjustment.

After five minutes Donald got restless. ''Ere, don't fancy a drop, do you? This is arrack what I've got. Not as good as fenny, mind, but it's all I could get. Hits the spot all right, mind. Not as if I'm complaining. You try it. See for yourself, like.' I warned him that it was illegal to drink alcohol on the train. I felt a bit of a prig but I could well imagine things getting out of hand and I didn't want to be embroiled. What's more the ticket inspector was due along at any moment. 'They won't bother us. Tell 'em we're bloomin' English. Well, it's in their interest to encourage tourists from richer countries, i'n't it?' Donald opened the rucksack, which seemed to be full of dirty clothes and loose bananas and rummaged about. He pulled out a plastic Bisleri bottle containing a clear filmy liquid that resembled turpentine. 'Are you sure that's arrack?'

'Oh arr. Mind you, it's like anything, see, no two batches the same. That's why it's, really, more moonshine, see?' The father touched Donald's knee. 'My friend. No drinky on train.'

Donald cackled. 'Go on! Don't harm nobody, does it?'

'Honestly, they've got quite a different attitude towards drinking.'

'Don't stop them then, does it? I can tell you.' He

uncapped the bottle and took a swig, then breathed out a terrible fuming gas.

The two women started clucking. The father extended his mighty forearms, crossed them, shaking his head and clucking as well to suggest that Donald was breaking a rule. Donald cackled and asked me, 'What the bloomin' hell's he making such a song and dance about? 'Ere, my son, don't you forget, you wouldn't have this bloody train or nothing if it weren't for people like me.'

'Don't be so sure he can't understand you.'

'I don't bloomin' care if he does. Just a bit of fun, a bevvy on the train. You get a bloomin' bar on an English train.'

'Why don't you drink it in the lavatory?'

'The bloody 'ell should I?'

'Because,' said the old man in the dhoti solemnly, 'you are behaving in an anti-social and brutish manner. You are deliberately breaking the law. From what I can gather you feel that you are entitled to do so. Believe me, you are wrong.' He'd closed the great book. His face was set in a mask of defiance, a slight trembling of the jaw betraying his courage.

'Who the bloomin' 'eck are you then? A bloomin' judge or what?'

'I myself am not a judge, sir, though I number several among my acquaintance. I am simply a passenger on this train and, on behalf of my fellow-passengers, I would ask you to refrain from drinking alcohol where to do so is prohibited.' Donald shuffled his feet – he was wearing fluorescent green trainers. He stuck his lower lip out and wiped the sweat off his bald pink head. Eventually he stood up and carried the bottle off to the lavatory. The old man turned to me. 'This is not good. When he returns he will, we can be certain, be drunk. Can you not persuade your compatriot to wait until he arrives at his destination?'

'I don't know him at all. It strikes me that he's an alcoholic, it'd be difficult to stop him.'

'There are children present. A drunken man does not set a good example.'

'I'll do what I can,' I said, wishing that Donald had been in another carriage.

I walked along to the lavatory and knocked on the door. 'Donald.'

'Bog off!' he called back.

'Listen, can I talk to you for a moment?'

'What are you, a bloomin' poof? Can't leave me alone in the toilet?'

'You're upsetting the other passengers. Please don't get blind pissed.'

'I won't get pissed. Relaxed, maybe. It's me routine, see? 'Bout this time at home I'd have a Special Brew. Tea-time, like? Stick to me routine, see? Stick to it and I'll be all right. You won't catch me blind pissed, not if I say so. Man of me word, me, see?'

I went back to my seat and told the old man, who told the family, Donald's promise. And when Donald came back, a few minutes later, the arrack had only gone down an inch. He put the bottle back into his rucksack and beamed.

'All right? All right? Am I drunk then? Tell me, am I drunk?' The old man opened the great book again. Donald sat with his hands on his knees and his legs spread to reveal the gaping flies. He was very pleased with himself. I returned to my book.

Two pages later, Donald tapped my knee. 'Know what your problem is? Shall I tell you, really?'

'Go on then. What's my problem?'

'You're trying too hard to fit in with them, like. I mean, there's not much point, really, is there? Just got to look at you and they know you're not one of them. What do you think, they'll mistake you for one of them? Come off it. Have some bloomin' fun, like. Take advantage of the situation. Don't go around saying I'm sorry I'm bloomin' English. It's daft.'

'I don't do that. I just try to respect their way of life, I don't want to offend people.' I realized as I said it that I sounded prissy.

'That's your bloomin' middle-class attitude, see? Who cares what people think?'

'It's not so much that. It's a question of not disrupting things.'

'Get on! What's there to disrupt? Have a bloomin' laugh.' The old man glared at Donald. Donald reassured him again that he wasn't drunk.

'There are stages of intoxication, sir. My opinion is that you are a barbarian, sober or otherwise.'

Donald was taken aback. ' 'Ere, steady. I'm from the civilized country, mate.'

'I have no wish to compare our civilizations. It is clear that you are not an educated man.'

'All right, all right.' Donald answered sheepishly. He turned to me. 'How'd he get so bloomin' clever, d'you think? Most of 'em can't read.'

'Literacy here in Kerala, sir, is higher than in United Kingdom.'

'What's that, then?' Donald asked me. 'What's he on about?'

'He's saying that a greater percentage of the population can read here than in Britain.'

'What? Stands to the reason that's a lie, don't it?'

'I assure you, that as a retired educationalist, I know what I am saying is correct.' Donald turned to the old man. 'All right, all right, you're bloody cleverer than me. So what?'

Two grey-uniformed stewards appeared taking orders for dinner – vegetarian or non-vegetarian. Donald ordered two non-vegetarian dinners. 'Haven't eaten all day. I'm bloomin' starvin'.' An old pedlar came along selling cigarettes, *bidis*, packets of pan (the ingredients other than the leaf) and cartons of Frooti from a tray. Donald bought some Charminar cigarettes and reached inside his rucksack for the arrack bottle. He stood up and announced that it was his custom – the custom of many civilized countries – to have a drink before dinner. 'Dinner won't be for some time yet,' I told him. 'Well, I'll take me time then. Relax, like. Have me aperitive.' The pedlar's eyes fell on Donald's bottle. 'What you lookin' at?' The pedlar grinned and raised a palm. 'You want a swig, mate? Come on then. Someone with some bloody sense!' The two of them headed towards the end of the carriage.

As the sun went down I heard Donald singing 'Drink Up Thy Cider'. Then another song: 'Blackbird, I'll Have 'Ee'. He was belting them out, thinking that the pedlar would be amused by his imitation of Adge Cutler, exaggerating his West Country accent. One of the women spoke nervously to the old man. He turned to me. 'She is worried that he has become angry. She hears him roaring like a lion.' I told them not to worry.

The pedlar came lurching through the carriage, dropping money and cartons of Frooti, trying to continue his rounds. Donald appeared, florid and laughing, and grabbed the pedlar by his collar. 'Come back 'ere, you bugger!' The Bisleri bottle was practically empty. 'I don't know what they put in it, I really don't.' Donald swung towards where he'd been sitting but missed and sat on his rucksack instead. The rucksack toppled over and Donald fell at the feet of one of the women, who shrieked. Donald reached into the rucksack. 'Would you believe . . . ? As it happens . . . Yes, we're in luck, see? There's another bloomin' bottle!'

'Now what will you do about this nuisance?' The retired educationalist man asked me. I didn't have the faintest idea. It certainly didn't seem as if Donald was going to sit quietly. The pedlar leant against the edge of the berth, swaying as if his legs were made of rubber. The train had stopped, as Indian trains will, between stations. Donald handed the new bottle to the pedlar, who gulped some down, letting out a loud sigh, almost a moan, as if it had been painful to swallow.

The father, who had remained remarkably calm so far, stood up and lifted Donald off the ground. Donald – no doubt used to being ejected from pubs – was curiously compliant. 'All right, all right. We're not going to drink it here, are we?' He steadied the swaying pedlar and they shambled back along to the end of the carriage. They reminded me of the Walrus and the Carpenter or characters from a Beckett play. Donald was singing 'Brand New Combine Harvester'.

That, mysteriously, was the last we saw or heard of either of them. Donald's rucksack remained on the floor at our feet. After an hour and a half, for want of anything better to do, I walked along the train to look for him. There were two Australian travellers a few carriages down. I asked if they'd seen a large red-haired drunken Englishman and an equally drunk pedlar but they hadn't. I went back to my berth.

'You don't think they fell off the train, do you?' I asked the retired educationalist.

'My suspicion is that the pedlar got off at his usual stop and that your compatriot accompanied him.'

'What shall we do about his rucksack?'

'We can inform the T.I. There are lost property offices at most stations.'

When the stewards came around with the dinner trays there was some confusion caused by the two extra non-vegetarian dinners. Eventually they were given to me (because we all look the same?) and, at Vadakkancheri Station, I handed the food to a tall striking-looking beggar; an aquiline face with piercing yellow eyes – if Donald and the pedlar had looked like Beckett characters, this beggar looked like Beckett himself.

A sweeper came down the aisle on all fours, two squares of cardboard as his broom. He was making a snuffling noise like a pig, presumably as a joke, because he spoke to the two little girls in a squeaky child's voice that made them laugh. I thought that, if the little girls hadn't been there, I'd have concluded that the man was mentally ill.

I remembered a story that I'd been told about an

American traveller on a rural bus in an Asian country. A man in the seat beside him passed the whole journey shouting frenziedly. The American decided that this poor man was, literally, raving mad and was impressed by the tolerance and compassion shown by the other passengers. Later he discovered the man was an official of the bus company teaching the driver a new route.

The train reached Bangalore Cantonment Station early in the morning. The rickshaw-wallah refused to believe that I wanted to go to Bhagpur Extension. 'No hotels there, sir.' It seemed ages since I'd seen the Trivedis. Anasuya made me a cup of tea and put three Horlicks biscuits on the saucer. A stack of letters had arrived for me. Mrs Trivedi handed them to me with her comic glare. 'From all your girlfriends.' I asked where Major Trivedi was. He had gone to the temple. 'World events are causing him such worry. This Gulf crisis. Often now he goes to the temple.'

Atul told me that he had a new George Michael cassette called *Listen without Prejudice*. 'Oh, it is too good,' he announced and proceeded to play it – so loudly that Mrs Trivedi spoke sharply to him in Hindi. 'Mum-mee!' Atul answered back. 'I know even Doctor-Sahib likes George Michael music.' But he did turn it down. Mrs Trivedi said, 'He doesn't think. It is much too early for this swinging music.' The adjective 'swinging' took on a derogatory meaning.

I asked how Dr Lal was and Mrs Trivedi answered, raising her shoulders, that he was always with Dr Stickney. 'This we cannot understand, she is not beautiful.'

'Maybe they're just friends.'

'How should I know this? Is it for me to ask the doctor his affairs?'

Major Trivedi returned from the temple. He immediately asked how my stomach had coped with Keralan food. I told him about my nausea at the beginning of the ferry journey and he nodded sagely. 'Oranges late at night, that is the cause, believe me.' When I told him about Donald, he shook his head slowly and asked if I'd read Spengler. He had vermilion powder on his forehead and it was the first time that I'd seen him wearing a kurta and a formally tied dhoti; I wondered if he'd passed from Garhasthya to Vanaprasthya. When I remarked on his outfit he waved his hand. 'No, no, no special occasion. Sometimes I wear this, as the mood takes me.'

But he was in a strange mood because later, at the breakfast table, he raised his hand, as if to halt the flow of conversation, and said, 'Surely some revelation is at hand.' I waited for the inevitable quatrain from Nostradamus but what followed was the second verse of 'The Second Coming' by Yeats.

'Surely some revelation is at hand;
Surely the Second Coming is at hand.
The Second Coming! Hardly are those words out
When a vast image out of *Spiritus Mundi*
Troubles my sight: somewhere in the sands of the desert
A shape with lion body and the head of a man,
A gaze blank and pitiless as the sun,
Is moving its slow thighs, while all about it
Reel shadows of the indignant desert birds.
The darkness drops again: but now I know
That twenty centuries of stony sleep
Were vexed to nightmare by a rocking cradle,
And what rough beast, its hour come round at last,
Slouches towards Bethlehem to be born?'

Major Trivedi finished the recital and there was an uncomfortable silence. He drummed a military tattoo on the table. I didn't know how to react. Mrs Trivedi said, 'Another *idli*. Plenty there are. Come on, Joe, take, take!'

I went to bed early that night. Just before I said good night to the Trivedis, Nagaraja Naidu came to the house and although Major Trivedi seemed pleased to see him, Mrs Trivedi was surprisingly inhospitable. She didn't even smile when he came in. Again I noticed the weird smell that came off him. It was clear to me that the Cobra King was seriously ill. Why didn't anyone else notice it? As I drifted off I could hear him growling away in the living-room. I woke up a couple of hours later, it must have been one o'clock, and he was still there.

Aswin

A change had come over the Trivedis. It wasn't particularly noticeable in their treatment of me but there was an uneasiness in their behaviour as a family. Mealtimes were tense and silent. Atul was always rushing out. The Major was preoccupied, I would have said anxious. On the surface Mrs Trivedi was as efficient and organized as ever but I sensed a quiet despair – or rather a carefully hidden struggle not to appear desperate. I saw that she turned to Mrs Sen for support and that they had long serious discussions in Hindi. I wanted to ask them what the matter was but I guessed it was something private, possibly financial. If they wanted to tell me, they would, I decided. But I felt inadequate all the same.

I went to Blue Jean Junction for a fitting. The suit Mr Haq was making was exactly what I wanted. The only minor disappointment was how long it was taking. I'd hoped to wash it a few times before I went home. Mr Haq was pleased to have his work appreciated. 'If only I could make such suits all the time I would be happy. But I have to make a living. If denim this and that I am asked to make, denim this and that I'll make.' I had bought more fabric than was needed. Mr Haq had given me what was left over and I'd taken it to Mr Prakash and asked him to make me a pair of gaberdine shorts. I'd given him a pair that I'd brought with me to copy. But, when a few days later, the shorts were delivered to the house, he'd gone wrong somewhere. The shorts were several inches too big at the waist, an inch too short in the leg and the bottom bagged out like a nappy. 'You must take them back,' said Mrs Trivedi. 'If he thinks you will accept, always he will do such work.' I said that I'd take them back when I went into town later in the day. After lunch I walked past the temple to the alley where Mr Prakash lived.

I knocked on the red door beneath the green-and-yellow board and a tall bearded old man, wearing a vest and a checked lungi, opened it. I assumed this prophetic figure was the *darzi*'s father or father-in-law.

'Excuse me, is Mr Prakash in?' The old man extended a bony hand and made a spiralling movement with his wrist. 'Prakasky?' he asked me, raising one bushy eyebrow.

'Prakash the *darzi*? Prakash, stitching?' I tried, holding up the shorts and wishing that I knew more Kannada.

The old man wagged his head. 'Acha, Prak*ass*, Prak*assss*,' he hissed, correcting my pronunciation of the *darzi*'s name. An old woman, certainly not Mr Prakash's wife, joined the bearded man. I asked if she spoke English. 'Ingriss, ha!' She clapped her hands. 'Ingriss!' echoed the man.

'Come,' beckoned the woman and I stepped inside. Roughly plastered walls painted light-blue. Finished garments hung on a rail; scraps of cloth surrounded the pedal-operated sewing-machine. A calendar from Windsor Shirtings showed Rama embracing Hanuman. A framed postcard-sized image of Rajiv Gandhi was draped with a garland of marigolds. I could smell cooking and sandalwood joss-sticks. 'City,' muttered the old man. 'Pleash, sheet,' said the woman pointing to the only chair in the room. The old man shouted to somebody (I assumed Mr Prakash) through the door that led to the rest of the house. But, a few moments later, instead of Mr Prakash, a girl in a flowered dress appeared and offered me a steel beaker of buttermilk and some bananas. The old woman gestured for me to eat. The old man sat on the floor and folded his hands in his lap. The buttermilk was thick and refreshing and the bananas had a subtle violet-scented taste. The old man closed his eyes and started humming a slow religious melody. After ten minutes a teenaged girl wearing school uniform came in. I asked her when Mr Prakash was expected back. She told me that her uncle was out of station, he had gone north to the Horsley Hills, visiting a sick relative. 'One week's time he returns.'

Dr Lal had been invited to attend a conference in Calcutta. The conference would last for ten days. Dr Stickney, it was decided, would stay in his flat while he was away. Major Trivedi approved of the idea. Dr Stickney had been living in an hotel room for months. 'What life is that? And it is not cheap.'

Mrs Trivedi was less enthusiastic. 'Softly, softly she catches her monkey.'

Mrs Sen clapped when she heard the news. 'Then I am all along right!'

Mrs Trivedi wagged her head dolefully.

Mr Shekhar cut my hair. 'You have wife in Britain?' When I said I hadn't, he asked if I intended to marry an Indian girl. He said he knew of a Christian girl whose parents were looking for a husband. 'Is her name Asunta?' I asked. 'Not Asunta. Teresa. Beautiful girl.'

Mr Shekhar looked in the mirror, rolled his lips into a kiss and made a poetic gesture with his hand, like a singer of *ghazals*. He scratched my head for a full minute before continuing. 'Fair skin. Teacher's certificate.'

'Thank you but I'm not really looking at the moment.'

'A man must have a wife.' He lathered my face. 'Who are more beautiful than our Indian girls?' He didn't talk as he concentrated on the shave but afterwards, as he was running the alum crystal over my cheek, he went on. 'English woman smoke a cigarette, drink liquor, this no good.' When I paid him he asked me, 'I tell the father of this girl?' and I said not to bother.

The time had come to confirm my flight home. As far as any of us (including the resourceful Mrs Sen) could work out, the nearest Golden Arrow office was in Madras. I decided to go there rather than telephone. So off I set on the afternoon train. Because the train ran in the day-time it had seats, like a European train, rather than berths. As afternoon turned to evening I stood at the open door and looked up at the sky that had taken on the shiny pink colour and quilted texture of an old-fashioned eiderdown. The rubbly ground streamed past me like a horizontal avalanche. I listened to my Walkman: A.K.C. Natarajan playing the 'Clarionet', then Ustad Alla Rakha and Ustad Zakir Hussain performing a tabla duet. When I reached Madras Central Station my white shirt was grey with dust. A beggar on the platform had a spongy mass, the size of a child's head, in his lap: testicular elephantiasis.

Near the railway station was a small bazaar. A group of six women were making a frightful racket, circling a coconut-wallah and chanting and clapping. There was something odd about them; I couldn't work out what it was except that their behaviour was lewd and raucous and that was unusual for Indian women. Their saris were made of flashy, glittering, tawdry material like net curtains covered with tinsel stars. I took them for gypsies of some kind but, drawing closer, I realized that they weren't women at all but *Hijras*, eunuchs. They didn't remind me of Western transsexuals (who should, after all, pass as natural women) nor trans-vestites (who often attempt a larger-than-life and super-glamorous femininity) so much as pantomime dames. Every movement was grotesquely exaggerated: a swaying sashay or an absurd hobble – like Mrs Thatcher's hen walk – hands coming to rest on hips or arms folded beneath great artificial bosoms. Their voices were straight from Monty Python. What the coconut-wallah had done to offend the *Hijras*, I couldn't tell. He was very embarrassed to be at the centre of such a spectacle; he just smiled at the ground or tidied his pile of coconuts with trembling hands. He obviously thought that if he ignored the *Hijras* they'd go away. The eunuchs circled his stall jeering menacingly, cackling or whooping like Apaches, and some of them gathered their saris up at the front to flash their scars at him. I was hoping to catch a glimpse myself, to see how thorough a job had been done[1]. I think they were making a nuisance of themselves so that eventually the coconut-wallah would pay them to go away.

I reached the hotel that I'd been to with Mrs Trivedi and the students. The receptionist was wearing the same grey silk suit as before but no rose this time. We talked about *Eyeless in Gaza*. He told me that he preferred the earlier books like *Antic Hay*. 'The frivolity appeals to me.' He preferred Michael Arlen to Aldous Huxley. 'Carl Van Vechten also, he is very good.'

'Then you must like Firbank?' The receptionist's face lit up and he clapped his hands. 'Oh, Firbank! Bravissimo!' He was afraid there were no vacancies but he recommended a modern medium-priced hotel.

The only room available at the modern medium-priced hotel was a conference room. The receptionist, a stout Muslim patriarch with hennaed hair and a beard like Abraham Lincoln's, was hesitant. I didn't mind.

'Does it have a bed?'

'Two bed.'

'And a bathroom?'

'Oh, yes, bat room.'

'So what's the problem?'

'Sir, is a wery big room.'

'Does that mean it's more expensive?'

'No, sir. I let you have him same price.'

'Sounds fine to me. All I want's a bed and a shower.'

'Sour?' enquired the receptionist.

'Bathroom,' I explained.

'Oh, yes, bat room.' He went back to his paperwork. After a minute or two, I asked if I could go to the conference room. 'Sir, is a wery big room.'

We were going round in circles. 'You said I could stay the night in the conference room. Please may I sign in.'

'Four nights you are staying?'

'No, just one night.' He signed me in and a bellboy in a tight red uniform appeared. The bellboy took my bag and I followed him to the lift, which stopped on the ninth floor. We walked up to the eleventh floor.

'Executive level,' said the bellboy. The room was vast. On one wall hung a screen for slide presentations and there was a long formica table with ten chairs around it. Crouching at the back of the room were two narrow wooden beds. 'Sir like me move table?'

'It's all right.'

'Television you like? In-house movie.'

'Yes please.' I sat on the bed and unpacked my sponge-bag. The bellboy staggered in with a huge television. 'Where you like, sir?'

'Anywhere down this end.'

The bathroom was very strange. A high tap served as a shower. A porcelain bowl without any taps at all was fixed to the wall at waist-level. The lavatory was Western-style but without any kind of flush. There was, however, a plastic bucket and a jug so water from the high tap could, when necessary, be tipped into the basin or the lavatory. There was a small half-open door in the wall. Expecting it to be a little cabinet, I opened the door fully – to discover a deep shaft, dropping all the way down to the basement. It was a sort of dumb waiter but without the lift. Disembodied voices drifted up from the depths. I stood beneath the tap listening to an argument that ended with both parties clearing their throats.

At the very top of the building was a revolving restaurant. It would have been more exciting if the whole thing had turned faster; what movement there was was imperceptible. Nor was there much of a view as the glass was tinted. I had *channa masala* (spiced chickpeas) and *pooris*. The only other person eating in the revolving restaurant was the hennaed receptionist. He was tucking into a biryani, a small spoon in each hand. The food wasn't bad. I couldn't think why, if the hotel was full, the restaurant was empty.

John Huston's *Freud*, with Montgomery Clift, was on television. I'd always wanted to see it but I fell asleep within ten minutes.

I was just down the road from the Connemara so I went there to have breakfast in the coffee shop. Then I dropped in on Giggles who was preparing to open a second bookshop (called 'Giggles and Scribbles' because it would also sell stationery) and was busy with the final arrangements. A young man, with a mouth shaped like the letter U, who wrote literary criticism for a 'little magazine', asked me about feminism. 'Can feminism be considered a branch of philosophy?' I replied that, as a movement, as far as I understood, its concerns were more social and political. There were feminist intellectuals, critics, historians, of course. I said that I didn't know enough about either philosophy or feminism to answer his question.

'The name, please, of the number one feminist philosopher in America today?'

'I couldn't tell you.'

'I will tell you. Her name is Gayatri Chakravarti Spivak.'

'Is she Indian?'

'Originally yes. She made her name translating Derrida.'

'*Of Grammatology*, we have it in stock,' Giggles said. 'I must order one for the new shop.' U-Mouth, who'd seemed a sober academic type, suddenly went into a crazed monologue about Nietzsche turning into a woman.

'Like a *Hijra*?' I suggested flippantly.

'Point taken!' retorted U-Mouth and launched into a speech about bodies without organs. I gathered up some English newspapers. 'There is no such thing as a newspaper,' proclaimed U-Mouth.

I chose some paperbacks including *Northanger Abbey*. I asked Giggles if she'd ever read it. 'Oh yes. I am a great Jane-ite.'

'There are no writers, there is only the text.'

'Hush now.' Giggles patted U-Mouth's arm soothingly. But U-Mouth was eager to engage me in debate. He picked up *Northanger Abbey*.

'What does this Jane Austen tell you of the means of production, huh?'

Outside the Connemara there was a snake-charmer wearing a huge Rajput puggaree. He didn't somehow have the authenticity of the Gonds I'd seen at Jabalpur Station; there was too much of the 'Mystic East' about his costume. In fact, I soon found out he wasn't very good, which was presumably why he hadn't drawn any spectators. He was out to fleece Western tourists. He opened a straw basket and pulled out a small docile snake. 'This snake kill seven men, poison,' he told me but I didn't believe him. Then he played a pipe made of a gourd and metal tubes. The snake remained in the basket. 'Isn't he meant to dance?'

'I send him to sleep. Now he don't bite. Give me ten rupees.'

'I'd rather see him dance.'

'He don't dance. Killer snake.'

'Have you got any other snakes? Any cobras?'

'No, sir. This snake, he kill cobras.'

'Well, it's not much of an act, is it?'

'No act, sir. Is real. Killer snake, I sent him to sleep.' I gave him two rupees.

'Sir, ten,' he urged; then, seeing he wasn't going to

get any more, he asked if I'd like to buy a snakeskin.

'No thank you.'

'Sir, wallet make, very nice. Killer snake wallet.' I considered the idea for a moment. It would cut a certain dash. 'No thank you.'

'You buy cobra pipe?'

'How much?'

'Ten rupees.'

'Five.'

'Acha, five.' He reached into his shoulder bag and produced a pipe just like his own. I blew through it. He hushed me. 'No sir. Killer snakey sleep.'

I was pleased with my cobra pipe. I was turning to walk away when he offered to sell me the killer snake as well. 'Supposing I got him back to England, what would I do with him?'

'Sir, Madrassi killer snake. People come see him, I promise, Indian people living London, England, Wembley. You say, he kill seven men, give me hundred pounds, cash sterling. They say no then you say he might kill you. Very good business.'

'I'll stick to the cobra pipe.'

To confirm my flight proved a long and tedious procedure – the telephone kept disconnecting – but I didn't leave the Golden Arrow office until I had the confirmation written down. Then I went back to my conference room and washed beneath the high tap. A peal of laughter floated up through the lift shaft. I sat down on the bed and blew the cobra pipe. I could only produce a squawking noise. Eventually, I thought to myself, I'll get quite good at this.

I decided to visit Mahabalipuram. It wasn't far from Madras, I could get there by bus. I went to the local bus stand. All the signs were in Tamil. There was straw everywhere, as if a number of bales had been torn apart and scattered; several cows had arrived to clear it up. I searched for an office. It was the lunch hour. Men were selling black grapes, coated in fine blue dust. A three-legged dog hopped past me. I asked a family, sitting on the ground eating from tiffin jars, if they knew which bus went to Mahabalipuram and they wagged their heads. 'This is the bus.'

'Mahabalipuram?' I asked the driver. 'Yes, yes, yes,' he answered impatiently. I paid for my ticket and found a seat. A man in a yellow shirt came and sat beside me. He was wearing a lemon-scented pomade in his hair. As we crept through Madras he told me that he wanted to move to New York. I told him that I'd lived there and knew that there was a large Indian community.

'Horatio Street,' he said. 'There my best friend lives.'

'That's in Greenwich Village.'

'Yes. My friend, he's a window dresser. Bergdorf Goodman.'

'Is he from Madras?'

'No, he came here on holiday. A long time ago. I met him in 1983.'

'So he's American?'

'Yes, American. His name is Troy.'

I was getting the picture. 'So you keep in touch?'

'I write to him. He never writes back.'

'Are you sure he still lives there?'

'How can I be sure? That is why I want to go to New York. To find him and make sure he is well. You remind me of him. That is why I chose to sit beside you. I miss him so much. Where are you going?'

'Mahabalipuram.'

'Oh. So far.' His eyes dropped.

Then he asked, 'Why not come to my house? It is near the next stop.' I didn't know how to tell him that I wasn't interested.

'Please, don't misunderstand my invitation. It is not homosex I am proposing. I am married now five years and happy. One daughter, light of my life. Friendship, that is all.'

'It's kind of you but I want to go to Mahabalipuram.'

'Would you like me to come with you?'

'I prefer travelling alone.' It was tricky not to hurt his feelings.

'Acha.' It was his stop. He got off the bus, then waved forlornly from the side of the road. Poor man, I thought. It was like *Madame Butterfly*.

We left the sprawl of Madras and headed down a wide dusty road, fine sand on either side. Sometimes the Bay of Bengal was to the right; sometimes it became an islet and the road a bridge. Sometimes the road curved quite far inland, away from the coast, through coconut plantations. We passed a white modern church of the kind that Texan television evangelists build with viewers' donations.

I asked the driver to let me know when we reached Mahabalipuram. 'Not yet, not yet, not yet,' he barked. All his concentration was on the road ahead. 'Soon now,' a passenger informed me, 'one half-hour.' There were painted advertisements for beach resorts. One, the Silver Fish, depicted a leaping marlin. I was just wondering if there was deep-sea fishing off this coast when we came to the resort itself. I asked the driver to stop and he scowled at me.

The gates of the Silver Fish Holiday Centre were open. I walked down a drive, stretching ahead at least half a mile, towards the beach and the office. Dhobi-wallahs had spread sheets on the ground to dry. An incinerator puffed black smoke. Cabins were set up among the palm trees. Two obese white men in bikini swimming-trunks waddled past me. An old woman with long grey plaits wore a batik kaftan; she looked like a very old squaw. I tried to work out what nationality she was. In the office was a portly young Indian who offered his hand and told me his name was Johnny Jolly Boy – later I saw it was spelt Jhalibhoi. He had a Rod Stewart hairstyle, layered spikes on top and long rats' tails at the back. He wore a snow-bleached denim beach suit; a short-sleeved (what Mr Prakash called 'half-arm') shirt and very short, obscenely tight shorts. On his feet were multicoloured flip-flops. The office was decorated with bamboo furniture and potted palms and a mural of a Polynesian island with a smoking volcano. A blown-up black-and-white photograph of, I assumed from the kurta and garland, a local politician, turned out to be a portrait of Johnny's father: Mr P.K. Jhalibhoi the proprietor. I asked if it was possible to rent a cabin for the night. 'No way,' replied Johnny with a grin. He was trying to see his profile in a cane-edged mirror.

'You're full?'

'That's right!'

I asked if I could walk down the beach to another resort instead of going all the way back to the main road. Johnny made a gesture that looked rehearsed, stretching his arms and raising his shoulders. 'Hey, hey, man! Whatever you like!'

As I turned around, in through the door came a familiar but none the less extraordinary figure. Elvis Presley was alive and walking about in Mahabalipuram! Petrol-blue oiled hair, sideburns, the great paunch like a bay window above the narrow hips. Elvis wore dark glasses, a black velour track suit. Around his neck was a red towel. 'Welcome to Silver Fish Holiday Centre. I am Berjiz Jhalibhoi.'

'Thank you but I'm afraid I'm not staying.'

'Why is that?'

'No room is available,' said Johnny.

'You would take a budget cabin?' Berjiz asked me.

'I'd prefer a budget cabin.'

'Budget cabin there is,' said Berjiz.

'Daddy says not for Western visitors.'

'That is an only peak-season ruling. Also Daddy says –always – an occupied cabin is better than empty.'

'I'm quite happy with a budget cabin.'

'Happy is what we aim at,' said Berjiz, exuding largesse. Johnny looked in the mirror and patted the sides of his hair while his brother signed me in. 'Daddy stayed in England five years,' Berjiz told me when he looked at my passport.

'One Englishman is here. Otherwise all Russians.'

'Tonight is disco night,' Johnny said.

The budget cabin, I felt sure, was not intended for commercial use by either Western or Indian guests. My guess was that it was used for putting up sales representatives. For a start, it was the whole drive's distance away from everything else, the nearest building was the *chowkidars'* shelter. It was very basic indeed: no ceiling fan, a hole-in-the-floor lavatory. Having said that, it wasn't uncomfortable at all. It was clean. There was a strong smell of disinfectant. I washed in the sink, then arranged my mosquito net over the hospital bed.

I walked back down the drive towards the beach. A narrow wooden bridge crossed a drainage ditch. A stout Russian woman elbowed past me. She was wearing a blue-and-yellow floral swimsuit and a white cellophane hat, woven like straw and decorated with plastic flowers; a Jamaican grandmother's 'Sunday-go-to-meeting' hat.

An expanse of fine, slightly grey sand; green wooden sun-loungers; a thatch-sheltered restaurant area. There were Russians everywhere in the weirdest clothes: swimming trunks made from unevenly cut-off track suit bottoms, string-vest T-shirts, ivory satin pyjamas. One red-haired man wore a brown shirt with an orange tie tucked into a pair of crimson Y-fronts, lace-up brown shoes and crumpled black socks; he looked as if he'd mislaid his trousers. Their faces, the strange mixture of Central European and Asiatic features, intrigued me. One or two of the younger Russians swam. The rest paced the beach in broad circles, stopping to talk to one another like prisoners in an exercise yard. Only the oldest ones sat down at all, the rest kept moving.

*　　*　　*

To the south I could see the shore temple, considerably further away than I'd expected. I drank a small pot of coffee, then set off towards it. There were hundreds of tiny crabs scurrying about. The beach was dirty and deserted. The sun started to go down, as quickly as it always does in India: a fleeting twilight, then semi-darkness, the blue half-light of the shining moon and the stars. The brightest light was the edge of the surf, a white string winding out ahead of me. I could still see the bulk of the shore temple, still some way off, and I could hear the waves pounding against its walls. It was the most romantic building I'd seen in India. The temple – a cluster of three shrines – was built at the beginning of the eighth century by Rajasimha, who also built the Kailasanatha Temple at Kanchipuram. The sea, I am told, has eroded much of the carved detail but it is still an elegant building. The temple was there for the sea to worship. I stood on the beach below the processional road for about ten minutes, listening to the waves booming their mantras. I turned around and walked back along the beach. Halfway back to the resort a pack of six dogs surrounded me. One was a bitch in season and the others were prospective mates, squabbling with each other, sometimes fighting quite viciously. The dogs took no notice of me but followed me, squabbling and panting, all the way back to the Silver Fish Resort where some Russian men pelted them with handfuls of sand.

The Russians ate, *en masse*, at long tables. There was a pile of sliced white bread in front of each place setting. I was seated at a small table and handed a menu. It was a big laminated card, like a menu in an American family restaurant. The spelling was rather wild.

Each section was given a heading: 'Soups and Such' (I decided against the 'Coromandel crap soup'), 'A Vist to China Town', 'Meat You Must Eat', 'Fried Corner'. I chose 'specal' fried fish and spinach, a lime soda to drink, 'fruity platter' from the 'Time for Pudding' section. The waiter came back with a flat serving dish. On the dish were round slices of white radish, trimmed to form letters that spelt WELL COME JOSEPH. A tall thin man with very thick glasses, whom I recognized as Mr P.K. Jhalibhoi, was talking to the Russians, in Russian. There were cheers and claps. Mr Jhalibhoi had a funny snuffling laugh. He slapped some of the Russians' backs then came over to my table, stretching to shake my hand. 'Please, don't get up. Relax . . .' he checked the radishes, 'Mr Joseph!'

He was quiet for a moment. 'Why did you come to Silver Fish Holiday Centre?' Because the bus had passed the gate. My answer seemed to disappoint him. 'So you had not heard of us in UK?'

I shook my head.

'That is bad. There is supposed to be advertising in the *Daily Worker*.'

'I think it's called the *Morning Star* now.'

'Yes, yes. You're quite right. In my day we called it *Daily Worker*. *Morning Star* now.'

'Not many people read it, that's the problem.'

Mr Jhalibhoi made a pained expression. 'You are wrong. Working classes are reading this paper.' This was clearly a belief that it would be unfair to shatter. I asked Mr Jhalibhoi about his time in England.

'Do you know Butlin's, Minehead? There I worked. Billy Butlin I would name as inspiration. He started out with hoopla stall. A man with visions.'

'You don't hear much about Butlin's any more. The Minehead one is called Somerwest World now.'

It was another shock, absorbed with dignity by Mr Jhalibhoi. He shuffled his feet.

'This cannot be right. What of Butlin's Beavers coming year after year? What of the space-age monorail?'

'You see, holidays abroad are more widely afford-able now than they were when Butlin's was thriving. People can be sure of sunshine in places like Majorca.'

Mr Jhalibhoi winced as I spoke but, I could tell, refused to believe my heresies.

'You have met Geoffrey?' he asked. 'Geoffrey's father I knew thirty years ago. Now he has a restaurant in Cromer, The Jolly Friar. You will know it.' Geoffrey was sitting between two elderly Russian women. The women were talking loudly to each other. He was a dim-looking teenager with a band of acne running across his forehead, a crucifix ear-ring and peroxide yellow hair.

Mr Jhalibhoi called over to him. 'Geoffrey! Here is another from Merry England. Mr Joseph!'

Geoffrey glanced over. 'All right then?'

'Second time Geoffrey comes here,' Mr Jhalibhoi told me proudly. 'Two weeks he spends, then home again.'

'Is this the only place he visits in India?'

'It is complete holiday break.'

'I'm sure it is . . .'

'It is.'

'It's just that, I'd have thought, coming all the way to India, he'd want to see more.'

'Mahabalipuram is world-famous heritage site, is that not enough?'

'Does Geoffrey speak Russian as well?'

'No, no, no. I don't think he speaks Russian.'

Johnny, who had changed into a shiny black shirt and green pegged slacks, asked his father if he should start the music soon. 'Yes, yes, start the music any time soon. First clear these unused tables.' Mr Jhalibhoi asked me if I had disco fever. 'My sons, they go disco crazy.' He snuffled. 'If you ask me, it is a fever.'

Johnny created sufficient space for a dance floor then went into a glass DJ's booth. He played three Madonna songs, sung in Hindi by Ayesha. 'All right! Lovely Ayesha, India's Lady Madonna! Ladies, you too are so lovely, please, come on!' By the third song four Russian women had taken to the floor. They danced by rocking from side to side on their heels, pointing their elbows outwards. Mr Jhalibhoi and several Russian men clapped to the beat. I wondered why the dancing women looked so strange. It was the constant bright lighting; most disco dancers are seen under flashing colours. Here was a steady operating-table glare. The next song was Stevie Wonder's 'Living for the City', followed by a sequence of film songs, some of which I recognized. In the middle of one of the film songs Johnny called out. 'You all know him well! Please, here he is, coming to you direct! My very own brother!' Berjiz (in dark glasses, a white satin cap with a matching scarf, a tight denim cowboy shirt and shiny red flares) appeared on the dance floor. He looked less like Elvis than he had 'offstage', more like a Bombay film star. There was a round of applause. Berjiz shimmied among the swaying women, working his hips like a belly-dancer. He took his scarf off and waved it gracefully. The dancing women started to clap. The song changed and Berjiz entered his stride. His hips continued to shake but, with the upper part of his body, he appeared to be miming the lyrics. Dabbing his eyes with the scarf, he signified sorrow. Then, looking upwards, he dropped to one knee and clutched his heart. Soon he was lying on the ground, to great applause, his hips still shaking. A dramatic expression, as stylized (and incomprehensible) as the *rasa* of a Kathakali dancer, played across his features. One arm lifted. He started to get up again. Now he was back on one knee and picking imaginary flowers. Soon his arms were full of flowers. Then he rose and presented the invisible bouquet to one of the women. Great applause. After this set piece, the ice was broken. Several Russian men joined in. Within ten minutes the dance floor was full. Even the gormless Geoffrey was dancing: his thumbs in his belt-loops, his torso bending forward at the waist, the classic Status Quo boogie. Berjiz remained the most accomplished dancer. He swirled through the mass of other dancers like Scheherazade.

But his thunder was soon to be stolen. A short Russian man in a white T-shirt and black trousers, a cigarette dangling from his lip, took to the floor. His dark hair was swept back, his muscular torso rippled under the white cotton, he was rather like James Dean. When he danced he emphasized, not his hips like Berjiz, but his small bottom. His sense of rhythm was stronger than Berjiz's. There was no need for him to mime. And, whereas Berjiz performed in front of, rather than with, his nearest partner, this Russian seemed to transform the lumpen women he danced with into beings as graceful and sleekly sexual as he was. One in particular, a tall fair girl, responded magnetically to each move he made, thrust for thrust, shimmy for shimmy, until the floor cleared around them. Fred Astaire was dancing with Cyd Charisse. Berjiz, hopelessly upstaged, holding his white scarf in his teeth, stopped dancing and stared Byronically out to sea.

I slept very badly. First a mosquito broke through my net and feasted on my earlobes and eyelids, then a column of ants marched across my arms and chest. When I did fall asleep I dreamt that I was back in England, a grown man forced to attend prep school. The other boys wore shorts made from track-suit bottoms, string-vest T-shirts and ivory satin pyjamas. I protested to Matron, who was conventionally dressed, that I was thirty-one years old. 'You must speak to Mr Bankes.' But I woke myself up rather than confront my old headmaster who loomed out of his study, wearing a cellophane hat decorated with flowers. The ants had eaten a hole in the gourd of the cobra-pipe. I had to throw it away. Just after dawn I walked down to the beach for a swim. The Russian dancer and the willowy girl were in the water. At first I thought they were swimming in the nude but they were, in fact, wearing white swimming costumes, perhaps underwear. They might just as well have been naked because the material was completely transparent.

A bus to Pondicherry passed the gates daily at eleven. I was exhausted from being awake most of the night. I decided, there and then, to catch it. So, after a breakfast of white bread and highly synthetic red jam, I paid my bill. Johnny was surprised that I was leaving, urging me to stay for the 'Miss Beauty Queen' and 'Mr Tarzan' contests that afternoon.

Pondicherry was much hotter and more crowded than it had been before; the streets around the bus station were congested with cycle-rickshaws, tongas, pedestrians, every kind of motor vehicle, bicycles, ox-carts, even a camel-cart. A fair of some kind was going on. There were tents everywhere, as there had been at Trivandrum, selling fabric and handicrafts. I saw a poster for Blake Edwards' *Ten*, retitled *Sex Ten*. I asked the rickshaw-wallah if it had rained at all yet. '*Si vous voulez mon opinion, on ne verra pas les pluies avant deux ou trois semaines. Qui sait?*'

I was drinking coffee in the refectory at the Integral Guest House. It was good to be back there. My room was next door to the one I'd had before. The only difference was a picture of the Mother instead of Sri Aurobindo. The Gauguin woman served me with a smile that turned into a yawn but gave no indication that she remembered me. The Rajneeshi was still around; I saw him doing t'ai chi exercises on the lawn. I was just wondering about the Lady of Shalott when she appeared, dressed in a shimmering sky-blue sari. The same smudgy lipstick and shining black eyes. She certainly remembered me. She sat at my table and looked me in the eyes and asked, 'Why did you come back?' I told her that I'd been just up the coast. 'You had to see me again.'

It was five weeks since I'd been there last. I asked the

sad girl (I still didn't know her name) if she lived at the Guest House. 'I have been sent here, you could say.' She took my coffee-spoon and played with the sugar. I asked her name. She hesitated before telling me. 'Oh. It's Rita. You may call me Rita.'

'Rita is one of those names, like Nina and Anita, that are equally Western and Indian.'

'That is why I chose it.'

'It's not your real name?'

'To your ears my real name would sound ridiculous.'

'Why should it? I'm used to Indian names.'

'It is Kunti.'

'Ah. I see what you mean.' I tried hard not to smile. 'Still, it's in the *Mahabharat*.'

'That is true. You know the *Mahabharat*?' She had dug a little hole in the sugar and now she was patting the walls of the hole with the back of the spoon.

'Only from the television.'

'All the same, I would prefer Rita.'

'What do you mean, you've been sent here?'

'I'm not a follower of Aurobindo. Nor are my parents. But here they know I am out of mischief and away from the eyes of their friends.' Rita was filling the hole in again. Now I was intrigued. I wanted to know what had happened but, wary of seeming nosy, which of course I was, I asked if she was willing to talk about it. Rita replied, 'I don't mind telling you but it's a long story.'

'Please don't think I'm prying,' I said hypocritically.

'I think I fascinate you,' she answered and a different light flashed over the black liquid.

'Would you like to have dinner with me?' I asked.

'When?'

'Tonight? We could go to the Aristo.'

'Ugh. That place I loathe! Why not the restaurant at the Alliance Française?' I hadn't realized there was a restaurant there. Rita said that it had been closed for a few months but had opened again a fortnight ago. I offered to meet her on the lawn at eight. 'Not on the lawn. People will notice us. I'll meet you in the restaurant at eight.' I didn't think my invitation merited such secrecy.

I had a shower, using the sandalwood soap provided, and walked down to the beach. Again there were tumblers cartwheeling down to the water and children shouting and clapping. The sky was cloudier than before, erasing the neat line of horizon. A pair of nuns led a party of schoolgirls on to the sand. They all sat down and opened aluminium boxes of food. A wild bearded man, not unlike Aurobindo to look at, but dressed in ragged brown pyjamas rather than saintly white, was gibbering frantically and, as I passed him, he shouted something at me.

The restaurant at the Alliance Française was a real surprise. I'd been expecting something along the lines of the Guest House refectory, with perhaps the merest nod towards French food: fancy pastries or filled baguettes. An informal snack bar for young people to gather after watching a Truffaut movie or while waiting for a French lesson. It turned out to be a proper French restaurant with starched white linen, the wine list and menu between leather covers, silver cutlery and candles. It was a long low room. The other diners were middle-class Indian families and elderly French people. A young *maître d'hôtel* showed me to a table for two. I waited for Rita and read the menu. There was shrimp soup. There was *vichyssoise*. Various salads: *salade niçoise, salade de tomates et poivrons, salade de carottes marinées*. There was *paté de foie de porc*, served with *cornichons*. There were *filets de maquereaux gratinés*. There were *paupiettes de boeuf*. There were *croquettes de volailles.* There was steak *au poivre*. Boiled potatoes or chips, green beans, carrots. For pudding there was *Saint Emilion au Chocolat* or *Tarte Tatin*. Just as the architecture was of a provincial French town, here was provincial French food. There was something slightly old-fashioned about the food, I thought. It was the sort of thing English travellers raved about in the 1950s, the world opened up by the early Elizabeth David books and Patience Gray's *Plats Du Jour*, perfectly delicious but definitely *ancienne cuisine*. I daydreamed about moving to Pondicherry, renting a large apartment, employing a cook. Rita showed up at half-past eight. I'd just about given up on her and was about to order. She didn't apologize. In fact, she seemed cross and distracted. I remembered how rude she could be and hoped that she wouldn't spoil the meal. 'Would you like some wine?'

'No. It's not really wine, it's port. It sends me to sleep.'

'How about beer?'

'I'll just have water.'

'This menu's extraordinary.'

'I'm not hungry.'

I ordered a steak *au poivre* with chips and vegetables and a green salad. Rita had a plate of chips. It was the first salad I'd had in India, apart from the slices of cucumber sprinkled with *garam masala* that Mrs Trivedi sometimes served.

For ten minutes Rita hardly spoke a word. Eventually I asked her why she had been sent to the ashram.

'OK. You'll probably think I'm stupid. Or a bad person.'

'Well, you don't know what I'll think. I don't even know what I'll think.'

'The other thing is I don't know where to begin.'

'Tell me about your childhood.' Rita told me about her parents.

She was the daughter of General Kapur of the Uri-Poonch Bulge, the soldier, swimmer and author of *Bring Me My Mule*.

'Crashy Kapur?' I asked, thinking how thrilled Major Trivedi would be when I told him.

'That stupid nickname none of his friends use.' He

was, Rita told me, a personal friend of Nehru, Mrs Gandhi and Rajiv Gandhi and All-Indian crawl champion. Her mother, twenty years younger than the General, was considered a great beauty; she was a musician, she played the vina. Kunti and her younger brother Ashish were privileged upper-class children, growing up in Madras. 'It was probably close to an English childhood. I mean, Beatrix Potter and all that.' Later she studied classical dance, Bharata Natyam. At eighteen Kunti was married to a handsome clever man, six years her senior, from a rich family. Her husband's name was Vinod. Very soon she was pregnant. Her son was called Ashok. Vinod was going to Stanford to study business law. It was before leaving for California that she changed her name to Rita. The young family took to American life. Rita found it 'a taste of freedom'. They were popular. 'Lots and lots of parties always.' She got on with American women. In India her friends had all been from much the same background. These new friends came from all across America, many different backgrounds. 'There was so much more to do.' The American women expected more from life than Rita had felt entitled to expect. They demanded and received freedoms that no Indian woman could have demanded. Vinod encouraged her to be like them. He had found a purpose, beyond just pleasing his parents, and he was excelling at his studies. The prizes on offer were within his reach. Ashok would grow up with real opportunities. Rita took an evening class in creative writing. She'd always loved poetry, as had her mother and grandmother. But she realized, when she tried to write her own poetry, that she didn't have anything to say. 'I was confused, I think. You know, I was between two cultures. I had no footing. You need to be calm and I was very dizzy.' Suddenly, although she'd considered herself perfectly happy with Vinod, Rita fell in love with her creative writing teacher. 'What, just out of the blue?'

'Well, it was a little more complicated. First of all, he

was in love with me. I thought to myself, he's crazy. And I knew he was married. He kept telephoning me. He said he couldn't live without me. I didn't even like him much, he was about forty-five years old. Then it was just like turning a switch. I was in love with him. I spoke about it to my girlfriends. Nearly all of them encouraged me.'

The steak came. It was very tough. 'What about Vinod?'

'You see, he didn't know. And it went on six months nearly. This poet – he was really a poet but he lived by teaching – Chuck his name was – he tells his wife. Then it all blows up.'

'So what happened?'

'Chuck says he will divorce Mary and marry me. I weigh it up. Then I tell Vinod I want to divorce. He goes quite mad.'

'I'm not surprised,' I said. Then I realized that she hadn't asked my opinion.

'He telephones his parents and my parents. Immediately I am flown back to Madras. To come back to India is like going back a hundred years. Also I was used to Rita and there I was Kunti again. I just keep saying I want to divorce. Ashok is taken away by Vinod's mother.'

'I was about to ask you about him.'

'He is happy. But I don't see him, that was the agreement. Anyway, Vinod comes back. Eventually, after such a long drawn-out weary struggle, and nobody in India on my side, I get my divorce. Then I write to Chuck but he has decided to try again with Mary. He says it was craziness due to stress. He has won a grant that means he is no longer obliged to teach evening classes. I am divorced in India, how can I get to America? Shame has fallen on both our families. My mother thinks this ashram might solve my problems. Why, God knows!'

'So that's why you're here?'

'Well, that is part of the story only.' My knife wasn't

sharp enough to deal with the leathery meat. 'One year I'm here, going to meditation, feeling quite calm, I suppose. I must be calm because I'm starting to write poetry. As for the teaching, I only take so much in. A lot of it's eyewash.' Rita finished her chips. 'One day in the refectory I meet an Australian, Peter's his name.'

'So?'

'So he asks me to marry him. And again, you see, I hadn't even thought of him in that way. I thought he was fairly typical, you know, on a spiritual quest and all that. But I ask myself, what have I to lose? In Madras we were married. I think my parents were quite happy.'

'What's happened to him?'

'Don't rush me, please. You see, I thought what would happen would be the same as before and that one day the switch would be turned on and I would be in love with Peter.'

'So where were you living? In Madras?'

'No, in Australia, of course. A very small town. It was like *Crocodile Dundee*. These people are as backward as Indians. But I suppose we could have moved to Sydney. That is a good city.'

'Why didn't you?'

'This is why you'll think me stupid. Peter had a brother, Simon.'

'Don't tell me, I can guess.'

'So you think I'm a slut?'

'No, not really, I think you should have followed your own instincts in the first place.'

'You have to understand. I don't come from a background of love-marriages. I don't know my instincts. What I mean is I have instincts but I can't always trust them.'

'OK. But it sounded as if you were fairly happy with Vinod.'

'When I think of him now I realize what a sweet man he was.'

'Where is he now?'

'He's in New York. He's a millionaire. Big corporate lawyer. Soon he is to marry an American girl and Ashok will go to them.'

'You shouldn't have trusted that Chuck character.'

'What, should I cry over spilt milk?'

'You're right. What about this Simon?'

'He was a silly boy but I was so lonely and there was nobody else. It was more that I hated Peter.'

'What did your parents say?'

'What could they say? They were struck dumb. All they could think of was back to Pondicherry.'

'Well, how do you live?'

'Daddy pays my bill. Otherwise I sell my grandmother's jewellery.'

'Couldn't you get a job somewhere?'

'What as? Bharata Natyam dancer?'

'No, you could do all kinds of things.'

Actually I wasn't sure what she could do. Off the top of my head I suggested she become an air-hostess. Rita laughed. 'Very funny, I must say!'

'Well, why not?'

'You don't realize that Daddy is very, very well known. Newspapers would get hold of the story. That is what he dreads.'

I finished the steak. It had been a disappointment. If I'd thought about it, the general condition of the cows, the improbability of decent butchers, I'd have chosen the mackerel instead. We both had *Saint Emilion au Chocolat*. 'What I want most of all,' Rita told me, 'is to get out of India.'

'How are you going to do that?'

'Cosimo.'

'What's that?'

'Cosimo Pirelli. He lives in Rome. He wants an Indian wife.'

'How do you know him?'

'I don't know him properly. He is in the leather business. Somebody I know here has done business with him. By post this mutual acquaintance introduces us. Now I've received three letters. Unfortunately he writes to me in Italian.'

'That's why you asked me if I could speak Italian.'

'Oh yes. I remember I asked you.'

'Did you find someone to translate?'

'Eventually I went to our mutual acquaintance.'

'So what are the letters like?'

'Nothing special. This mutual acquaintance is a problem. He says if I marry Cosimo, he will ask my father for a fee.'

'Tell him to get stuffed.'

Rita laughed. 'I think Daddy would tell him that.'

'Do you want to marry Cosimo.'

'What choice do I have?' I felt her toe brush against my anklebone and then the black eyes fixed on to mine. 'Tell me about England.'

After dinner we walked northwards along the seafront and then stepped down on to the beach and turned back towards the Integral Guest House. The sea was rough and the wind blowing in from it was somehow charged; occasionally there was the heat lightning that I'd noticed when I was last in Pondicherry. I'd probably acted somewhat guardedly, I simply didn't want Rita to pin any hopes on me, and had tried, successfully, to keep the conversation on impersonal things. Rita continually surprised me with what she'd read – not because I'd presumed she was ignorant – but because it would have been difficult to come across the books in India. 'My parents had a library. That was all I did with my time. Read, read, read.' She'd been talking about Swinburne, another poet she admired. She asked if I'd read Max Beerbohm's account of visiting Swinburne, when the poet was an old man kept on the straight and narrow by Watts-Dunton. A weird ragged creature scuttled towards us. It was the man who'd shouted at me earlier. He was absorbed in a garbled monologue but, seeing us, he broke off to mutter harshly at Rita. 'What did he say?' I asked as he shambled on his way. Rita replied that the man was a lunatic. 'For some reason he always insults me.' Just before we got to the Integral Guest House, it started to pour with rain. 'The monsoon!' I shouted. Rita said not to count on it. 'It could be just a shower.' But it was coming down very heavily and soon we were soaked. I called out, 'This is like a Hindi musical!'

'Do you know what the monsoon symbolizes in a movie?' she shouted. I'd thought it was just a cliché, an extravagance in a dry land, possibly an excuse to get the heroine wet and show off her curves. I shouted back that I didn't think it symbolized anything specifically. 'You wouldn't!' Rita's mood had soured. She snapped, 'This could have been just like a movie if you'd been interested in anyone beside yourself!' That was an absurd statement, I thought, as I'd spent most of the evening listening to her stories but I didn't say anything. Rita flounced on ahead and I walked back on my own.

At one in the morning there was a knock at my door. I got up, winding a towel around my waist, to see who it was and there stood Rita in her wedding sari. She smiled. 'I have decided to forgive you.'

'Oh, right. Well, thank you.' I was still half asleep.

'Let me in please.'

'I'm sleeping.'

Rita hissed, 'You are a pig! I don't forgive you at all!' and spun down the passage.

'Good night,' I yawned after her and closed the door. At three there was another knock. Oh no, I thought. This time Rita was wearing the red silk *salwar-kamiz*. It was obvious that she wasn't wearing a bra. Her hair was no longer tied back.

'I can't sleep at all. Can I come in?'

'OK, for a while. I'm really tired.' As soon as she got into the room she said, 'You do realize I'm not leaving, don't you?'

*   *   *

It was a rainy morning. At eight o'clock I went to the refectory. The Gauguin woman giggled as she served me and a few moments later one of the kitchen staff came out and she nodded in my direction. He flashed a broad grin and rested his hands in the small of his back. I walked past the Alliance Française towards the shops to buy some toothpaste. When I came back, the two *chowkidars* at the gate slapped each other and laughed as I passed them. At nine-thirty there was a knock on my door. Expecting Rita, I was surprised to find a stern-looking middle-aged woman.

'You are Mr Robert?' She demanded and I nodded. 'I am proprietrix. You are not official ashramite. This guest house gives priority treatment to ashramites, that is ruling. Please vacate room by twelve so that official ashramite may stay in it. Thank you for your co-operation. The blessings of the Mother.' I was leaving anyway.

Mrs Trivedi told me that Mr Shekhar had come to the house asking questions about me. He'd wanted to know how much money I had, what my professional qualifications were. She had sent him packing.

'Believe me, it's not wise to get caught in his schemes.'

'But I'd told him I wasn't interested.'

'You probably weren't firm enough. He sees money in it.'

'Do you think he's been to this girl's parents?'

'That you can be sure of. Probably before he even mentioned the idea to you.'

'I hope they don't take him seriously.'

'These people are serious. To them you present hope.'

'I've no intention of marrying this Teresa,' I stated.

'This you must make clear to Shekhar.'

'I have.'

'Clearer then.' As we were talking, a buffalo lumbered along the street and attempted to feed on Mrs

Trivedi's plants. She shouted '*Ket! Ket! Ket!*' and there was an uncharacteristic hysteria in her voice.

It was the festival of Dussehra. Everywhere I looked I saw trucks, buses, even auto-rickshaws decorated with leaves and flowers. The post-office counter was a riot of foliage. On the street white pumpkins had been smashed open and dye drizzled over the pale inside flesh.

Major Trivedi had more or less given up wearing Western clothes. He usually wore the white kurta and dhoti, sometimes he draped a bright orange silk scarf, printed with Devanagari lettering, around his neck. I asked what it said on the scarf and was told that it was a passage from the *Bhagavadgita*. He rose as early as usual but went to the temple instead of praying in front of the row of gods in the alcove. He seemed even more distant and tense. Mrs Trivedi said, 'It is the same in all our lives. We have periods when we must pray more than at other times.'

I looked at the photograph of Rita's father. There was only a faint resemblance. Major Trivedi asked why I was interested and I hastily replied that I'd seen a magazine article about General Kapur. 'Very likely. He is a national hero still. Nowadays he leads a quiet life. It's rumoured that he has problems within his family.'

'Oh, really?' I asked, trying to sound ingenuous.

'Yes. Yes. I believe that his son is addicted to gambling.'

'He has a daughter as well, hasn't he?'

'A daughter, no. One son only.'

Then the Major asked what I'd read about him and where. 'Does the poor man have more trouble? Newspapers hound him.'

'Well, I skimmed through it.'

'You must surely remember the tenor of the article?'

'I'll try to remember.' I was intrigued by the possibility that Rita had been lying to me.

*　　*　　*

Atul, who'd been there when Mr Shekhar called, told me that he knew Teresa. Her family lived on the airport road, not far from the Hotel Pushpa. I asked if she was pretty.

'Pretty? Teresa? No way!'

'Apparently she has a teacher's certificate. She can't be stupid.'

'That Shekhar tells you! Don't believe it.'

'Mr Shekhar is a troublemaker. I told him I wasn't interested.'

Atul chuckled. 'It takes more than that to discourage him.'

'Yoohoo!' There was a knock on the screen door. It was Dr Stickney. I noticed that she'd finally learned to tie her sari. There were no visible safety pins. 'Come, Beryl Didi,' Mrs Trivedi smiled, 'you will take tea or coffee?' As I'd understood that Mrs Trivedi didn't like Dr Stickney I was surprised at her hospitality. They sat and chatted together (sometimes switching to Hindi, which Dr Stickney could speak well, making me feel inferior) like close friends. Anasuya brought Dr Stickney her coffee and was thanked in Tamil. That's not so difficult, I thought, but then the doctor rattled off what must have been a witticism, causing Anasuya to smile. 'Ah, Beryl. You will eat with us, I hope,' the Major said, returning home from the temple.

'Where's Atul?' I asked.

'He stays tonight with Ajay.'

Besides Dr Stickney we were joined by Nagaraja Naidu who looked and smelt slightly healthier. He'd lost some weight. His wig was lower on his head – more like hair, less like a hat. If Mrs Trivedi's attitude towards Dr Stickney had changed, it had also changed radically towards the Cobra King. She hardly spoke to him at all. Nagaraja Naidu, I'm quite certain, was aware of this change but he was the type of man who enjoyed a little hostility. He sat and chewed his inner cheek and the greenish light intensified in his eyes. Mrs Trivedi produced chapattis, *lobia dhal* (black-eyed peas) and rice, bitter gourd and a very good dish that was like curried hash browns. I asked what it was called and she answered, 'Dry Potato.' Major Trivedi was sticking to his fleaseed gruel.

The Cobra King had also taken to Dr Stickney; he almost seemed to flirt with her in his gruff way and, if a button-eyed wooden puppet can twinkle, Dr Stickney twinkled in his presence. He was perhaps more forthcoming towards me than he had been. Halfway through dinner, he asked me, 'You are prepared, then, for Tuesday?'

I had no idea what was happening on Tuesday.

'October the Second. It is the birthday of the Mahatma,' Dr Stickney explained. 'Gandhi Jayanthi, it's a national holiday. It's usually observed as a quiet day of prayer and spinning. Sometimes Bapu's favourite hymns are chanted and passages from the *Bhagavadgita*. Bapu, of course . . .' (for some reason I didn't feel that Dr Stickney was entitled to call Gandhi Bapu; it sounded presumptuous, like a visitor using a family nickname) '. . . loved all religions. Muslims read from the Koran. You and I can read from the New Testament. I've marked out the relevant passages.'

'That was very thoughtful of you.'

'We are going one step further,' announced the Cobra King, 'using Gandhiji's teachings to help the world of today. We are planning a fast, starting Tuesday. To continue until peace is restored.' He jabbed at me with a grey finger. 'You are prepared?'

'I'm leaving a few days after that. I wouldn't be able to join you for very long. I'll be very busy packing.' (I felt like saying, 'Don't prod your finger at *me*.')

Mrs Trivedi cleared some dishes off the table. 'There are people who should not fast. Not all have the health. Those who choose to take such action should not force others to join them. Did Bapu make others fast?' The

Major glanced nervously at his wife, urging tact. Nagaraja Naidu gave a dismissive snort. 'What is the health of one man beside the health of the world?' The Major pushed his steel bowl away. He was quite upset.

Late at night, after Nagaraja Naidu had gone, Mrs Sen came to the house with a shopping basket. The Major had gone to bed. Mrs Trivedi was excited. 'Did you get it?'

Mrs Sen said, 'Acha, don't worry. I have a good one.' Out of the shopping bag she brought a small hairy coconut.

'That is just right,' whispered Mrs Trivedi. Anasuya took the coconut from Mrs Sen and went with Mrs Trivedi into the kitchen. I asked what the coconut was for. Mrs Sen told me it was to make a *kalasam*, a special puja offering for Dussehra. I watched as Anasuya filled the mouth of a copper vase with betel leaves. Then the coconut was placed on top of the leaves. Anasuya draped a short garland of yellow chrysanthemums around the neck of the vase. The vase she then placed on a banana leaf on a wooden tray and scattered raw rice around its base.

'And then you'll take the tray to the temple?'

'No, no, no. It stays here. Household puja.'

'Can I join in?'

'Unfortunately not this time. Only women. Go to bed now,' said Mrs Sen. Anasuya took the tray from the kitchen and placed it in front of the row of deities. I went to bed but I was intrigued by the bizarre goings-on in the corridor and couldn't sleep. The women's puja was led by Anasuya; that was odd in itself – two Brahmin women attending and a Sudra woman officiating. And it struck me that what was going on was peasant Hinduism; closer to the bowls of yoghurt placed beneath trees and decorated stones by the roadside. I listened to Anasuya's low incantations and smelt incense and later camphor. It seemed rather furtive, performed in whispers, and it lasted for several hours.

*   *   *

I went to Blue Jean Junction to pick up my suit. Mr Haq rubbed his plump hands and said, 'I have a surprrrise for you.' He fetched the suit and I saw that he'd lined the jacket in red-and-green-check silk. It looked magnificent – I hadn't considered a lining at all. 'No charge for the lining. This makes it special. You can tell your frrriends in England, if everrr they should come to Bangalorrre – Blue Jean Junction.' He'd sewn a patch on the inner pocket: M.A. HAQ, FASHION CREATIONS, BANGALORE.

I went over to M.G. Road and ordered a pot of coffee at Chit-Chat. ''Ere! I know you!' A familiar voice called out from behind me. It was Donald. He'd lost a lot of weight and he was wearing an immaculate white kurta. His tousles of hair, that had looked so clownish, were swept back into gleaming copper wings. He still wore the fluorescent green trainers but otherwise he was barely recognizable. 'You look well,' I told him.

'Bloomin' feel well and all.'

'What happened to you? Did you fall off the train?'

'No, I bloomin' didn't! I'd had enough, that was all.'

'But you left your rucksack.'

'Weren't nothing valuable in it, really. I had me passport and traveller's cheques, didn't I?'

'So what are you doing in Bangalore?'

'I've come to live 'ere, 'aven't I?'

'Where do you live?' I asked, hoping that it was sufficiently far from Bhagpur Extension.

'Well, just outside, really.'

My coffee arrived. Donald announced proudly that he was receiving spiritual instruction. 'A course, like.'

'What, from Sai Baba?'

'No, mate. Kalki, i'n'it?'

'Kalki?'

'Yeah, he's the real thing, he is. What I mean is, he's not really a man or nothing. He's what you call the Tenth Aviator of Vishnu.'

307

'Avatar,' I corrected him. It all sounded far-fetched.

'That's what I said.'

'Where did you meet him, this Kalki?'

'I was called to him, like.'

'What do you mean?' I was fairly sure that Donald was pulling my leg.

'Can't explain it, really. It's all a bit mystical. Don't fit into words or nothing, see? It came over me, more. I was in this small town, see, and me bloody guts were awful, I was weak as a kitten. Suddenly I goes light-headed, you know? Like the whacky baccy? 'Cept I hadn't had none. All bloomin' colours, pink and green, all spinning about in my head and like all shapes and that. I thought, Whoa Donald, steady now, boy! Next thing is I'm sittin' on the back of a scooter with a string of yellow flowers round me neck. And the thing was, see, the remarkable thing, see – you don't have to bloomin' believe me but it's the truth, I tell you – I knew, *knew* like, if you get my meaning, that I was meant to be going wherever I was being taken on that flippin' scooter, see. Me whole bloomin' life up to that point, like, had prepared me for that scooter that would take me to Kalki.'

'Who was driving the scooter?'

'He was a priest, he said, but I haven't seen him again.'

'Where did he take you?'

'It's just a small house. On the road to a place called Hosur. Nothin' special, really. But I was made welcome, all right.'

'Who was there?'

'Only Kalki and a few priests. Always a few of them around. Come and go, see.'

'Is this something to do with the BJP?'

'What you on about? I've told you, it's the tenth aviator, Vishnu and that.'

'How did you know it was Kalki?'

'I didn't at first. One of the priests told me. Explained it all, filled me in.'

'What does he look like?'

'He's just a man, well to look at, like. He looks like me, I s'pose. Only coloured, of course. Little bit pudgy. He don't eat much really so I can't see why. He's gearing up, see.'

'What for?'

'A bloomin' new age, like! Everything different! The renewal of creation! The destruction of evil! Restoration of flippin' purity!'

'Are you sure this guy's not a con man?'

'I told you, didn't I? He's not really a man, even. He's just taken human form, like, while he's in training.'

'How many disciples does he have?'

'Disciples!' Donald laughed. 'It's not bloomin' Galilee!'

'Followers, then?'

'Only me, like. And the priests, I suppose, 'cept they're not really his followers. As I said, they come and go. Bring us food and that.'

'Are you giving him money?'

'Course I bloomin' ain't.'

'So why've you joined him?'

'Didn't I tell you? I was called, chosen. By God, like. I'll be there when it happens, see?'

'Why you?' I asked – realizing that it was a rude question – but Donald smiled beatifically. 'I s'pose I was lucky. I mean, it's all a mystery, really. But now, like, I can see how everything I'd said and done in me whole life was preparation for this stage, if you get what I'm saying. It was pre-ordained, wa'n'it? That's God for you.'

'Well, good luck. I'm about to fly home.'

'I wouldn't go back there, mate. Not if you paid me. Doubt I'll ever go back, really. Shan't miss it neither. This is me home now.'

Mrs Trivedi admired the jacket. 'You have struck a real bargain.'

Atul said that he would have chosen a more exciting

fabric than beige gaberdine. I asked what he'd have chosen and he thought for a while. 'Perhaps black denim, lining neon.'

'Neon isn't a colour.'

'I mean any of those very bright colours, the new dye technologies. They make ace linings.'

The next day there was frightful news: Nagaraja Naidu was dead. Mrs Trivedi told me that it was all quite mysterious. 'When did he die?' I asked.

'Late on Friday night, that is all we know so far.'

'Do you know what he died of?'

'Not even a doctor can work it out.' Mrs Trivedi told me that after he'd left their house, instead of going home, he'd driven out along the Hosur Road. Where he'd been off to she had no idea. At dawn a milkman had found his car parked beside the road and his body face down in a ditch. His watch and shoes had been pilfered before the police arrived.

'That's terrible.'

'Yes. It is terrible.'

'Do they suspect foul play?'

'That, who can say? He was a powerful man and such men have enemies, of course.'

'It could have been an accident. He wasn't at all well.'

'That is true as well.'

Dr Lal returned that evening. He came to dinner but he wasn't his usual breezy self; he looked tired and ungroomed.

When I asked if he had heard about Nagaraja Naidu, he shrugged.

'Where's Dr Stickney?' I asked and Mrs Trivedi caught my eye and frowned.

'Where is Dr Stickney?' I asked Atul the next morning. 'I don't know, OK? Why do you ask me?' He sounded defensive. So, later on, when the family were out, I asked Asunta who asked Anasuya. She reported back that 'Dr Stickney has returned to her hotel. Doctor-Sahib and this lady have argued. Big row. As soon as he reaches Bangalore, she is talking, talking, talking of the late Nagaraja-Sahib. Dr Lal is not a fan of this fellow. Big row right here downstairs. Nobody must talk about her.'

There was a change in the Major over the next few days. He kept on going to the temple and wearing the orange scarf but his mood lightened and he seemed relaxed. The family drew closer together; mealtimes were chatty again. It was as if a cloud had lifted.

I looked for a notice about Nagaraja Naidu in the *Deccan Herald*; Indians go in for poetic announcements. I felt sure that the demise of such a big shot would receive enormous attention but there was nothing. I asked Atul why the Cobra King should die unnoticed and he asked me, 'Who were his closest friends?'

'Perhaps he didn't have any close friends?'

'Oh, he did. Others just like him. There is a network of such fellows.'

'Do you mean politicians?'

'They are not exactly politicians.'

'Do you think he was murdered?'

'Not exactly murdered.'

'So what do you think?'

'Between you and me, OK? I think this old fellow had powers and such powers maybe he would use over people and there are others with powers also and people who were scared of this fellow banded together and asked the other powerful ones to set them free.'

'So you mean gangsters?'

'Not gangsters! Did I say gangsters?' Atul was slightly irritable. Perhaps I was being dim.

'Well, you don't mean magic, do you? Come on!'

'Magic is the wrong word. A foreigner like yourself – no offence – you would probably walk past such things. It's not magic in that sense. But it is on a different wavelength, yes.'

A hand-delivered letter had come for me. On the outside of the envelope was written *Mister Joe* in rounded letters. Inside was a printed sheet that read:

IS YOUR LIFE CRISIS GREATER THAN GULF CRISIS?
MURDERS! SUICIDE! SICKNESS! POVERTY! DIVORCE! DRUGS!
WORLD IN 2000
EVERY 10 SECONDS 43 BABIES ARE BORN
EVERY HOUR 15,480 ARE BORN
EVERY HOUR 6050 DIE
BY YEAR 2000, THE WORLD'S POPULATION WILL REACH
6 BILLION 157 MILLION
EVERY PULSE BEAT ONE PERSON DIES IN ASIA
The Answer For Every Crisis & Failure
Is Your Creator
YOUR DISAPPOINTMENTS ARE GOD'S APPOINTMENT!
Come and Receive Blessings

On the back of the card was an address that I recognized as not far from Bhagpur Extension. Under the address was written in the rounded hand, *Please we welcome to you to join with us and Praise One Lord Jesus, Holy Saviour. Then welcome to visit to Sebun family at home.*

'That is the family of this Teresa,' said Mrs Trivedi. 'You will go?'

'Of course not.'

'That is a pity!' laughed the Major. 'I thought that would be just your cup of tea. Keep tambourine a-rolling.'

'No, you must go!' Atul was teasing me. 'I know, maybe you will come back next year and marry her?' He translated what he'd said for Anasuya who cackled.

*   *   *

Gandhi Jayanthi came and, although Major Trivedi went to the temple for a long time in the morning, no mention was made of a fast and we ate as much as we always did. I spoke to Dr Lal in the afternoon. We were standing outside drinking from green coconuts. Had he heard about the fast for world peace?

'I heard that that big shot was planning such an exhibition of piety. Do you think he himself would have fasted? I doubt it, I doubt it.'

The next-door ayah came out with a box of waste-paper. She grinned at both of us. That was enough to set the doctor off. As she walked down to the concrete bin, he muttered, 'Hubba, hubba, hubba,' and did a little twisting dance movement.

Packing my bags took a long time. All the books that I'd bought at Gangaram's I put in a box; they were to go to Krishnarayan's school. Mrs Trivedi made me a picnic for the flight. I told her that it wasn't necessary, that the airline provided meals. 'What would such food be? How could it be healthy, you tell me?' The Major said that I should rest on the plane, try to sleep, to avoid jet lag. Stimulating foods would prevent me from sleeping.

In the morning I put on my suit. 'This is a pukka suit,' said the Major. Mrs Sen and Dr Lal came to the house to see me off. They stood at the gate with the Trivedis and Anasuya and waved. It was hard to know what to say, there was so much to thank them for. Perhaps I should have prepared a speech.

Atul came to Bangalore Airport with me in a taxi. The last thing he said to me was, 'All right, my friend, stay cool.'

There was a four-hour delay at Bombay Airport. I picked around in Dowson's *Hindu Mythology and Religion*, passing my time in the company of heroes and demons. When I went to board the plane, a secur-ity officer tried to confiscate my Swiss Army knife.

Later on, high above the Persian Gulf, I unwrapped my food parcel: a *paratha* stuffed with fenugreek leaves, two boiled eggs, a piece of *burfi* and a custard apple.

Notes

JAISTHA

1. There is a lot of fanciful nonsense spoken about Jains; Western Vegans and New Age types claim affinity with them and will tell you that all Jains walk along with a little broom clearing insects from their path, a practice confined to a few extreme ascetics.

Jainism is historically similar to Buddhism; it originated in East India at much the same time. The sixth century BC was a time of religious upheaval in India. The Kshatriyas (the military and aristocracy) were resentful of the increasingly powerful Brahmin priesthood. The Brahmins derived their authority from the Vedas. Both the Buddha and Mahavira (usually referred to as Jina, 'victorious over Karma'), the founder of Jainism, were noblemen by birth; both refuted the infallibility of the Vedas; both rejected the caste system. Buddhism had the backing of the great emperor Ashoka and spread alongside his power. Jainism, on the other hand, while taken up by the Kshatriya and Vaisya (mercantile) castes, never had that kind of push. It didn't catch on among the lower-caste Sudras (cultivators, small farmers) because of its insistence on *Ahimsa* (the reverence for all life) which forbade tilling the soil lest earthworms should be injured. Royal backing of a kind did come with the Mauryan emperor, Chandragupta, who converted to Jainism in his old age and Ashoka's own grandson, Samprati, was a great patron of the Jain faith. Jainism reconciled itself with Hinduism far more than Buddhism did; both religions, for example, celebrate Divali.

There are some two million Jains in India, dividing into two main sects with monks and clergy: the Digambaras and the Swetambaras. Digambara means 'sky-clad' or naked, Swetambara means 'white-clad'. The very holiest of

Digambara monks do creep about in the nude but the ordinary monks and nuns wear clothes.

2. This is the legend of Gomateshwara, a prince in the first century AD: Gomateshwara's kingdom was usurped by his brother but Gomateshwara fought and regained it. Back on the throne, he found no happiness in being a prince and peacefully handed the kingdom over to his brother. Then Gomateshwara renounced worldly fortunes and became a Digambara monk. His brother, out of gratitude, had a vast statue made of the monk, to be placed at the top of a hill for all the world to see. But the centuries passed and most people forgot the story of the magnanimous prince and even the whereabouts of the statue. A tenth-century warrior-king, Chamundaraya, encouraged by Kalala Devi, the mother of one of his ministers, decided to find the great statue. Nobody could tell him where it was. An ethereal being visited Chamundaraya and told him to shoot an arrow at the Vindhyagiri Hill. The rock cleaved apart to reveal the head of Gomateshwara. A monk with a jewelled hammer chipped away the rest of the rock and there stood the statue, restored to all its earlier glory.

Every twelve years an eccentric ritual takes place called Mahamastakabhishekha; the statue is surrounded by scaffolding then anointed with various substances – thousands of pots of coconut milk, yoghurt, ghee, bananas, treacle, dates, almonds, poppy-seeds, milk, gold coins, saffron and sandalwood. Mahamastakabhishekha draws pilgrims from all over India.

3. From infancy these women were given tiny doses of poison, either from a snake or a scorpion; over the years they developed immunity. Having reached maturity, they became secret weapons. They would visit the Hoysalas' enemies disguised as courtesans; the enemies fell for their charms and perished from sexual contact.

4. The twelfth-century Moroccan traveller Ibn Battuta (1304–1369) wrote: 'Three days after leaving Fakanur we reached Manjarur (Mangalore), a large town on the inlet called ad-Dumb, which is the largest inlet in the land of Mulaybar. This is the town at which most of the merchants from Fars and Yemen disembark, and pepper and ginger are exceedingly abundant there. The sultan of Manjarur is one of the principal rulers in that land and his name is Rama

Daw. There is a colony of about four thousand Muslims there, living in a suburb alongside the town. Conflicts frequently break out between them and the townspeople, but the sultan makes peace between them on account of his need of the merchants.'

5. The Sanskrit word *'jangala'* from which our word 'jungle' derives, actually means 'uncultivated land'. And *'jungli'* is the Hindi word for 'uncouth'.

6. This isn't such a dreadful brew as one might think. Barley grows abundantly on the slopes of the Himalayas and there would once have been plenty of genuine Caledonian expertise. The brand names are wonderful: one is called 'Prince Phillips', another 'Peter Scot'.

ASADH

1. Hanuman's mother was Anjana, an *apsara* (celestial handmaiden) married to a monkey called Kesari; his father, however, was not Kesari but Pavana the Wind God. Hanuman inherited enormous muscular strength from Pavana and the ability to fly. As soon as he was born he amazed his parents by leaping into the sky to grab hold of the sun – which he'd mistaken for an orange. Hanuman is certainly not your average macaque or langur – according to the entry in Dowson's *Hindu Mythology and Religion*, he is 'as vast as a mountain and as tall as a gigantic tower; his complexion is yellow and glowing like molten gold. His face is as red as the brightest ruby and his enormous tail spreads out to an interminable length. He stands on a lofty rock and roars like thunder. He leaps into the air and flies among the clouds with a rushing noise, whilst the ocean waves are roaring and splashing below.' At one point Ravana set Hanuman's tail alight but Hanuman used his burning tail to torch Ravana's capital city, Lanka. His bravery in battle was extraordinary. He not only fought but acted as a medical officer as well, flying to the Himalayas to gather medicinal herbs with which he restored the wounded. Hanuman is also known as Yogachara for his magical powers of healing and as Rajatadyuti which simply means 'the brilliant'. His great abilities are attributed to his strict celibacy. His principal mental relaxation was the study of grammar.

317

2. Lambadis, known as Banjaras outside the Deccan, are the Indian gypsies. Whether they are related to the gypsies of Europe (who certainly descend from a nomadic Indian tribe) is uncertain. Lambadis are widespread throughout the South but are particularly established in the Bellary and Hospet districts. In fact the Lambadis claim descent from Sugriva; rather than outcasts and gypsies, they consider themselves the rightful aristocracy of Kishkindha. Their origin, according to this legend, is with Mola, a famous gymnast and Sugriva's grandson. Mola married a local beauty called Radha who played the drums while Mola (with the innate agility of his monkey race) tumbled and flipped and tied himself in spectacular knots. This union, however, was marred by infertility. One day the couple were performing in front of three neighbouring rajahs. The rajahs were so impressed by Mola's skill and Radha's beauty that each one offered a son of his own for them to adopt. The three boys were called Chavia, Lohia Panchar and Ratade. Ratade was the father of Bheekya, the first Lambadi.

Before the railways, transportation in this part of India was difficult; there wasn't a navigable river on the Deccan peninsula and many of the roads were unfit for wheeled transport; the Lambadis went into the haulage business using pack-bullocks to carry supplies such as grain and salt. Several thousand Lambadis were employed by the British army in their war against Tipu Sultan. A black market emerged when certain Lambadis discovered that the soldiers would pay for food and goods that they had pilfered from the villages the Army passed through. Thus the Lambadis fell into disrepute and, after the advent of the railways, while the majority took to small-scale cultivation and enterprises such as the gathering of firewood, others fell back on petty crime as a livelihood. One of the most exhaustive studies of late-nineteenth-century Lambadi life and customs is in F.S. Mullaly's *Notes on Criminal Classes of the Madras Presidency.*

A Lambadi marriage is still a fairly bizarre ritual. The couple walk seven steps around a rice-pounding pestle while the Lambadi women chant hymns. A Brahmin priest is in attendance, mainly as a witness, though from time to time he calls out *'Sobhana, sobhana!'* – best wishes. After the ceremony the priest is ritually groped, sometimes even stripped naked, by the women.

3. Hindus believe that a guardian deity presides over each of the eight compass-points: Indra (east), Agni (south-east), Yama (south), Surya (south-west), Varuna (west), Vayu (north-west), Kuvera (north) and Soma (north-east). Each deity has an elephant to ride while on sentry duty and Indra's eastern elephant is called Virupaksha. Virupaksha has several nicknames: Abhramatanga ('the cloud elephant'), Arkasodara ('the brother of the sun'), Nagamalla ('the fighting elephant'), Madambara ('dripping with ichor') and Sadadana ('always sexually excited').

4. Narasimha means 'Man-lion' and is the fourth avatar or manifestation of Vishnu. The god appeared on earth to rid the world of a tyrannical *Daitya* (demon) called Hiranyakashipu who claimed that he had been granted protection from Brahma so that neither beast nor man could kill him. Hiranyakashipu had a son who was a devotee of Vishnu, which so displeased the *Daitya* that he tried to kill the boy. His son warned him that Vishnu was omnipresent and Hiranyakashipu, scoffing, banged on a stone pillar, asking sarcastically if Vishnu could be hiding inside it. Out of the pillar sprang Vishnu to avenge the attempted murder, and bearing in mind the tyrant's protection, he chose a form that was neither beast nor man to slay Hiranyakashipu: the head of a lion on top of a man's body.

5. Buchanan, who also visited Sravanabelagola but failed to see the colossal statue because of an eye infection, was the author of the concisely titled *A Journey from Madras through the Countries of Mysore, Canara and Malabar, performed under the orders of the Most Noble the Marquess of Wellesley, Governor-General of India, for the Express Purpose of Investigating the State of Agriculture, Arts and Commerce, the Religion, Manners and Customs; the History, Natural and Civil, and Antiquities in the Domains of the Rajah of Mysore and in the Country acquired by the Honourable East India Company, in the late and former Wars, from Tippoo Sultan.*

6. I came across a recipe for Head Curry in *Delights from Goa* by Aroona Reejhsinghani. It specified, 'One head of goat exclusive of brain.' It didn't sound at all unpalatable, bearing some resemblance to the Jamaican Goat's Head Soup. And don't forget that old Scots standby, Sheep's Heid Broth.

7. The Club is a lovely building, more redolent of Company days than the Raj. A low, white, classical structure with an Ionic pillared portico, it spreads its graceful wings above a sloping garden. It was built in 1831 as a private house by Sir William Rumbold, a partner in the Hyderabad banking firm of Palmers, the financiers to the ruling Nizam. The house had just been finished when the firm collapsed and at much the same time Lady Rumbold died. The mournful baronet spent just three years in Ooty, in a state of financial anxiety, before dying at the age of forty-six. Then the house was run as a private hotel by Rumbold's butler, Felix Joachim. Joachim welcomed some very distinguished guests including, in 1834, the Governor-General, Lord William Bentinck. Bentinck, in his turn, welcomed Thomas Babington Macaulay who had just been appointed, by the Supreme Council of the East India Company, to head the commission to reform the law. So the very first notes towards the great Indian penal code were drawn up in this building. In 1843 the premises were taken over by the Club.

8. This is an old Toda song, in honour of the arrival of the Maharanee of Mysore who spent her summers at Fernhill:

All us Todas go to her house and dance.
She pays us fifteen rupees.
She chats to the women.
She gives us some cloth.
Next day we deliver milk.
Eight bottles in the morning, four in the evening.
She sets up a monthly account.
Before she returns to Mysore, we line up in front of her
and are given presents. More cloth and three rupees each.
The women have their hair done for the occasion.

Todas may not be the most scintillating songwriters but they are splendid to look at. The men are tall with long leptorhine Biblical faces, jet-black hair and curling beards. They often have thick hair growing from the helix of both ears, an outcrop they put down to drinking too much buffalo milk. Toda women are shorter and lighter-complexioned. They wear their hair in Nell Gwyn ringlets. Both sexes wear poncho-like mantles called *putkulis*, white with blue and red lines at the border. Rancid ghee is used to weather-proof the *putkulis*. The women also rub ghee into their feet and sometimes have blue snake designs tattooed about their ankles. Women's feet are considered very sexy.

The Todas claim to have lived for ever on their high plateau and deny that their ancestors came from elsewhere. Over the years anthropologists, amateur and professional, have come up with all sorts of theories to refute this claim. The Lost Tribe of Israel? Descendants of palanquin bearers to the kings of Kandy, having fled from Sri Lanka after an insurrection in the palace? Macedonians who accompanied Alexander? Roman soldiers? As recently as 1951 Prince Peter of Greece declared the Todas to be of Mesopotamian origin.

Madame Blavatsky, who didn't visit Ooty, nevertheless wrote about the Todas in *Isis Unveiled*. Among several wildly erroneous declarations (she stated, for instance, that they were white-skinned) she was adamant that, 'Nobody has seen more than five or six at one time; they will not talk with foreigners, nor was any traveller ever inside their long and flat huts . . . nobody ever saw the funeral of a Toda, nor very old men among them . . .' in order to make her point that the Todas aren't really a tribe at all but members of a mystical super-caste. 'They are not born of Toda mothers, nor of Toda parentage; they are the children of a certain very select sect, and are set apart from their infancy for special religious purposes. Recognized by a peculiarity of complexion and certain other signs, such a child is known as what is vulgarly termed a Toda, from birth.' Even Phineas T. Barnum was intrigued by them and a Toda family was enticed into joining his travelling show. Many, many years later an old Toda man returned alone to Ootacamund, having visited Europe, America and Australia. He wore a white top hat and told his relatives about a beloved elephant called Shumbu.

Their complicated religion involves buffaloes. Their priests (Palols) are sacred milkmen, their temples are dairies. But it isn't as pastoral as it seems; until well into the last century unwanted baby girls were ritually stamped to death by the cattle.

The buffaloes may appear as vague and dreamy as the Todas themselves but woe betide the European who approaches, only Todas can go anywhere near them!

Todas consider it beneath their dignity to cultivate land. In the nineteenth century a mistake about the ownership of some buffaloes committed an old Toda to jail. Nothing could induce him to work with the other convicts so, to save face and keep the peace, the authorities made him an overseer.

9. The South Indian Bharata Natyam is named after the *Natya Shastra (Textbook of Dance, Drama and Music)* which is attributed to the sage Bharata and was written at some point in the second century BC. The *Natya Shastra* holds that all the arts were created firstly for the amusement of the Gods.

The original performers of the Bharata Natyam were Devadasis (literally 'Slaves of the Gods'), dancing-girls, attached to the Tamil temples, who made ends meet by sanctioned prostitution. This tradition of temple prostitution flourished up until this century and, though now officially illegal, probably still goes on. It would be naïve to imagine that any kind of prostitution is without its share of exploitation and misery but equally wrong to merely regard the Devadasis as indicative of a corrupt and lascivious priesthood. The first Devadasis were possibly the female offspring of inter-caste unions, left at the temple gates. In many cases it was a profession passed from mother to daughter. Boys born to the Devadasis often became temple musicians or wandering minstrels.

To be a Devadasi was to be a respectable member of the temple staff. The Devadasis fanned the deity with *chamaras* (yak-tails), they carried the sacred *kumbarti* lights and they sang and danced in front of the deity whenever it was carried in a procession. Prostitution nevertheless remained their principal livelihood. Some, rather like the *cocottes* and *grandes horizontales* of nineteenth-century Paris, amassed sizeable fortunes and even became public benefactors, financing the construction of bridges and water tanks. As Devadasis were officially married to the temple deity they could never be widowed and consequently they were considered propitious guests at Hindu weddings; the *tali* or marriage necklace was often threaded by a Devadasi and sometimes she was asked to lead the wedding procession – her unique semi-divine status would repel evil omens. The Devadasis were cultivated women, they could read and write and play musical instruments as well as dance. An early objection to the education of women was that they would become too similar to Devadasis to be marriageable.

10. A Makara is a sort of crocodile with a fish's tail. Sometimes, even weirder, the fish's tail is the root of a lotus plant. Inside the Makara's mouth there is a pearl. Any man brave enough to extract this pearl can be assured of the love of any woman he desires. The Makara also contains a sac of aphrodisiac fluid. The sea-god Varuna rides a Makara.

SRAVANA

1. I hereby endorse a wonderful Indian toothpaste called *Vajradanti* which means 'Lightning-Flash-Teeth'.

2. The river that runs through Jabalpur is also called the Nerbudda but Narmada seems to be the older name and the mention of it is said to be a charm against snake-bite.

3. Lear arrived in India in November 1873, a guest of the Viceroy, Lord Northbrook. He spent thirteen months travelling all over the subcontinent, painting and sketching. He found the formality of viceregal life somewhat stifling and preferred to stay in hotels, railway retiring-rooms, private houses and Dak bungalows. He travelled with his manservant, Giorgio. Like nearly all Western visitors, Lear swung between adoring India – 'Colours, & costumes, & myriadism of impossible picturesqueness!!!' – and loathing the place – 'I am half wild when I think of the folly of coming to India at all. The only thing now is to make the best of a miserable mistake.'

4. The Indian way of making tea is quite different from ours. To begin with, it's made in a saucepan rather than a teapot. Milk and water are brought to a slow boil. Tea leaves are then added and lots of sugar and the brew goes on bubbling gently until it turns the desired colour. *Masala chai* is made the same way but cardamom, cinnamon, a little black pepper and ginger are dropped into the pan along with the tea leaves. I find it a delicious and restoring drink but it's best not even to think of it as tea as we know it. When I've made it at home I've found that Kenyan tea gives the best strength and colour. Chai-wallahs at railway stations shout '*Chai! Chai! Garum, garsala!*' which means 'Tea! Tea! Hot and fresh!'

5. Apparently there are over two million Gonds. All Adivasis are outside the caste system but not in the same way as the Untouchables. The Gonds have their own royalty and these rulers in the past were great soldiers. In the thirteenth century there were as many as four Gond kingdoms. The area around Jabalpur, Eastern Madhya Pradesh, was once the powerful state of Gondwana. In Jabalpur there is an ancient Gond fortress called Madan Mahal. It is on the top of an enormous boulder. The city of Nagpur was founded by Gonds who ruled until the eighteenth century. A northern Gond queen, Durgavati, fought and lost a famous battle against Akbar's army. A fierce Gond army called the Tarvels prepared for battle by chomping on wild orchids. In other words the Gonds are a proud and ancient race if somewhat adrift in the modern world. The unflattering legend of their origin is attributed to Shiva. He created the Gonds in the Himalayas but forgot to teach them to wash. After six months he started to find their 'BO' too much to bear and decided to get rid of them. Out of his own sweat he fashioned a magic squirrel which the Gonds, like a pack of hounds, chased. The squirrel ran into a cave and the Gonds followed it and Shiva blocked the entrance with a boulder and thought that that was the end of his problem. But four Gond brothers had not joined the chase and, when they saw what their creator had done with the rest of the tribe, they decided to head south, away from the mountains. When they got to Central India they met a giant who found their pong far from repugnant – in fact he found their smell so delicious that he wanted to eat them! However, the brothers came to an understanding with the giant and, instead of eating them, he offered them his four daughters in marriage. It is from those brothers and their giant wives that all Gonds claim descent. Traditionally Gonds are buried with their feet pointing north towards the Himalayas, their ancestral homeland. The Gonds have adapted Hinduism to fit their own sylvan religion of spirits and fairies, where the principal evil spirits are diseases, smallpox and cholera.

6. The Thugs were a hereditary guild of highwaymen and assassins who strangled their victims, hapless travellers, with a silken cord in order to please Kali, the Hindu goddess

of destruction. Under Sleeman's authority, over three thousand Thugs were convicted and, those that weren't hanged, put to work making carpets. Thuggee caught the British public's imagination. Three popular books came out during the 1830s. Sleeman's own *Ramaseeana* in 1836 (Ramasee being the secret cant of the Thugs), Thornton's *Illustrations of the History and Practices of the Thugs* in 1837, and in 1839 the enormously successful novel *Confessions of a Thug* by Philip Meadows Taylor, which Queen Victoria herself enjoyed. Taylor was a police officer in Hyderabad and his novel was based on his own interviews with convicted Thugs. His fictional confessor is a Muslim called Ameer Ali. Apparently, despite the devotion to Kali, Muslims could also practise Thuggee. Both Sleeman and Taylor were heroes to the Britons who read their books. It has to be remembered that early Victorian Britain was in an evangelical frenzy. The London Missionary Society had been founded at the very end of the previous century and by the 1830s was going strong; indeed the empire was primarily regarded by many Britons as an enormous mission. All three of the popular books on 'Thuggee' emphasized the religiosity of the assassins, making it seem that the Thugs were following a set of rules and ancient traditions never far from the mainstream of their non-Christian faiths. The official attitude to both Islam and Hinduism was not as open-minded and tolerant as it had been in the eighteenth century. Increasingly, districts were governed by men with evangelical notions and even the army officers had become eager to convert their sepoys to Christianity. This attitude was one of the factors that led to the Great Mutiny of 1857. When Queen Victoria, thereafter, was proclaimed Empress of India, a promise was made to the Indian people that there would be no official interference with their religions. Missionary work did continue, of course, but it was always completely separate from the Government and the Army. But in the 1830s to portray Islam and Hinduism as mindless and evil religions, little more than witchcraft, was shrewd. It was exactly what the public wanted to read. Certainly the murder of innocent citizens was a heinous crime in itself but the reality of the Thugs, taken away from this context of Christian outrage, was probably less dramatic. The first forty years of the nineteenth century were a time of political chaos in Central India. The Mogul Empire was falling apart and the local rajahs were fighting among themselves and against the British. Highway robbery would have been a frequent occurrence, perhaps the only option left to gangs of defeated soldiers who'd lost their jobs and their land and become brigands. Perhaps, as was the case in the Scottish border country at the time of the 'reivers', there was little point in cultivating land that was so frequently used as a battleground. A certain loose confederacy might have existed between different gangs, united by common interest, but a religious movement that included both Muslims and Hindus (and Hindus of many different castes) seems unlikely. Perhaps certain Hindu gangs did claim the patronage of Kali but, in India, religion enters all aspects of life. The significance of this religiosity was probably much less than contemporary accounts would have us believe. It seems that the British took 'heathen religion' to be the very *raison d'être* of Thuggee. The Hindi word from which Thuggee derives is the verb *thagna* which, fittingly, means no more than 'to cheat' or 'to deceive'. Sleeman and his colleagues estimated that over the previous three centuries the Thugs had committed at least 40,000 murders every year. Yet very few records point to incidents before 1799. This scarcity of evidence was regarded as proof of complicity among co-religionists and the sinister and all-pervasive professionalism of Thuggee. Then, as now, people believed what they chose to.

7. The long-suffering King Harischandra is the Hindu equivalent of Job. Harischandra was a popular monarch, known by his subjects for his fairness and courtesy. One day, when out hunting, Harischandra heard wailing female voices and, in his role as defender of the distressed, rushed to their rescue. But Harischandra had misinterpreted the cries. In a clearing of the forest he discovered the austere Brahmin sage Viswamitra, a grim and merciless figure. Viswamitra had obtained great powers; just at that moment he'd managed to conjure up Science in its purest form, as an embodied being. Science was squealing as her secrets were pulled from her like teeth. Harischandra, not realizing what was going on, saw an old man mistreating a woman; with drawn sword, he interrupted the experiment. Science vanished and Viswamitra was furious. Harischandra apologized and promised compensation. Viswamitra demanded

all the king's land and belongings. Harischandra handed them over. Then Viswamitra remembered a stipend that it was customary for a king to pay to a Brahmin (the payment is called *rajasuya dakshina*) and demanded that as well. How could Harischandra pay it when he'd already given all that he owned to the sage? Viswamitra was relentless. The king, having promised to give Viswamitra whatever he demanded, set off for Benares, wearing a garment of tree bark, where he sold his wife and son into slavery. Then Harischandra sold himself into bondage with the Doms, the ritual cremators who work the burning ghats. He laboured on the cremation grounds for a year until the day his wife, broken down by hardship and misery, came with the corpse of their son who had been poisoned by a snake. She couldn't even afford a blanket to cover the boy's corpse. The queen recognized her husband and begged him that they might throw themselves on to their son's funeral pyre. Harischandra, maintaining his honour even in tragedy, hesitated; after all, he hadn't repaid his Dom masters yet. He went to discuss the matter with his supervisor who suddenly turned into Yama, the divine judge of the dead. Yama told Harischandra that he and his family were welcome to reside in heaven. But Harischandra asked that his subjects should be released from slavery under Viswamitra and should ascend to heaven with him. This wish was granted and Harischandra and his family and subjects, found themselves in a beautiful aerial city. This city, according to popular belief, is sometimes visible, on a clear day, in the sky above Benares.

8. There was once a male *rakshasa*, a fiend, called Durga (which means 'the unassailable') whose powers were so strong that he challenged the authorities of the gods. The gods went to Shiva to complain of this usurper and Shiva commissioned Devi, the greatest of all goddesses, to deal with this nuisance. Devi sent Kalaratri ('black night') as a messenger to warn Durga that the gods were angry and to ask for his surrender. But, instead of being afraid of Kalaratri, Durga ordered his attendants to capture her and put her in his harem. Insulted, Kalaratri burned the impudent servants with the fire of her breath and returned to Devi. Devi then declared war on the demon who stood his ground and accepted the challenge. Mobilizing an army of demons, he actually attacked the goddess first. But Devi had

an almighty secret weapon, unlimited *Shakti*, and this divine energy instantly wiped out the demon's army. This left Durga to fight on alone and he used every trick he could think of. He uprooted a mountain and slung it at the goddess who chopped it into pebbles with her sword. He turned himself into an elephant and charged the goddess who lopped his trunk off. Then he became a bull, but to no avail. He was wounded by Devi's trident and then pierced through the heart with her arrows. When the demon finally died there was great rejoicing and Devi, the great goddess, took the name Durga, 'the unassailable', herself as a spoil of the battle.

9. The story of the young prince Siddhartha Gautama is well known: how he left his father's palace to solve the mysteries of sickness and old age and death; the years he spent in the forest, practising asceticism, learning from spiritual teachers; how he left the teachers in search of 'a middle way', sitting and meditating under a bo tree in a place called Bodhgaya where he found enlightenment; having become the Buddha (the 'Awakened One'), he walked to the holy city of Varanasi, some two hundred miles away; and there, in the deer park at Sarneth, he preached the sermon of the Four Noble Truths and the Eightfold Noble Path. That was in the seventh century BC. For some three hundred years after the Buddha's death, his teachings remained more or less confined to Eastern India. Then, in the fourth century BC, Ashoka came to the throne of the Mauryan Empire. Ashoka had been converted to Buddhism and conceived the notion of converting the rest of the world as well. Ashoka's empire was enormous, covering virtually all the subcontinent; missionaries went from India to other Asian countries and, though it took centuries, Buddhism spread. In different countries it evolved in different ways but, by and large, Ashoka's efforts were successful and, from the time of his reign right up until the rise of Islam, Buddhism was certainly the most important religion in Asia. In Sarnath and other sites, the emperor had great *stupas*, bell-shaped monuments, constructed. Deep inside these tumuli of bricks were a selection of the Buddha's mortal remains. To circumambulate these shrines was an act of worship and pilgrims travelled all over India to do so. At Sarnath, Ashoka also put up his own famous pillar, now

used as the state symbol of India, its capital four lions, back to back and all-seeing. Monasteries were built, more *stupas*. For centuries Buddhism flourished and Sarnath was one of its most important centres – the others being Lumbini, the Buddha's birthplace, Bodhgaya and Kushinagara, where he died. In the late eighth century, Sankara, the philosopher saint, revived the Hinduism that had been bubbling up for centuries and is generally considered responsible for driving Buddhism out of India. By the time the Muslim suzerainty was established, Indian Buddhism hardly existed apart from a few communities up in the Himalayas that were closer to Tibet. Most of the shrines had been converted into Hindu shrines. The Buddha himself was declared an avatar of Vishnu. Sarnath and its splendours were neglected and, that favourite Muslim pastime, iconoclasm, left it all in ruins.

10. B.R. Ambedkar was Nehru's Minister for Law. He chaired the committee that drew up India's Constitution. He had a doctorate from Columbia University. He was also an Untouchable, the great champion of his people. Ambedkar felt that it wasn't enough just to rename Untouchables Harijans, the whole concept had to be abolished. Article 17 of the Constitution formally did so. However, the vast majority of high-caste Hindus chose to ignore the article. Disillusioned by this, Ambedkar became a Buddhist and encouraged half a million of his fellow Harijans to follow him in this conversion to a religion that was fundamentally Indian (unlike Islam and Christianity, both of which had attracted Harijan converts) but without a caste system. In the census of 1961, three million of these neophytes were counted. According to rather sneery Brahmin opinion, most aren't proper Buddhists at all, keeping their old Hindu way of life and celebrating the birthday of Dr Ambedkar as a holy day.

11. The origins of Raksha Bandan are fairly vague. In the Puranas there is a story about Indra, the Lord of the Firmament, gathering an army of gods to fight an army of demons. The word came to him that the demonic army was extremely powerful and, for a moment, Indra doubted that the gods would win. Indrani, his wife, tied a charm to his wrist and assured him that the charm would scatter his enemies – which it did. But the legend of Indrani's charm is

not referred to by the majority of Hindus at Raksha Bandan – just as the majority of Christians don't consider the symbolism of eggs at Easter – and it's about as secular as a festival can be in India.

12. The life of Sabu the Elephant Boy seems unbelievable, almost far-fetched. Sabu Dastagir was born in the Karapur jungle in January, 1924. A penniless and illiterate orphan, he decided to follow in his father's footsteps and apply for work in the Maharajah's stables. He was taken on as a groom and started to train as a mahout. In 1935 Alexander Korda decided to make a film of the Kipling short story 'Toomai of the Elephants'. The documentary film-maker Robert Flaherty was put in charge of the outdoor scenes to give the production authenticity. Flaherty's cameraman, Osmond Borrodaile, discovered Sabu the eleven-year-old trainee-mahout and both men were impressed by his natural charisma. Before long Sabu, who'd neither acted nor seen a movie before, was the star of the film (retitled *Elephant Boy*) and, because the interior scenes had to be filmed in the studio, Sabu went to England. He was sent to school in Beaconsfield and soon picked up English. His great charm, athleticism and eagerness and his ease with animals and other actors ensured stardom. *Elephant Boy* was a hit and was followed by *The Drum*. Offscreen, Sabu adopted an image straight from the pages of *The Magnet*: he wore an old-fashioned public school uniform and a brilliant red turban. *The Thief of Baghdad* was being filmed as war broke out. It was arranged that the production would be completed in Hollywood. So Sabu went to California (where he found the climate agreeably similar to Mysore's) and remained there after the film was completed. In 1941 he became an American citizen. Then he joined the United States Army Air Force as a tail-gunner and flew on 42 missions. He was demobilized as Staff-Sergeant S. Dastagir with a cluster of medals (including the Distinguished Flying Cross) and a presidential citation. Sabu made several films after the war in both Britain and America. Powell's and Pressburger's poetic *Black Narcissus* (based on the novel by Rumer Godden) cast him, against type, in an adult role, surrounded by sexually hysterical Anglican nuns in the Himalayas; this unlikely role established Sabu's reputation as a serious actor but, nevertheless, he continued with the jungle pictures that the public preferred. Sabu bought a mansion in a suburb called Chatsworth, married the actress Marilyn Cooper and fathered a son and a daughter. He died of a sudden heart attack not long before his fortieth birthday.

BHADRA

1. Sri Aurobindo (Aurobindo Ghose) was born in 1872 in Calcutta. He was educated at Manchester Grammar School and King's College, Cambridge, then joined the Indian Civil Service in Calcutta. He became active in the Free India movement and in 1908 was sent to prison. Upon his release in 1910 Aurobindo left Calcutta and headed south, attracted to Pondicherry because it was a French enclave and away from British interference. As soon as he got there his energy transferred from the political to the spiritual; he took up the study of Sanskrit and devoted himself to the spiritual discipline of Yoga. Aurobindo's basic philosophy was Integral Yoga, a form that encompassed all previous yogas and was intended to prepare man for a great evolutionary leap, to herald a transcendental dawn: the divinization of all humanity. By practising Integral Yoga, man reaches up to Brahma, the supreme soul of the universe. Brahma in turn reaches down (a process of Grace) and, where the two forces meet, gnostic man is created. In 1914 a Parisian woman called Mirra Alfassa arrived in Pondicherry. She had dabbled in painting and music and had experienced a string of psychic and spiritual revelations; as soon as she met Aurobindo she felt drawn to him as a mentor. For nearly a year, she sat at his feet, then she went back to Paris. In 1920 Mirra Alfassa returned to Pondicherry and spent years perfecting the discipline of Integral Yoga. In 1926 Aurobindo withdrew into a prolonged meditation and his disciples turned to Mirra Alfassa, whom they named the Mother, for guidance. An ashram soon grew around the Mother. Disciples swarmed to her from all over the world. Sri Aurobindo died in 1950. In 1968, the ideal city of Auroville was founded as an extension of the original ashram. The Mother died in 1973. Auroville and the Pondicherry ashram still thrive – though a certain tension exists between the civil administrators of Pondicherry and the Aurobindians.

2. As a wise man with magical powers who befriends a heroic king, Agastya is a figure comparable to Merlin; he features in many Puranic legends. He is sometimes called Vindhyakuta because he ordered the Vindhya Mountains to prostrate themselves before him and Samudrachuluka ('Ocean-drinker') because he swallowed the sea to reveal the hiding-place of the Daityas who fought the gods and interfered with sacrifices.

Agastya used his powers to make himself the perfect wife. He combined the most graceful attributes of various creatures – the eyes, for example, he took from a doe. Then he placed the assembled child in the palace of King Vidarbha who assumed that the beautiful creature was his own daughter. As soon as the girl reached a marriageable age Agastya demanded her hand. Vidarbha was reluctant until Agastya revealed the girl's unusual origin. Then the girl was known as Lopamudra – which means 'Lost Beauties', implying that the animals surrendered their beauty on the girl's behalf.

3. Mount Kailasa, north of the Manasa Lake, is Shiva's paradise. It is sometimes called Rajatadri which means 'the silver mountain'. Shiva sits on top of a tower of ice. His popularity is probably greatest in Southern India and when the god is in residence at Mount Kailasa he is known as Dakshinamurti or 'Looking Southwards'. As Nataraja ('Lord of the Dance') he set the universe spinning from Chidambaram in Tamil Nadu.

4. It was, however, not Hanuman but Nala, another prominent monkey and the son of Visvakarma the Divine Architect, who constructed the bridge over which the army marched. Hanuman, as a solo advance guard, had already leapt the straits.

5. Ganesh, the jovial elephant-headed god, is the most popular Hindu deity. He is the son of Shiva and Parvati. According to one legend, after her marriage to Shiva, Parvati remained sterile and appealed to Vishnu to grant her a son. Vishnu was pleased with her devotion and deference to his status and decided to get himself born as Parvati's child. Parvati held a feast to celebrate the birth of her son and invited all the gods. Each guest praised the child's beauty and congratulated Parvati – except Sani (the planet Saturn) who shuffled in in black rags and displayed no interest at all in the mother and child. Parvati was offended by this discourteous behaviour and asked Sani the reason. Sani replied that he daren't look at the baby because there was a curse upon him – everything he looked at with pleasure shattered. Parvati dismissed Sani's curse, saying that, as the child was an incarnation of Vishnu, it was unlikely that a minor deity like Sani could harm him. So Sani looked at the bonny baby and smiled and, immediately, the baby's head shattered into hundreds of pieces. Parvati panicked but Brahma, who was present, pointed out that the body was still alive, all that was needed was a new head. Outside in the courtyard was a sleeping elephant, whose head was placed on the baby's shoulders. Parvati protested that it was far from an ideal arrangement – who would respect such a figure? Shiva, to reassure his wife, promised her that he would appoint the boy commander of the Ganas, his personal troop of attendant gods. So the elephant-headed boy was called Ganesh 'Lord of the Ganas'. Another legend concerning the elephant-head is that Parvati was alone in the palace and getting ready to bathe and so she fashioned a living being out of clay to stand guard over the bathroom door. She was very pleased with her handiwork. When Shiva returned, the clay sentry refused to admit him, which made Shiva so indignant that he lopped his head off. Parvati was most upset so Shiva fetched the head of a favourite elephant as a replacement and, as a reward for the creature's single-minded vigilance, he made him commander of the Ganas. Ganesh is the remover of obstacles, the arranger of miracles, a harbinger of good fortune. Sometimes he is known as Lambodara ('the pot-bellied one') and he does have a roly-poly, almost Santa Claus-like reputation. Any new business venture is inaugurated with prayers to Ganesh. The prayer or 'mantra' to Ganesh (said to be effective against writer's block) goes '*Om Sri Ganeshaya Namah*'. Ganesh is also believed to have written down the *Mahabharata* from the dictation of Vyasa and consequently many Indian books open with a salutation to Ganesh. A seated Ganesh usually has four arms; when he dances he has eight – as Heramba ('The Boastful') he has five faces and ten arms.

Ganesh has been known to take human form. In 1640, a Brahmin from Poona called Muraba Goseyn, after a long regime of prayer, abstinence and mortification, was visited by Ganesh one evening while he was bathing at Chinchoor, a few miles outside the city. Ganesh told Goseyn to grab hold of the first tangible object he came across. Goseyn found a pebble on the river bank and Ganesh told him that as long as he possessed the pebble he would be the deity's human incarnation. The pebble gave Goseyn miraculous powers and he was able to heal the sick, see into the future and grant the wishes of pious supplicants. Goseyn bequeathed the pebble to his son, who left it to his son and so on; this way Ganesh's human incarnation lasted for six generations. The powers of Goseyn's great-great-grandson (who was visited by an early nineteenth-century Indologist called Captain Moor) were rather diminished: he was unable to work miracles and was considered unworldly and childish, something of a holy fool. His sleep patterns, on certain auspicious nights, were closely monitored by other priests; a calm night indicated peace and plenty; a lot of tossing and turning, war; wakefulness, famine. After the sixth generation, Ganesh abandoned human form. Perhaps the pebble was lost.

6. These *yugas* are Puranic divisions of 'Divine Time'. One day of this Divine Time is equal to one mortal year. Thus a divine year is three hundred and sixty-five mortal years. The *yugas*, then, are enormous measures. There are four of them, which together extend to twelve thousand divine years: the Krita, the Treta, the Dwapara and the Kali – which is the present. The Krita Yuga lasted four thousand, eight hundred divine years. It was the Great Age, the time when creation had been completed. It was Paradise. Without disease or hunger or even old age. The decline began with the Treta Yuga, which lasted three thousand, six hundred divine years. Sacrifice, to buy the favour of the gods, commenced. The simple righteousness of the previous *yugas* gave way to righteousness as a means to an end, men sought rewards for their goodness. However, they remained devoted to their duties and religious ceremonies. Things got steadily worse in the Dwarapa Yuga, which lasted two thousand, four hundred divine years. There was religious confusion, that eventually led to ignorance, with people not knowing what to believe. There was disease. Now we are living in the Kali Yuga when, according to the Vishnu Purana . . . 'Unable to support their avaricious kings, the people will take refuge in

334

the chasms between the mountains and they will eat honey, vegetables, roots, fruits, leaves and flowers. They will wear ragged garments made of leaves and the bark of trees and they will have too many children and they will be forced to bear cold, wind, sun and rain . . .' The one consolation is that it's the shortest, lasting only one thousand, two hundred divine years. Or four hundred and thirty-eight thousand mortal years – which doesn't seem such a consolation after all. What's more, I could never find out how far into the Kali Yuga we actually are. But once we've stuck it out, our minds will become 'as pure as flawless crystal'. Kalki, the tenth avatar (Vishnu riding a white horse and wielding a flaming sword), will redeem us, the great wheel will turn and the Krita Yuga will start again.

7. The word *Moplah* (or *Mappilla* as it's sometimes spelt) originally meant 'bridegroom' and could refer to any foreign settler who took a local wife; its more specific meaning came later. It might also derive from the local mispronunciation of the Arabic *muabbar* which means 'from over the water'. Legend has it that the local ruler, Cheraman Perumal, though a Hindu, had a dream about Mecca. He saw the full moon split in two and one half fell to the foot of a hill called Abu Kubais. Around that time, a party of Muslim pilgrims, on their way to a sacred shrine in Sri Lanka, were put up and entertained by the Perumal at his palace in Kodungallur. The ruler told the pilgrims of his dream and was told that such a miracle had indeed occurred at Mecca. So the Perumal was converted to Islam and travelled with the pilgrims back to Arabia where he died. But before he died he sent letters to the various local chieftains that he'd appointed to rule in his absence, requiring them to welcome settlers from Arabia, to give them land and for mosques to be built and endowed with funds from his own coffers. Nine mosques in Kerala do date from this period though the story of the Perumal and his conversion is apparently fanciful. What is certain is that, most likely for commercial reasons, there was an Arab settlement on the Malabar Coast at that time. By the end of the fifteenth century, when the Zamorin of Calicut formed an alliance with the Arab traders in his war against the Rajah of Cochin who'd joined forces with the Portuguese, the Moplahs fought alongside their cousins and, in consequence, held considerable power in the

Zamorin's court. Today the Moplahs are generally fishermen though, inland, they farm. Over the centuries the
Moplahs have converted low-caste or untouchable Hindus
(in particular, other fishing communities) to Islam. In the
process they've picked up a whole host of folk-beliefs
(including an almost shamanic approach to medicine) that
make their variety of Islam, like so many religions on the
Malabar Coast, somewhat unorthodox. The Moplahs that I
met were fine-featured, almost Latin-looking, much fairer
than most Malayalis.

8. Marco Polo visited Quilon. He complained of the heat and
found '. . . the sun so powerful that it is scarcely tolerable.
For I assure you that if you put an egg into one of the rivers
you would not have long to wait before it boiled.' The flora
and fauna of the Malabar Coast, however, enchanted him:
'There are black lions with no other visible colour or mark.
There are parrots of many kinds. Some are entirely white –
as white as snow – with feet and beaks of scarlet. Others are
scarlet and blue – there is no lovelier sight than these in the
world. And there are some very tiny ones, which are also
objects of great beauty. Then there are peacocks of another
sort than ours and much bigger and handsomer, and hens
too that are unlike ours. What more need I say? Everything
there is different from what it is with us and excels both in
size and beauty. They have no fruit the same as ours, no
beast, no bird. This is a consequence of the extreme heat.'

9. Ibn Battuta wrote: 'On the tenth day we reached Kawlam
(Quilon), one of the finest towns in the Mulaybar lands. It
has fine bazaars, and its merchants are called *Sulis*. They are
immensely wealthy; a single merchant will buy a vessel with
all that is in it and load it with goods from his own house.
There is a colony of Muslim merchants; the cathedral mosque
is a magnificent building, constructed by the merchant
Khwaja Muhazzab. This city is the nearest of the Mulaybar
towns to China and it is to it that most of the merchants from
China come.' Ibn Battuta had already come across Chinese
traders in Calicut and had unsuccessfully attempted to sail
away with them to China.

10. Saint Thomas, it is widely believed, landed on the
Malabar Coast in AD 52. The port is said to have been
Maliankara which was situated at the mouth of the Alwaye
River. This would have been a feasible place to disembark

for it was a port frequented by the Phoenicians and the early European spice traders, a place to stock the ships with provisions and fresh water for the voyage home. For a long time scholars argued that the apostle would have arrived in India by the route Alexander the Great had taken and that the countries in the north-west would therefore have come into contact with Christianity before Kerala. But now it is accepted that the commercial links that Palestine had with Alexandria, then the principal trading post between East and West, would have offered Saint Thomas a comparatively straightforward passage to Southern India, by way of the Persian Gulf. Once ashore he set about converting the Malayalis and founded seven churches in the region. His method seems to have been the performance of miracles. At Chavakad the apostle visited a Hindu temple. There he threw some water into the air and it remained there, suspended, defying gravity. The Nambudiri Brahmins were so impressed that they abandoned the temple there and then and let the Christians have it as a church. There is a church there still. Then Saint Thomas moved across country to the Coromandel Coast where, after making many converts, he was speared to death by some Brahmins in Mylapore, an area of Madras.

In the middle of the fourth century another Thomas, Thomas Cana, a Syrian merchant, visited the Malabar Coast and became concerned that the descendants of the original converts were dwindling with neglect. He returned to the region with a number of Syrian settlers including a train of clergymen. The Malabar Christians then became the concern of the Eastern Patriarchs who were a schismatic bunch, bristling with heresies, continually splitting into opposing factions. Oblivious to all this, the Malayalis would appeal from time to time for a bishop, unconcerned about the finer points of his doctrine nor what side of the latest dispute to rage through Christian Asia Minor the bishop was on. A traveller from Constantinople, Cosmas Indicopleustes, who visited 'the land of pepper' in 522, reported a fully organized church, with its bishops consecrated in Persia. Another early visitor was, surprisingly, an Englishman, the Bishop of Sherborne, who, during the reign of Alfred the Great, made a pilgrimage to the apostle's tomb at Mylapore.

When the Portuguese arrived the Malabar Christians were

overseen by the Nestorian Patriarch of Mesopotamia, an arrangement that the Franciscan and Dominican Friars, and later the Jesuits, didn't approve of at all. All correspondence between the Patriarch and his bishops was carefully intercepted; several of the bishops were imprisoned, some even executed. In the 1570s the Jesuits built a church and a Christian school at Vaippacotta near Cranganore. In 1584 a seminary was established to teach the Malabar Christians theology in Latin and Portuguese. The Malabar clergy, however, refused to ordain students trained in the seminary and this angered the Jesuits who sent for the formidable Alexes de Menezes, Archbishop of Goa. Menezes was invested with the spiritual authority of the Pope and wasn't afraid to use the terrors of the Inquisition to enforce this authority. He set off on a tour of the Syrian churches, burning any books that he could find in the Syrian or Chaldaean languages. Book-burning is always shocking but the loss of those ancient texts seems particularly awful. The Malabar Christians, many of whom had been tortured, desperately appealed – to any Eastern Patriarch who would listen – for a bishop as quickly as possible. Envoys were sent to every ecclesiastical head from Babylon to Alexandria. A bishop called Mar Ignatius was duly sent out from Antioch. Quite what became of him nobody knows except that he fell into the hands of the Portuguese. Some believe that he was drowned in Cochin harbour. Others say he was burned to death in Goa. Outraged by the murder, thousands of Malabar Christians gathered at the Coonen Cross at Mattancheri in Cochin and formally renounced any allegiance to the Church of Rome. While, on the one hand, this gathering was an important gesture of autonomy, on the other, it was the beginning of the divisive tendency that would characterize the Syrian Christian Church in Kerala. The majority now called themselves the Jacobite Syrians (after Jacobus Zanzalus, a patriarch who had united various divisions into a fairly consentient whole in the sixth century, thus founding the Jacobite Church in Antioch). They placed themselves under the supremacy of the Patriarch of Antioch and followed the rites of that church alone, while maintaining the Syrian language and appointing native bishops called 'Metrans'.

A smaller group, weary of arguing with the Portuguese,

compromised by becoming 'Romo-Syrians'. They kept the Syrian language for their services but acknowledged the supremacy of the Pope. Pope Alexander VII, unhappy that such a schism should exist and favouring a more complete conversion, sent the Carmelites to India to solve the problem but he made the mistake of failing to consult the King of Portugal who claimed absolute possession of the Indian missions and their progress was hampered because of this slight. The Romo-Syrians were still smarting from their earlier treatment by the Jesuits and, when the Carmelites eventually made contact with them, they were welcomed as an alternative. And, yet again, there was a split among the Romo-Syrians, with a faction becoming mainstream Roman Catholics while the rest stuck to the original compromise. From that point on the story gets increasingly complicated and would certainly strain any reader's patience. Suffice to say that political arguments in Europe and a series of internal ecclesiastical disagreements – and the growing conflict between the Portuguese and the Protestant Dutch over trade on the Malabar coast – caused countless problems for both branches of the church. In the nineteenth century the British and their Church Mission Society attempted to gather the Jacobite Syrians into the Church of England. Faced with a crisis, the reaction of the Syrians was always to divide, creating a disunion that persists to this day. While it is true that a fifth of present-day Kerala's population is Christian, literally hundreds of sects and subsects thrive within this 20 per cent; a situation that Mormons, Jehovah's Witnesses, Seventh Day Adventists and the like have only exacerbated.

The majority of Syrian Christians, from whatever faction, claim descent from Nambudiri and Nair converts. Nambudiri families that became prominent Christian clans were the Callys, Calliankaras, Sankarapuris; perhaps the most illustrious of all Syrian Christian families were the Pakalomattams who insisted that they were ordained as priests by Saint Thomas himself; every Metran of the Jacobite Syrians from 1653 to 1815 was a member of this dynasty. One is tempted to think of Malayali Borgias.

Indian Christians of all varieties have been known, from time to time, to make offerings to Hindu deities and likewise some Hindus (though not as a rule Brahmins) are reportedly quite happy to worship at Christian shrines (the Virgin Mary, for instance, is a favourite deity of certain Goan fishermen, otherwise resolutely Hindu). Some crossover is bound to happen when religious communities exist alongside one another. Among the Syrian Christians, a surprising number of Hindu traditions remain. The Syrian Christians, like all Christians, exchange rings at a wedding but in a traditional marriage the bridegroom also ties a *tali* around the bride's neck. This is a cord – holding, it must be said, a small golden cross – but otherwise identical to the *talis* worn by high-caste Hindu wives. When the husband dies, it is the custom for Hindu wives to remove the *tali*, indicating widowhood; some Syrian Christian widows also follow this custom. A period of strict vegetarianism follows the death of a near relative. This corresponds to the Hindu *pula* (death pollution) laws though the Christians have given the period a symbolic duration of forty days. A low-caste or untouchable Hindu, even if a convert to Christianity, is no more welcome in a Syrian Christian household than he would be in a Nambudiri or Nair household.

11. Perhaps as a warning against over-indulgence, there is described, in the *Mahabharat*, a terrifying demon called Mada; a great open mouth with jagged teeth, ready to chew up anyone who comes under its spell. Mada's spell is drunkenness.

12. An avatar means 'a descent' and is different from an incarnation in that an avatar is a worldly form chosen by a god in which to descend to earth; it is a manifestation and need not be subject to normal biological limitations. An incarnation, on the other hand, is born of woman – and takes the standard mortal path from infancy to senility – but is endowed with miraculous powers. The avatars of Vishnu, so far, are generally reckoned to be nine. The standard sequence is: 1. Matsya ('the fish'). 2. Kurma ('the tortoise'). 3. Varaha ('the boar'). 4. Narasimha ('the man-lion'). 5. Vamana ('the dwarf'). 6. Parasmurama. 7. Rama. 8. Krishna. 9. The Buddha. The tenth and final avatar, Kalki (somewhat Wagnerian; Vishnu on a white horse, wielding a blazing sword to smite the wicked and restore purity), has yet to appear.

13. Tradition has it that Nambudiris have been in Kerala since the Treta Yuga. They were brought down from the

north by the god Parashurama, Kerala's founder, who, having reclaimed the land from the sea, called it 'Karma Bhumi' – the country in which salvation depends upon man's individual actions. What better settlers than the devout Brahmins who understood Karma so well? Parashurama recruited some Brahmins from the banks of the Krishna river that runs through Andhra Pradesh, offering them his new lush land of heavy rainfall and no famine. They stayed for a while, then went home again, complaining of snakes. So he looked further north and eventually he gathered a selection of suitable Brahmins. To prevent the second wave of settlers from running away, Parashurama decreed the cobra a sacred creature; a small snake shrine exists, to this day, in most Nambudiri compounds. This shrine is called a *sarpakkavu* and is either a patch of artificial jungle or, in some older households, a tiny relic of the authentic primeval jungle, in the middle of which stands a stone image of Naga the serpent. Sometimes real cobras are encouraged to nest in the *sarpakkavu*. Nambudiris are generally small landowners whose two chief characteristics are orthodoxy and simplicity. Unlike other Brahmins (who have established themselves as scholars, administrators, intellectuals of all kinds) most Nambudiris prefer to turn their backs on worldly achievements. Very few Nambudiris ever had much to do with the British government, shunning the opportunities for employment, in the Civil Service or the legal profession, that so many other Brahmins seized. The Nambudiris held back, distrustful of Europeans. Wasn't it, after all, widely known that white people had tails? They chose to ignore the Western-style schools and universities that were set up in the nineteenth and twentieth centuries. New agricultural methods, technology in general, passed them by. Gradually their hold on the land slipped, their large estates shrunk to little more than houses standing in groves. Their lack of material values made them prey to fraudulence and intrigue but, more often, they just allowed their own affairs to get in a muddle. A languorous genteel poverty pervades a Nambudiri's existence in contemporary life as does a sustaining belief in divine providence.

The Nambudiris are mild people. If anyone insults them they retaliate by asking him to take it back a hundred times over. That is, apparently, their strongest rebuke. Nambudiris are great Vedic scholars. From the age of seven to fifteen, every good Nambudiri boy studies the Veda. Should anything interrupt these studies (illness, for example) then the whole course has to start all over again from the beginning. Nambudiri men used to shave their heads and bodies, leaving only a knotted strand on the top of the head which hung down over the forehead. But shaving the entire body meant that the hair kept growing back. Whenever their wives were pregnant, custom forbade them to shave at all. As a rich Nambudiri could have up to four wives, he might spend many years of his adult life in a state of great hairiness. They used to wear wooden shoes, leather being a distasteful substance to them. Nowadays they wear rubber flip-flops. Nambudiri women wear undyed saris. Their bracelets are made of brass, never silver or gold.

Some Nambudiris are sorcerers. A group in Southern Kerala were forcibly converted to Islam during Tipu Sultan's invasion. Within a generation they returned to their true religion but a stigma had attached to them. These Southern Nambudiris were considered slightly *déclassé* and discouraged from sacerdotal work so they became warlocks instead. A spell for the destruction (*marana*) of an enemy involves burying a coconut shell in the enemy's garden or work-place. Inside the shell is a live frog or lizard with pins stuck into its eyes and stomach. The creature eventually dies in a great deal of pain. So does the enemy. Nambudiri magicians are helpful to treasure-hunters. Hanuman, even Kali, can be invoked with special prayers and asked to locate buried loot. Some of them keep a pet demon called Kuttichchattan ('Boy Satan') who looks like a very dark-skinned servant boy with a quiff like Tintin's. Mainly he guards the property but, if asked to, he can make an enemy's life intolerable. Kuttichchattan does no real harm but torments his victim with a series of tricks: the victim's clothes catch fire, turds materialize on his dinner table, thorns sprout in his bed – that sort of thing. Kuttichchattan is paid with food and his appetite is so immense that many families can't afford his services.

14. All Nambudiris are superstitious. Good omens include overheard music, a prostitute, a virgin, an elephant, a horse, a tethered cow or bull, yoghurt, uncooked rice, sugar-cane, a water-pot, any flower, any fruit, honey or two strangers who turn out to be Brahmins (though not necessarily Nambu-diris) as well. Bad omens, particularly if seen first thing in the morning, include a crow on one's left, a kite on one's right, a cat, a jackal, a hare, an empty pot, a smoky fire, a bundle of sticks, a widow, a one-eyed man or a man with a big nose. Any of these bad omens encountered at the beginning of a journey is enough to make the traveller turn back. But if, having turned back, he should see a lizard on the eastern wall of a house, then he may proceed again. To sneeze once means good luck, twice bad. A Nambudiri often clicks his fingers when he yawns to prevent an evil spirit from entering his mouth.

In the old days a Nambudiri would walk along the road shouting. This was to warn those of lower caste that he was on his way, that they should allow him to pass unpolluted. Likewise those of the lower castes shouted to warn nearby Nambudiris of their polluting presence. The roads of Kerala must have been as noisy with human voices as they are today with motor horns. There used to be graded distances that other castes had to keep from a Nambudiri. For instance, a Nair (the Malabar equivalent of the Kshatriya) was allowed within six paces but a Pulayan (an agricultural serf) had to keep at least ninety-six paces away.

15. Nayadis, it would seem, have been generalized into the untouchable masses or have converted to Christianity; their specific traditions and characteristics have faded. They were always mysterious, as would befit 'Unseeables'. A late nineteenth-century Malabar Manual, drawn up by the Civil Service, reports: 'Of the Nayadis, or lowest caste among the Hindus – the dog-eaters – nothing definite is known.' The great Edgar Thurston filled that void with a fairly long entry on the Nayadis in the fifth volume of *Castes and Tribes of Southern India*. It was to Thurston that I turned to find out what I could about these extraordinary people so the following titbits are, quite possibly, eighty years out of date:

A traveller in Kerala might come across a rag spread out on the side of the road with a few coins on it – the begging-cloth of the unseen Nayadi. If one missed the begging-cloth or failed to grasp its purpose, shouts might be heard from the Nayadi's hiding-place. It was considered unlucky not to give alms. Near Kollatur there is a stone called the Nayadi Parai; it is believed to be a hard-hearted traveller turned to stone for ignoring a Nayadi's plea. Not all Nayadis lived by begging. Some were nightwatchmen, guarding crops from deer; some were employed as labourers in the paddy-fields. Traditionally, Nayadis collected honey and bees-wax which they could exchange for liquor. They also gathered gum from the mattipal tree which was used as a temple incense; this gum they could sell and with the money they could buy provisions (such as salt, chillies and dried fish) and tobacco and liquor. Nayadis made ropes from the malanar plant and the bark of the kayyul tree. At Onam the Nayadi rope-maker presented four ropes to the nearest Nambudiri household and two ropes to the nearest Nair household. In return he was given a supply of rice. Despite their reputation Nayadis didn't eat dogs. Nor did they eat cats, snakes, land-crabs, shellfish or beef. They *did* eat monkeys, rats, mongooses, pigs, deer, parrots, cuckoos, doves, quails, jungle-fowl, paddy-birds, hares, tortoises, lizards, crocodiles and all kinds of fish. They were great hunters. Yams and aroids were favourite vegetables.

Nayadis were able to heal the sick. When a villager was seriously ill, a bundle was made, from a black blanket, containing sesame seeds, mustard, turmeric and coconut. This bundle was passed three times over the patient then presented to a Nayadi, together with a palm-leaf parasol, a stick and a cucumber. This was called a *kala-dhanam*, an offering to Yama, the god of death, with whom the Nayadis had some rapport. The Nayadi accepted the gift and prayed for the long life and prosperity of the giver. Then he offered the gifts in turn to his own family god and prayed that the life of the sick person be spared.

16. There was never a clearly defined trading caste in pre-Christian Kerala. The Nambudiris, of course, were the Brahmins and the Nairs were the close equivalent of the Kshatriyas; both castes held considerable wealth and, when the occasion demanded it, would dabble in trade. A regional version of the Vaisya caste doesn't seem to have existed and perhaps, because of this absence, foreign traders found it easy to get a foothold on the Malabar Coast. As soon as Malayalis were converted to Christianity, they started to fill the traditional Vaisya role and, because they had abandoned the rigid inheritance laws of their own castes (male primogeniture for the Nambudiris, matriliny for the

Nairs) entire families were able to prosper. The Christians, strengthened by the Syrian influx, set up plantations to grow spices and hard woods, supplying the foreigners' demands and growing richer and richer all the time. On their estates they built sturdy mansions called *tarawads* (rather similar in concept to the fortified farmhouses one comes across in Cornwall) where they lived the bourgeois life of the landed gentry. Despite Kerala's Communist government, most of these estates still belong to Syrian Christian families.

17. The first Jews arrived in India a long time ago, at the time of the Babylonian diaspora. The story goes that two groups arrived in India around the sixth century BC. One group, the Ben-E-Israel, made it to the Colaba District (in what is now downtown Bombay) and from there to several regions of Maharashtra. Another group landed, to the south, at the ancient port of Cranganore in what is now Kerala. Six and a half centuries later, this southern group was joined by a second wave, fleeing after the Romans had destroyed the temple in Jerusalem. These newcomers were called 'Pardeshis' (foreigners) but they soon referred to themselves as White Jews and the older community, darkened by centuries of Malabar sunshine and intermarriage with non-Jewish inhabitants, as Black Jews. The two communities existed alongside one another, trading as spice merchants and generally prospering. Preserved in the synagogue are some copper plates known as the Sasanam (charter) dating from the end of the tenth century, inscribed with a grant from the local ruler, Bhaskara Ravi Varman (962–1060) to a Jewish merchant (it's not clear, and a sore point, whether he was Black or White) called Joseph Rabban. The plates are inscribed in the ancient Vatteluttu character which had once been the prevalent Tamil character but, at the time of this grant, was only used for drawing up documents by Hindu rajahs. Compared to the restrictions of European Jewish life, the grant affords us a glimpse of the privileges and acceptance enjoyed by the Malabar Jewry at the time. Here is the translation made by Dr Hultzch (in volume 3 of *Epigraphia Indica*, 1894–95): *Hail! Prosperity! This gift was made by him who had assumed the title 'King of Kings', His Majesty the King, the glorious Bhaskara Ravi Varman, in the time during which he was wielding the sceptre and ruling over many hundred thousands of places, in the thirty-*

sixth year after the second year, on the day on which he was pleased to stay at Muyirikkodu. We have given to Isuppu Irappan (Joseph Rabban) the village of Anjuvannam, together with the seventy-two proprietary rights (viz.), the tolls on female elephants and other riding animals, the revenue of Anjuvannam, a lamp in day-time, a cloth spread in front to walk on, a palanquin, a parasol, a Vaduga drum, a large trumpet, a gateway, an arch, a canopy in the shape of an arch, a garland and so forth. We have remitted tolls and the tax on balances. Moreover we have granted with these copper leaves that he need not pay the dues which the other inhabitants of the city pay to the royal palace and that he may enjoy the benefits which they enjoy. To Isuppu Irappan of Anjuvannam, to the male children and female children born of him, to his nephews, and to the sons-in-law who have married his daughters, we have given Anjuvannam as an hereditary estate for as long as the moon and the world shall exist. Hail! (It is then witnessed by a variety of officials.)

The arrival of the Portuguese, at the very beginning of the sixteenth century, disrupted this rather stately existence. The two main rulers on the Malabar Coast, the Rajah of Cochin and the Zamorin, whose capital was Calicut, embarked upon a war for the supremacy of the region. Calicut had grown under the patronage of Arab traders and the older port of Cranganore was waning in importance. The Zamorin had been warned against the Portuguese by the Arabs – all the more reason for them to be welcomed by the jealous Rajah. Soon a new phase of the war developed: an Arab-Zamorin offensive against the Cochin-Portuguese alliance. It was a long war and eventually Cranganore was sacked by the Arabs in 1524. Furthermore, the sea broke through and blocked the harbour entrance with silt. It was decided not to rebuild Cranganore but instead to move all trade further south to Cochin itself, which was flourishing under Portuguese patronage. So what remained of the trading population, including both groups of Jews, moved to Cochin where they established Jew Town in the Mattancheri district.

When Thurston's *Castes and Tribes of Southern India* was first published in 1909, the Jewish population must have been a large one. Thurston refers to the Reverend J.H.

Lord's 1907 publication, *The Jews in India and the Far East*, which lists four synagogues in Cochin, three belonging to the more numerous Black Jews. Only the White Jewish synagogue remains today. Bickering between the two groups seems to have been constant throughout their history. This seems surprising at first. One would imagine that the similarities between the two would prove greater than the differences but, in that their history unfolded in India, where the word for caste is 'varna' which more accurately means colour, it ceases to be so surprising. Thurston quotes from a letter written in the middle of the nineteenth century by Canter Visscher: 'The blacks have a dark coloured Rabbi, who must stand back if a white one enters, and must resign to him the honour of performing the divine service in the synagogue. On the other hand, when the black Rabbis enter the synagogue of the whites, they must only be hearers. There has lately been a great dispute between the two races; the Black wishing to compel the White Jewesses to keep their heads uncovered, like their own women and trying to persuade the Rajah to enforce such a rule. The dispute ended, however, with permission given to every one, both men and women, to wear what they chose.'

The Black Jews even set up divisions within their own community, wanting to be distinguished as Brown Jews and Black Jews. The Brown Jews claimed racial purity, to be *M'yukhasim* (of ancient lineage), true descendants of the Cranganore originals. These Brown Jews regarded all the still-darker-complexioned Jews as racially impure, probably descended from Dravidian slaves owned and converted to Judaism by their ancestors.

ASWIN

1. A hundred years ago the castration operation was generally performed by barbers. The patient, drugged with opium or bhang, was made to sit on an upturned pot. Here I quote from an article published, in 1873, in the Journal of the Anthropological Institute by Dr Shortt: 'The entire genitals being seized by the left hand, an assistant, who has a bamboo lathe slit in the centre, runs it down quite close to

the pubis, the slit firmly embracing the genitals at the root, when the operator, with a sharp razor, runs it down along the face of the lathe and removes penis, testicles and scrotum in one swoop, leaving a large clean open wound behind, in which boiling gingili oil (sesame oil) is poured to staunch the bleeding and the wound covered over with a soft rag steeped in warm oil. This is the only dressing applied to the wound, which is renewed daily, while the patient is confined in a supine position to his bed and lightly fed with *conjee* (rice gruel), milk, etc.' Nowadays the operation is performed by another eunuch. *Hijras* eke out a living as dancers and prostitutes, though in some states they lead a religious life, performing temple duties. In Rajasthan they are sometimes faith-healers, with gynaecological matters as a particular forte.